Hey Charlie —
It's a plez
an honor to
story with 2 2-7 Marin.
Semper Fidelis,
gary Harlan

"There are only two kinds of people
that understand Marines:
Marines and the enemy. Everyone else
has a second-hand opinion."

-General William Thornson, U.S. Army

ALWAYS FAITHFUL

Returning to Vietnam

Gary Harlan

M. Harlan, Publisher

Book Layout ©2017 BookDesignTemplates.com

Always Faithful/ Gary Harlan. —1st ed.

ISBN 978-0-578-71554-4 (paperback)

ISBN 978-0-578-71554-4 (e-book)

Contents

i

Foreword

By Christopher Sawyer-Lauçanno

Gary didn't look much like a Marine when we met at South-western College in January 1969. Tall and lean, with longish hair, mustache, round John Lennon-like eyeglasses, he appeared to be a card-carrying member of what we termed the counterculture. Within a few days we began talking. I wasn't particularly surprised when Gary told me he's just gotten his discharge from the Marines. At that time, Southwestern had probably as many veterans as fresh-faced recent high school grads. I remember telling him straight off that I totally opposed the war. His response was this: "So do I."

And so began a friendship that has lasted a half-century.

As Gary and I got to know one another we discovered, despite our different paths and backgrounds that we had a lot in common. Among our mutual interests were philosophy, history, jazz, literature, alcohol and weed. We also joined forces in protesting the war. As he states in Always Faithful, his reasons for opposing the war were highly personal, the result of two tours in Vietnam. There was nothing abstract in Gary's reasoning. It was propelled by raw emotion, by witnessing slaughter, by realizing that young men were dying because a government, far removed from the reality of battle, even from Vietnam itself, believed (maybe) that they were upholding some notion of American might.

I was ardently anti-war, at least in part, because by September '68 I'd already lost two cousins and a high school classmate. Within a year three more friends would be dead, and another permanently damaged physically and mentally.

And so Gary and I, along with a number of others, spent time strategizing protests, getting chased by cops in Oceanside, and helping to organize campus moratoriums against the war in the fall of 1969. Gary was active and out-spoken. He was also an accomplished tactician. Part of that came from having been a Marine; his pursuit of philosophy helped, too.

In his "Introduction" Gary mentions using facts and figures to debate a college professor about the war. I vaguely remember the event, though I don't recall Gary stumbling, as he thought he did. But I do know that had Gary confronted Dr. Henderson by recounting some of his own personal experiences, there would have been no doubt who would have "won" the match.

That he didn't talk more from his heart was understandable. Gary wasn't initially very willing to talk to anyone about his time in Vietnam. But over time, usually late at night after a joint or two and a bottle of something or other, he'd open up. I didn't say much. I just listened. The APA hadn't yet diagnosed PTSD. But neither of us really needed a sanctioned definition. I knew Gary was suffering. He knew he was suffering. And while we both knew why, neither of us knew what to do about it.

In no small way, Always Faithful is a book about overcoming the lasting effects of PTSD through action, through embracing trauma, and through finally having those unfinished conversations about what the war was and what it had done to so many. Gary's mission to reunite with as many of his former Marines as possible, and to tell their stories about the war and its aftermath, is an act of exceeding generosity. It allows each man to finally recount how he viewed combat, and how he dealt with coming home.

But Gary went even farther than just reuniting with his fellow Marines. He also organized a trip back to Vietnam, the second for him, where he and his group could also walk on the soil where they had fought and friends had fallen. But likely even more important, these veterans had the unique opportunity to meet a few of their former enemies. This wasn't about reconciliation as the Americans had never been friends with the Vietnamese. But it was about recognizing one another as human beings, not just as the enemy.

What began as simply an opportunity for Gary to get together with a few with whom he'd served a half century ago, soon became something more: a chronicle with varied voices, multiple stories and differing perspectives. But this book is far more than a handful of guys reminiscing: this is a powerful tale of the human experience that speaks about the ordeal of an entire generation. And while the focus is on Vietnam and its aftermath, Gary's training as a philosopher pushes him to extrapolate a larger whole from specifics. As such, Always Faithful is a powerful statement about the consistent and destructive desire on the part of the U.S. to engage in wars without definable outcomes. This book is an extremely valuable resource for anyone, of any age, who is trying to make sense of what the cost truly is of "endless wars."

Charles Phillip Alexander

Killed by a sniper's bullet February 21, 1967

Introduction

In all fairness I should have a special acknowledgment page devoted to George W. Bush and Dick Cheney. Had it not been for their successful effort in persuading Congress and the majority of Americans that invading Iraq was in our country's best interest, I would never have had the time nor the resources to complete the project you will read about in these pages. I'd be just another guy struggling to make a living, all the while pissed off that America learned nothing from the debacle known as the Vietnam War.

Beginning in the 1980s, friends encouraged me to file a disability claim for PTSD with the VA, and each time I would reply with the old expression from the Nam: Never happen! Formally acknowledging a history of depression, divorces, alienation, estrangement, suicidal thoughts and substance abuse would, to my mind, amount to casting myself in the role of victim. My attitude changed when our president, who spent the war years flying jets in Texas, and our vice president, who skated the war with a slew of deferments, used the tragedy of 9/11 and the bogus threat of Saddam's weapons of mass destruction as the pretext for invading Iraq. That's it! I'm filing that claim!

The process began with a drive from my home in rural Southwest Missouri to Fayetteville, Arkansas, the location of my regional VA hospital. There I had my first appointment with Dr. Hiett, a pleasant female psychiatrist whose ultimate assessment of my emotional and mental health would determine my future. Her office was located on the first floor of the building. "Please, come in and take a seat," she said. Her desk was located against the wall on the side of the room closest to the door. The nearest available chair was located in the center of the room, in front of a window, several feet from where she would be sitting. The only other option was a chair located in the far corner. I chose the nearest chair.

"A lot of veterans don't want to sit in front of the window," she said.

Knowing what she meant by that, I seized the opportunity to properly introduce myself.

"Well, doctor, it's like this," I began. "I have absolutely no reason to think that someone has followed me down here from Missouri with the intention of doing me harm. I could have arrived here unshaven, wearing a grungy field jacket, and slunk over to the corner. I'm not that guy. Nor am I the guy who hits the deck when he hears a car backfire. I'm a reasonably intelligent man whose life has been screwed up as a result of his experience in the Vietnam War."

It was an honest beginning resulting, months later, in a positive outcome. My disability claim was successful, and now I live comfortably with free health care. Instead of feeling annoyed by strangers thanking me for my service when they clearly have no understanding nor interest in understanding the nature of my service, I should say, "You are thanking me for my service. Every day."

Though I cannot say the same about three ex-wives whom I caused much aggravation and heartache, I still don't feel like a victim of war. In fact, I feel as though I'm being compensated for learning some important life lessons the hard way, one of which is the essential meaning of the Declaration of Independence where it states, "all men are created equal."

The combat zone was the only environment I've ever known in which one's status in the group had nothing to do with one's socioeconomic background, level of education or skin color. It was a group comprised of Whites, Blacks, and Hispanics, the numbers of which were proportionately the same as the demographics back home. There was only one membership requirement: the willingness of each man to risk his life for the others.

Over the course of meetings with the VA, a narrative emerged of the person I became as a result of my combat history. This narrative was based, in large part, on what Dr. Jonathon Shay calls "indignant rage," which he identifies as the primary trauma underlying PTSD symptoms in Vietnam vets. "It is," he writes in his book, Achilles in Vietnam: Combat Trauma and the Undoing of Character, "the kind of rage arising from social betrayal that impairs a person's dignity through violation of 'what's right.'" This is precisely what is triggered in me each and every time I hear expressions of racism both overt and tacit.

There have been many such incidents over the years, one of them occurring a few years ago during the height of the Ferguson demonstrations. I was at my health club in Springfield when my friend invited me to take a five mile walk outside with him and another member. Less than a mile into our walk the subject of Ferguson was brought up, and this other fellow said, "That guy (Michael Brown) deserves to be six feet under." I lost it. I immediately confronted him, calling him an asshole. They were both stunned. I was enraged, prepared to fight him right then and there. Thinking about it later, I knew what provoked that reaction. It was the loss of a friend during my first tour of duty. His name was Charles Alexander. We called him Alex.

Like Michael Brown, Alex was a black teenager. He turned 19 a month or two after joining our outfit. In the ensuing months he became far and away the most likable person in the platoon. Not because he was funny and entertaining. We had plenty of guys like that. Alex's impact went much deeper. Alex stood out as a source of light in a very dark world. His very existence served as a reminder of our humanity. Unlike most of us, he never treated the civilians harshly, which was saying a lot given the area in which we operated, Quang Nam Province, an especially nasty place that, as Guenter Lewy rightly observed, "defied meaningful pacification," and where over 6,000 Marines were killed in less than four years.

For his friends, the day Alex was killed by a sniper's bullet was the first day of a lifetime of grieving.

In his classic work A Theory of Justice, philosopher John Rawls introduced a device with which one can determine the morality of issues. It's called the "veil of ignorance." We, the decision-makers, in an effort to arrive at principles of justice and fairness, are asked to imagine that we do not know where we stand in terms of class, gender, race, or any other defining characteristics that might influence our decisions in favor of one group over another. As indicated, living day-to-day in the life and death world of the Marine combatant rendered this exercise unnecessary. I returned home knowing that Black Lives Matter, just as I knew Hispanic lives and White lives matter, no more, no less.

If that was all there was to it, I would not have been sitting in the office of Dr. Hiett. After all, I had good reason to feel proud of having risked my life for my fellow Marines, to have met the demands reflected in our motto, Semper Fidelis—Always Faithful.

The lesson that came close to destroying my life was one that Alex apparently knew from the start: the knowledge that Vietnamese lives matter as well.

It has been estimated that as many as two million civilians on both sides were killed during the war. But then, according to General Westmoreland, "The Oriental doesn't put the same high price on life as does a Westerner. Life is plentiful. Life is cheap in the Orient." Perhaps we felt that way too, at first. But the longer you spent among the peasant population out in the bush, the less likely you were to believe such racist garbage.

Introduction

Witnessing my first funeral in the Quang Ngai Province was enough to permanently disabuse me of the notion that life meant nothing to those poor rice farmers. Their wailing and abject sorrow left an indelible image in my brain.

During the decade following my discharge I was not familiar with the concept of survivor's guilt, though I was suffering from it, mainly as a consequence of the deaths of two Marines: Charlie Alexander from my first tour and Nate Lee, whom I discuss in chapter 19, from the second tour. It took years of reflection to realize that the greatest impact the war had on me was neither the fighting nor all the casualties we sustained: it was the suffering of the Vietnamese civilians. I experienced my first hint of this during my second semester of college when I made the misguided decision to challenge Dr. Henderson, the conservative, pro-war political science instructor to a debate on the Vietnam War two weeks hence in the student union. It was the absolute dumbest decision of my life. The notion that a Marine grunt could be capable of taking on a Ph.D. head-on in a debate on the war less than a year after he had crawled inside a tunnel and killed two VC was, in and of itself, insane. But I was sufficiently naive to think I could compete with my opponent in a contest of ideas, advancing facts and arguments in support of my antiwar position. In other words, an objective examination of the issue.

I began by reciting all the facts and historical considerations I had memorized, such as the Geneva Convention and so forth. Then suddenly I was literally overwhelmed by the subjective reality of the Vietnam War—a flood of flashbacks of death and destruction with images of Vietnamese peasants caught in the middle. That was it for any chance of presenting a coherent point of view. My body was in the student union of Southwestern College, but my mind was 10,000 miles away, back in the war, alone and unarmed.

Despite three marriages to three supportive women, I stayed alone for nearly three decades struggling with an issue the French philosopher Albert Camus details in his essay, "An Absurd Reasoning":

"There is but one truly serious philosophical problem, and that is suicide. Judging whether life is or is not worth living amounts to answering the fundamental question of philosophy." All the rest, he claimed, were just games.

Recalling a conversation I once had with my friend Bud back in the 80s suggests that neither of us had judged that life was worth living. Bud had been a Marine captain, a tank commander in Vietnam. We were having a beer together when Bud said, "Those guys on the Wall? They're the lucky ones," to which I instantly replied, "You've got that right."

In the pages that follow I discuss two life-affirming decisions that managed to turn things around: I reached out to Marines I served with in the combat zone; and I returned to Vietnam—twice.

My first trip back was in 1994. It included five days in Hanoi, three days in Saigon, and then back to the old neighborhood, Quang Nam Province, where I met with former Viet Cong cadres. Twenty-five years later, in March 2019, I returned with six men—four fellow Marines and two of our Navy Corpsmen that I served with in 1966 with Lima Company, 3rd Battalion, 1st Marines.

We were accompanied by a film crew from Carbon Trace Productions, a non-profit documentary film company based in my hometown, Springfield, Missouri. Documenting our journey, they produced A Vietnam Peace Story. A month before our departure, the group came to Springfield for pre-trip interviews organized by Carbon Trace director, Andrew Cline.

In a general sense I knew the trip would have a healing effect on each man, but I had no clue as to which of them needed it most—that is, until Andy shared the interviews he shot. I was stunned to discover that the one man who stood out as a veteran displaying symptoms of PTSD was the one I would have least suspected, Bob Detty. Bob is a psychological counselor, which is how he comports himself—cool and detached. But he was anything but that during the interview. From the opening introduction in which he explained how he had started out as a private serving as a member of a fire team, later becoming a squad leader, and then platoon guide, it was obvious Bob was having a difficult time holding it together. That only got worse as the interview continued.

Bob Detty and Charlie Alexander were best friends. Talking with Bob at a unit reunion in the 90s, he admitted he snapped the day Alex was killed. Watching that interview, there was no doubt in my mind that he had never gotten over the loss of his friend. As A Vietnam Peace Story was in post-production, I sent Andy an email asking about his observations of Bob Detty. Here is his reply:

"While all the former Marines had emotional moments during the pre-trip interviews, it was Bob Detty who was the most distraught of the group. He sat alone and crying in an empty office adjacent to our studio set up. When we finally sat him down and got the cameras rolling, he was unable even to identify himself without breaking down. But he was one of the most articulate of the group in dealing with his feelings about his service in Vietnam. I found his observations particularly insightful regarding incidents that happened to him and their psychological impact. Toward the end of his interview he said something that struck me as important and thematic. In fact, what he said helped me create the meaning I hoped to create with the documentary. When we asked him why he wanted to return to Vietnam, he said, "I left a piece of me in Vietnam, and I want it back. I want me back." And, thus, the idea of a documentary about the inner journey of returning to Vietnam – Vietnam as a place and people rather than just a war—became clear. Bob's experience in Vietnam was, by his own recounting, profound. And in the final interview the day before we flew home, I think he might agree he had found himself. There were no more tears."

One of the Marines I reached out to in the early 90s was First Lieutenant Simon Gregory, who was Lima Company's XO (Executive Officer) when we landed in Vietnam, and became the company commander when our CO, Captain Sehulster, was nearly blinded by white phosphorous. For the past two-and-a-half decades Simon's friendship has been invaluable. In Simon I discovered a man possessing what Viet Thanh Nguyen describes as a "just memory." That is, someone whose concern is not limited to our own losses, but also to the losses suffered on the other side, losses substantially higher than our own. By Nguyen's calculation, "The body count in Vietnam for all sides was close to one-tenth of the population, while the American dead amounted to about 0.035 percent of the population."

Establishing a friendship with Simon, combined with the return visit to Vietnam, produced the emotional catharsis necessary for leaving behind thoughts of self-annihilation once and for all. In 1997 I met Marissa, the woman who would become my fourth wife. Determined to make this my final marriage, I gave up a decades-long pot habit a couple of months before we married. Last month we celebrated our twenty-second anniversary.

The rage I lived with for decades was brought back to the surface by the Iraq invasion. That, plus the War on Terror in general, is what inspired me to write this book. As I will discuss in the final chapter, there is a direct connection between Vietnam and these endless wars. There is also a tragic similarity between the two wars in terms of the suicide rates among the veteran population. When I hear that twenty young veterans a day take their own lives—veterans who are constantly thanked for their service—it confirms what I knew all along from my own experience, that the cause of the suicidal thoughts runs much deeper than the reaction of the folks back home to one's service.

To those acquainted with veterans of the War on Terror, let me say this: instead of the cursory "Thank you for your service," take the time to listen to what the veteran has to say about his or her service. To the veteran who thinks the guys who didn't make it home were "the lucky ones," I say this: you have your own Simon—someone you admired and respected when you were overseas. Get in touch with that person and all the others who once had your back.

This book is about my experience in Vietnam and the long aftermath of suffering from PTSD. But I'm not the main character. Vietnam is the main character, and this book is about what happened to a good many of my fellow Marines and Vietnamese, not just what occurred on the battlefield, but how the war changed all of our lives long after the last shots were fired. I spent several years reuniting with those I could. This book tells their stories as well as remembrances of the men we lost. And because a group of us were able to travel back to Vietnam, we were honored to reunite in peace with a people who never cease to amaze. This is their story, which includes recounting the stories of those whom we fought against, and of their astonishing ability to forgive.

Lima Company veterans meet with three of the NVA soldiers they fought in 1966. Top: Ron Clay andBob Detty; Center: Gene Cleaver, Doc Reyerson, Bob Boland, Doc Hastriter; bottom: Gary Harlan, Nguyen Van Nuoi, Bui The Nhoi, Nhu Van Liet.

CHAPTER 1

Returning to Vietnam

It was summertime in California, 1967, the famous "Summer of Love." For me, it was the summer of alcoholic escape. Life consisted of dragging myself out of the rack for morning formation, still inebriated from the massive amount of Bacardi and Coke consumed the night before, going through the motions of whatever training was scheduled for the day, and heading to the NCO club sharply at 1630 to get refueled.

There were some occasional variations to the routine. One morning a lance corporal asked, "Why were you looking for an M-14 round last night, Corporal Harlan?" I told him I didn't remember. But I knew. What was the point of dragging out this exceedingly boring process of self-annihilation by alcohol when, with one pull of the trigger, the whole thing could be over and done with?

Back home in Missouri, my folks would have been devastated. Just when they thought their son had safely come back in one piece and life returned to normal, Mom working as a nurse, Dad making a living in the insurance business, taking my little brother to the newly constructed Busch Stadium to watch the Cardinals on their way to a World Series championship; just when they thought the Vietnam War was no longer their problem to agonize over, their son, had he locked and loaded for the last time, would have informed them that for him the war was finally over, but for them it would never be over.

As things turned out, it would take decades for the war to wind down for me. "All wars," writes Viet Thanh Nguyen, "are fought twice, the first on the battlefield, the second time in memory." Beginning my college career the week after my discharge, I was determined to skip the second part and forget about the Marine Corps and the war, both my own involvement in it as well as its continuation. The latter was somewhat manageable in that I watched no TV nor read any newspapers. The community college I attended was located in a somewhat conservative area of San Diego and had no antiwar activity. I began classes with one and only one goal in mind: become a philosophy major, complete the requirements of the two-year college, transfer to a four-year college where I would earn a bachelor's degree, then go to graduate school to earn an advanced degree.

As for forgetting my own involvement in the war, that was another matter altogether. For one thing, Jose Perez, Jr., my best buddy during my first tour, was serving his second tour up at the DMZ with the 9th Marines.

Besides being conscious of my best friend still being in the thick of it, there were other reminders of the war, such as a dream I had one night which was so vivid, so compelling it seemed more like a vision than a dream.

I was standing alone beside the narrow bend of a stream. It was dusk and somewhat foggy. But I had no difficulty recognizing the dozen or so men standing on the other side of the stream. They were all Marines I had served with, each of whom had been killed in action, some from my first tour and some from the second. Now they appeared to be a closely knit group of friends, all of them in high spirits.

Naturally, Sergeant Nate Lee was standing in front of the group. He was my platoon sergeant. I had been one of his squad leaders. A wide grin appeared on his handsome Italian face. He was gesturing for me to join them.

"Come on, Sergeant Harlan! Get over here!"

I was getting confused and agitated, which seemed to contribute to their merriment.

"I can't!" I shouted back in frustration. This prompted a burst of laughter from the group. Richard Turner, a black guy in my squad who came from Washington, D.C., who was killed in the same ambush as Sergeant Lee, motioned for me to cross the stream. "Come on, Sergeant Harlan!"

Again, I yelled, "I can't!"

The more upset I got the more jubilant they became. Charlie Alexander was bent over, slapping his right leg, laughing uncontrollably.

Instead of feeling a sense of relief that it was only a dream, I woke up depressed. Part of me wanted to join them. The other part was determined to establish a new identity. One thing was certain. The notion of effecting self-imposed amnesia was not going to happen. As Viet Thanh Nguyen put it, "Memory is haunted, not just by ghostly others but by the horrors we have done, seen, and condoned. Haunted and haunting, human and inhuman, war remains with us and within us, impossible to forget but difficult to remember."

Apparently, I thought Kurt Vonnegut was correct when he stated you are what you pretend to be, and to a certain extent he was. Prior to the fighting on Hill 50, I was pretending to be a Marine grunt. After that, I became a Marine grunt. But to suppose that in the course of pretending to be an academic I would eventually transcend the identity of a combat veteran was naive at best. In my junior year at Sonoma State, one of my professors loaned me his copy of *The Warriors: Reflections on Men in Battle* by the philosopher and World War Two veteran, J. Glenn Gray. "The soldier," Gray wrote, "who has yielded himself to the fortunes of war, has sought to kill and escape being killed, is no longer what he was. He becomes in some sense a fighter, whether he wills it or not. In a real sense he becomes a fighting man, a *Homo furens*, a subspecies of the genus *Homo sapiens*."

Once I accepted this fact about myself what I was not about to do was conform to Nguyen's notion of fighting the war on the battlefield followed by fighting it in memory. After all, the war was still going on, with people dying every day—Americans and her allies, Vietnamese from both sides, civilians in the north and south, Cambodians, and Laotians. And for what? To stop the spread of communism? The folks living in the places in which I served demonstrated no aversion to the communists. What they had an aversion to were outsiders—invaders who traveled 10,000 miles to prop up a corrupt regime in the south to impose our will on a Third World country. Fight the war in memory? Bullshit! There was only one option available, and that was to join the effort to fight the war machine back home. By my second semester I became acquainted with like-minded students, veterans and non-veterans, and we organized. Following the Kent State shootings, we were among the hundreds of universities and colleges to suspend classes.

I was not one of those protesters who chanted, "Ho Ho Ho Chi Minh, the NLF is gonna win!" Not because I had no respect for the NLF. I had a healthy respect for them which doubtless contributed to my staying alive. But I did not idolize them or Ho Chi Minh.

And I was not one of John Kerry's "Winter Soldiers," characterizing myself and my comrades as war criminals who, in Kerry's own words, "had personally raped, cut off ears, cut off heads, taped wires from portable telephones to human genitals and turned up the power, cut off limbs, blown up bodies, randomly shot at civilians, razed villages in a fashion reminiscent of Genghis Khan, shot cattle and dogs for fun, poisoned food stocks, and generally ravaged the countryside of South Vietnam in addition to the normal ravage of war and the normal and very particular ravaging which is done by the applied bombing power of this country."

Which is not to say that we were perfect. There were isolated instances of low-level atrocities. Early on in 1966, after being fired at from a village, I shot and killed a water buffalo. During my first tour, I also participated in an act of retaliation after enemy fire from a village that killed and wounded several Marines: Some of us burned down the thatched huts from which we received the fire. An order was subsequently issued from above that torching hootches would not be tolerated.

One of our Navy corpsmen, Doc Ingraham, also recalled an incident, of which I was not aware:

"The next thing that happened was we received one round of sniper fire. The Marines in that column expended hundreds of rounds of counter-fire. No one was injured, and we continued the march. We went around a bend and on a trail on the other side of the rice paddy we could see an elderly man with a white beard carrying a walking stick. A machine gunner opened up on him. You could see the tracers. First you could see the rounds striking a wall in front of him. Then he went down. And nobody did anything."

The distinction I want to make is this: I didn't serve in an outfit whose leadership considered all Vietnamese as the enemy. No matter how ambiguous the situation, our leaders drew a clear distinction between civilians and combatants. But when you've got an environment in which it is not at all clear as to who your enemy is, and you have 19 and 20 year-olds getting extremely pissed off about their buddies getting killed and wounded, it doesn't take a genius to figure out that some bad shit is going to happen from time to time.

But rape, cutting off heads, torturing civilians? I cannot speak for the actions of every American unit during the war, but if Kerry's list of crimes was an accurate summary of actions committed by me and the Marines depicted in this book, that our leaders carried out a mission reminiscent of Genghis

Khan, I would not be inclined to attend a Marine reunion. And I have attended many reunions over the years, and plan to attend more in the future.

I shared these thoughts with Simon Gregory, our executive officer when we landed, and then our commanding officer our second month in-country. His reply: "Well put. We all had to deal with conflicting emotions, especially early on. As time went on, our basic humanity took over and overall, we acted with kindness and dignity."

I protested the war for one reason: It was the country of the Vietnamese, and I could see no justification for our being in their country.

The idea of returning to Vietnam for a third time never entered my mind until 1993 when Larry Rottmann presented the opportunity. Larry was a local Vietnam veteran and poet who taught at Missouri State University in Springfield. Even though the U.S. Embargo on Vietnam was still in effect, he was organizing a group to travel to Hanoi to attend an art exhibition, *As Seen By Both Sides*, a collection of work depicting the Vietnam War by twenty American artists and work depicting what they call the American War by twenty Vietnamese artists.

My decision to go back to Vietnam had less to do with an interest in the exhibition and everything to do with my mental health. Mentally, I had never left Vietnam and consequently had never completely come home. I lived in the country north of Springfield. Riding my motorcycle into town, there was a curve that went around a large rock formation. Many times, I imagined how easy it would be to end my life by smashing into that huge rock at 80 or 90 mph. So, when this Army veteran presented the opportunity to return to the Nam, I thought, why not? What the hell have I got to lose?

The group stayed in Hanoi for five days before returning to Missouri. I made other plans. From Hanoi I would travel to Ho Chi Minh City, formerly called Saigon, which was hundreds of miles from where the Marines operated. From there I would return to the place with which I was most familiar, Quang Nam Province, outside Danang. Not only did I want to see what the area was like after nearly two decades of peace, I was hoping to meet some veterans who were once my enemy. Modeled after the art exhibition, my mission could be called *Both Sides Meet*.

I was especially interested in contacting fellow survivors of a battle that took place in March 1966, in Quang Ngai Province, south of Quang Nam. Code named Operation Utah, the fighting took the lives of 98 Marines and nearly 600 Vietnamese. In hopes of securing the cooperation of the Vietnamese veterans, I arranged a meeting with officials at the Veterans Association located just a few blocks from the Central Prison, formerly known as the Hanoi Hilton. The day before I met with Colonel Tran Gia Thiet and his interpreter, Huynh Van Trinh, I dropped off a cover letter and a copy of the after-action report of Operation Utah.

Colonel Thiet and Mr. Trinh were the perfect good guy-bad guy team. The meeting began with what felt like an interrogation. Facing the intense, thoroughly unfriendly Colonel, I felt like I was in a time warp. I had to remind myself that America's involvement in the war, including my own participation, was well documented, that I was not restricted to giving my name, rank and serial number.

"The Colonel wants to know the exact dates and locations of your service in Vietnam."

"January 1966 to April 1966, Quang Ngai Province. April 1966 through November 1966, Quang Nam Province. February 1968 to May 1968, Quang Nam Province."

Questions regarding the after-action report and my letter followed.

"The Colonel wants to know exactly how many battalions participated."

"Elements of four U.S. Marine battalions."

"Is the 1st Marines a regiment or a division?"

"A regiment."

"The Colonel wants to know, do your plans include the soldiers who were called ARVN?"

I anticipated that issue would come up since a battalion of ARVN (Army of the Republic of Vietnam), who the North had always referred to as "puppet troops", were mentioned in the report.

"That would not be my decision to make."

"The Colonel says there will be no ARVN at the meeting. The ARVN do not exist."

That was pretty much how we felt about them during the war, doubtless unfairly, but I would never have given the Colonel the satisfaction of saying so.

At that point we moved on to the reeducation portion of the meeting.

"The Colonel wants you to know that even though the Americans identified us as two groups, we were only one group."

I could have asked him if he didn't mean to say two groups with a single command structure. Clearly, there were differences between the regulars from the north and the Viet Cong in the south—as there were differences among insurgency groups in the south. But at that point I was certain the Colonel had served as an interrogator at the Hanoi Hilton during the war and a reeducation camp instructor afterward.

Our meeting ended with my receiving a valuable contact down south, but not before some very tense moments. Tense and bizarre. The Colonel's harshness suggested he would like nothing better than to strangle this audacious American who showed no remorse about the deaths of 600 of his comrades while Mr. Trinh translated his words with the cheerfulness of a hotel concierge informing guests of available tours.

"The Colonel wants you to know we are a generous people."

I nodded respectfully, thinking maybe he was lightening up a bit.

"The Colonel wants you to know why we are a generous people. You committed crimes against our country, and yet we are willing to be friends."

I had the distinct impression my new-found friend would have liked to see my trip cut short with an extended stay at the Hanoi Hilton. But as the saying goes, in for a penny, in for a pound.

"May I say something?" I asked Mr. Trinh.

"Of course," he answered with a smile while the Colonel fumed.

"I am proud of my service in Vietnam. I am also proud of having publicly opposed the war following my honorable discharge from the Marines."

When my words were translated, the Colonel nodded. Though he probably had difficulty processing such a paradox, I had told him the truth. Yes, I had arrived at the conclusion that it was *their country*, that Washington's decision to wage war in Vietnam was a horribly tragic mistake, and that I had fought in an unjust cause. But it was equally true that when we arrived in Vietnam, we believed what we had been told, that we were there to help the South Vietnamese. And as this book will demonstrate, in the words of men I served with, we did help them. We may have been duped, but contrary to John Kerry's statement to the Senate Foreign Relations Committee, we were not war criminals.

Before our meeting ended, Colonel Thiet told me about another Marine who had visited the Veterans Association several months earlier. He was in a wheelchair. He was raising funds with which to build schools in Vietnam. I later learned the identity of that Marine: Lew Puller Jr., son of the legendary Marine Chesty Puller. Nine months after his meeting with Colonel Thiet Lew Puller took his own life.

19

A couple of days later in Ho Chi Minh City I was sitting across from my contact in the south, General Tran Van Tra, a legend in Vietnam. Happily, General Tra and his interpreter, Colonel Tran Doan Toi, were cordial. No interrogation and no reeducation. The two of them had served together since the days of fighting against the French.

Born in 1918, General Tra grew up in the Quang Ngai Province. At 19 he left his job with the railroad to join the Vietminh French resistance. In 1954 he was sent up north, where he trained in China and the Soviet Union. In 1963, in his mid-forties, he made the journey south down the Ho Chi Minh Trail to assume responsibility for organizing the Viet Cong in the Mekong Delta region. He commanded the attack against Saigon in the Tet Offensive of 1968, and was the strategist of the series of opening attacks in the Final Offensive of 1975.

Thinking about it now, I find it very odd that Colonel Thiet, a man who followed the party line to the letter, would introduce me to a man with a history of standing up to the Politburo. The General published a book in 1982 in which he placed the blame for the disastrous Tet Offensive of 1968 solely on the leaders in the north:

"The Tet objectives were beyond our strength. They were based on the subjective desires of the people who made the plan. Hence our losses were large, in material and manpower, and we were not able to retain the gains we had already made."

General Tra's stance toward national reconciliation revealed someone more inclined toward nationalism than communism. On 7 May 1975, exactly one week after the Saigon government's surrender, General Tra gave his first speech as chairman of the Military Management Committee, assuring the South Vietnamese people that "Only the U.S. imperialists have been defeated...All Vietnamese are victors...The grandchildren and children of all strata of the new society will from now on be able to grow up with a spirit of national pride, hold their heads high, be happy, be provided for, and be able to work in the most brilliant period of development of this country."

As the thousands of Vietnamese who escaped Vietnam to settle in America will attest, harsh retribution was widespread. Hundreds of thousands of southerners were sent to long-term "reeducation camps"--a euphemism for forced labor camps. Both they and members of their families were denied basic rights as citizens including decent employment, education, or any hope for advancement.

As for Colonel Thiet's assertion that there were not two groups fighting the Americans, but one, that was contradicted by the founding of The Club of Former Resistance Fighters (CFRF) in 1986 in which General Tra served as a senior adviser. The CFRF accused the party of imposing a reign of terror on the whole population including those who fought with the Viet Cong against the Americans. "The whole population lives in terror of the Party, exactly as they lived in terror of the emperors and feudal rulers of yore."

General Tra wrote a letter on my behalf to the Veterans Association in Danang, which was my next stop.

"Here is your passport," he said with a smile as he handed me the letter.

After presenting the General's letter to a man who had served as a NVA liaison officer during the war, I was afforded the opportunity of meeting my former enemy. Unlike the situation with Colonel Thiet in Hanoi, there was a feeling of mutual respect between us. With the translating services of Muoi, an English-language teacher, I met former guerillas and regulars all over the province. I also met a number of civilians who had worked for us while helping the enemy.

One woman who owned a small noodle stand near Marble Mountain with her husband was quite excited to hear I had served there as a Marine. She even remembered the 3rd Battalion, 1st Marines. That was not surprising since she was employed at the PX in Danang, where she could easily keep tabs on every outfit in the area. Such information was highly useful to her husband. While she smiled and spoke to the Marines serving in the rear, he was out in the bush trying to kill Marine grunts like me. Now he was serving me a twenty-cent bowl of noodle soup. Guenter Lewy, author of the book *America in Vietnam* certainly got it right about Quang Nam Province when he wrote that it "defied meaningful pacification." Twice before I had left Vietnam thankful to be alive. Now I found it amazing any of us got out alive.

Yet as vicious and formidable a place as it had been, I detected absolutely no animosity from anyone in Quang Nam Province. And it went much deeper than simply an absence of hostility. I realized that early on in my first meeting, sitting at a table sipping tea with a group of former VC regulars. I provided the maps which enabled us to recall exactly where and when we had met before. It was similar to being at a Marine reunion. Who, after all, could appreciate the fact of our mutual survival more than each other, the men who had once spent their days trying to kill the other? Who but the other really understood the sacrifices that made our mutual survival possible?

The lessons I learned during my first two experiences in Vietnam were the hard lessons of survival and comradeship, paid for with the lost lives and lost limbs of others. The lessons learned this time were not hard, but they were humbling. My ethnocentric attitude at nineteen was simple: America was so much more advanced than this primitive culture. What I discovered upon returning in peacetime was that in some very basic ways, Vietnam is more advanced than America. For instance, they would be utterly bewildered to hear their leaders preaching family values, something the Republicans had been doing a lot of at the time. The Vietnamese *live* family values. No one I met asked me, "What do you do for a living?" They asked about my family, did I have a wife and kids back home.

22

Their social interaction is certainly superior to ours. They tend to treat one another with respect and courtesy. They observe the importance of *saving face*. I was somewhat taken back my second day in Hanoi when I realized the people I saw in those crowded streets looked much happier than the folks I'd see back home in the mall. Clearly, *saving face* has advantages over our preferred *in-your-face*.

For years I had recurring nightmares of pursuing and/or being pursued by shadowy figures—ghostly others—some dressed in black, others in green, all of them armed and dangerous and all of them faceless. In the 24 years since I revisited Vietnam, I have not had a single nightmare about Vietnam combat. I met the enemy. I saw his face. I could see he was no longer my enemy.

In my last meeting with the VA psychiatrist, when it appeared likely I would receive compensation for PTSD, Dr. Hiett offered some sound advice: "Don't just take the monthly payments and get lazy. Be productive."

Though I cannot claim to have consistently followed her advice, I decided in 2017 to give it my best shot ever. I enacted a project resulting in three separate stages.

The first stage involved traveling around the country meeting with Marines and Navy Corpsmen I served with my first tour in 1966 in Lima Company, 3rd Battalion, 1st Marines. I wanted to hear their stories and learn how the war impacted their lives. Truth be told, I was curious to know if our mutual experience, beginning with the amphibious landing in the Quang Ngai Province that rainy morning in January 1966, was as big a deal for them—particularly those whose accomplishments in civilian life exceeded my own—as it was for me. To a man, it was.

After his discharge from the Navy, our platoon corpsman, Doc Reyerson, completed medical school and became a pediatrician. "I think I went into Pediatrics partly because I enjoyed helping the little kids in Vietnam," he told me. He pointed out that his email address was l311, standing for company L, 3rd Battalion, 1st Marines, 1st platoon.

I was especially excited about spending a couple of days with Gunny Gingrich at his home in Alabama. Before his promotion to gunnery sergeant landed him the assignment of company gunny, he was my platoon sergeant. I have looked up to no one as much as Gunny Gingrich. Not only was I interested in hearing his recollections of Vietnam, I was eager to hear about his service in the Korean War.

Those are two of the nine men whose stories are told in this book.

The second stage evolved naturally from the first. During my conversations with the Lima Company veterans, when I mentioned the trip I had made back to Vietnam in 1994, it was obvious that some of them were intrigued by the idea of making the journey. I contacted everyone I had met to find out who would be interested in making the journey back to Vietnam. Some declined for health reasons, two who were adamantly opposed to the idea, some immediately agreed, and some were interested, but were doubtful they could afford it. Thanks to the support of a Marine with whom I had become acquainted years earlier, the trip was made more affordable.

After visiting with our company commander in New Orleans followed by a two-day stay with Gunny Gingrich, in Alabama, I drove to Memphis to meet with a gentleman with whom I had corresponded for over a decade, Frederick W. Smith, founder and CEO of FedEx. The first thing Fred did after showing me into his office was something any Marine would have done, break out a box of photos from his time in the Nam. Like Simon, Fred had received the Silver Star medal for his leadership during a battle with an NVA battalion. And, like Simon, Fred gives all the credit to the Marines he led. After sharing stories and explaining what I was trying to accomplish with the book and the trip to Vietnam, he asked if he could help. I gratefully accepted his offer of support. Fred made it possible for five Marines, two Navy corpsmen, and two spouses, to make an extraordinary journey to Southeast Asia.

Thanks to the vast network of contacts of our guide and translator, Kyle Horst, our visit was unlike the usual battlefield tours most veteran groups are limited to. To begin with, we were not issued tourist visas. Our visas stated that we were invited guests of the government. We were accompanied by an official with the Ministry of Foreign Affairs whose presence alone opened all doors.

In the following chapters the reader will become acquainted with both the veterans with whom I reunited but were unable to make the journey, those of my comrades who made the trip, and some very interesting Vietnamese veterans we met. Three of those veterans, who served with the 21st Regiment, the NVA unit with whom we fought on Operation Utah, will be introduced in chapter seventeen. Even for Kyle and his contacts, locating surviving 21st Regiment soldiers who fought in 1966 was no easy matter. For one thing, the NVA soldiers, unlike the Marines, did not serve 13-month tours of duty. They were in it for the duration. Those who survived Utah continued to fight for another nine years. On the eleventh day of our journey we were fortunate to meet three Utah veterans from the other side who made it home alive, though one of them, a 12.7mm machine gunner who shot down four of our helicopters, returned home with a missing right arm.

HOTEL CONTINENTAL SAIGON
SINCE 1880
A member of SAIGONTOURIST
132 - 134 Dong Khoi St., District 1 - Ho Chi Minh City

CHAPTER 2

Mister Dao

Our group arrived in Ho Chi Minh City, which I shall henceforth refer to as Saigon, on separate U.S. flights around midnight on the 2nd of March 2019. The members included Bob Boland from Arizona; Gene and Kathy Cleaver from Pennsylvania; Ron Clay from Ohio; Bob Detty and his wife, Kristina Houser, from Ohio; Mike "Doc" Hastriter from Utah; Don "Doc" Reyerson, from Iowa; and me, Gary Harlan, from Missouri.

Our guide/translator was Kyle Horst from Virginia. Kyle's mastery of the Vietnamese language is nothing short of amazing. For instance, one member of the four-person film crew that accompanied us, a young lady from Hanoi, called Kyle prior to our departure to confirm scheduling details. Twice during their conversation, she asked, "You're not Vietnamese?"

Since all of us had served in I-Corps, commonly referred to as eye-corps, the northernmost area of the four corps comprising South Vietnam, no one in the group other than myself, who visited the city in 1994, had ever been to Saigon. As the person responsible for our itinerary, I booked the Hotel Continental because of its historical significance. Constructed in

1880, it was a popular gathering spot for journalists during the Vietnam War. *Time* and *Newsweek* magazines had their bureaus set up on the second floor. One of the correspondents for *Time* was H.D.S. Greenway.

There was a time when Greenway was not only a correspondent, he became one of us. In February 1968, he and two other correspondents—Alvin Webb, covering the war for *United Press International*, and Charles Mohr, for the *New York Times*—were covering the battle of Hue City. They carried Marine-issue M-16s, which they used. They were working alongside Marine Sergeant Steve Bernston, a combat correspondent.

On 19 February, during a fierce firefight, a young Marine took a round through the throat. The four correspondents carried him through a bamboo thicket to safety. Greenway, Webb, and Bernston were also wounded. The group was eventually picked up by a truck. The young Marine died. Bernston was later awarded the Bronze Star medal, but the three civilian correspondents never received recognition for their efforts at Hue.

That changed twelve years later. In 1979 Marine commandant General Robert H. Barrow heard about what took place at Hue from Peter Braestrup, who had been the *Washington Post* Vietnam correspondent. General Barrow instructed his staff to check out the story, and if it held up, do something about it. The story was verified. What was done about it was something rarely, if ever, done by the Marine Corps for civilians.

On 13 June 1980, Greenway, Webb, and Mohr, along with dozens of guests and Marine Corps officials, gathered in the garden of the commandant's home. They were each awarded a Bronze Star.

H.D.S. Greenway has reported from 96 countries, and covered conflicts in Pakistan, Afghanistan, Bangladesh, Lebanon, Israel, Iraq, Vietnam, Cambodia, Laos, and the former Yugoslavia. In 2009, in a series on war hotels, he reminisced about his days at the Hotel Continental. Greenway was in Saigon until the very end of the war, when helicopters were picking up Americans on the roof of the embassy which was surrounded by thousands of Vietnamese desperately trying to escape the communist takeover.

"It was dusk when I left," Greenway recalls. "A squall had just passed, and as my helicopter was racing away and out to sea, below I could see the rain-swept streets and the red roof of the Continental where I had lived, off and on, for eight years. The friends I made there would remain friends for life, while those who died are never far from my mind."

The hotel had been renamed the Continental Palace during the Vietnam War years. It was closed in 1976, reopened in 1986, and fully restored by 1989 under its original name, the Hotel Continental. And that was where our group gathered on the afternoon of our first full day in Vietnam.

We spent several hours in the hotel lounge conversing with a gentleman who grew up in Saigon and was twelve when the war ended in 1975. Learning that we were accompanied by a film crew, he stated his unwillingness to be on camera, but agreed to my recording our discussion. In our email exchange following the trip, he asked that he not be quoted in my book. He did not explain why, but I assured him I would respect his wishes. We reached a compromise when I suggested including our conversation in the book but identifying him as Mr. Dao.

Mike Hastriter, one of the two Navy Corpsmen in our group, was the first to ask Mr. Dao a question:

Hastriter: I was amazed this morning to see people smiling at me. I'm wondering, among the people our age is there much animosity toward Americans?

Mr. Dao: I can't speak for everyone, but I remember watching a PBS interview when they came back here for the anniversary of My Lai. They spoke to survivors of the massacre, asking them if they had hatred or animosity toward the Americans. I remember one lady saying she did not hate the American people. She hated the regime that caused all the casualties.

Gary Harlan: While she had good reason to place blame on the regime, it was not the regime that murdered all those men, women, and children. It was a group of undisciplined soldiers who chose to murder civilians.

Mr. Dao: The fact you have come over here, that other groups have come over here, I feel it's a very good experience for healing, not only for veterans, but for our people as well. During the fight you are fighting for your own side. No one would expect you to do otherwise. But afterwards, we have time to reflect. How did we deal with it? Could we have done it better? Could we have done it in a different way? But it's all in the past. So, it's more important what we are doing now, and what we're going to do in the future so mistakes will not be repeated.

I'm glad you have time to walk around the city, and particularly if you have time, sit down at an outdoor cafe and simply observe the people. I think you'll get a sense of how dynamic the local population is nowadays and how they are going after their own things. If you ask them about the past they would say, OK, the past is something we won't forget. But we have to put it aside and move on. We cannot cling to the past.

Gene Cleaver: How were the veterans treated after the war, particularly the disabled veterans?

Mr. Dao: We always revere and respect our veterans. But there was only so much we could do, so many of them went through difficult times, especially after 1975 when we were under the embargo and did not have relations with many international economies. So it was not only hard times for the veterans, but for everyone.

Gene Cleaver: So, there wasn't the money to do everything you could do for them?

Mr. Dao: We always believe we haven't done enough for them. Always.

Gary Harlan: You've spoken about the people. What is your government's present attitude toward the U.S.?

Mr. Dao: We have a comprehensive agreement in place with the U.S.

Gary Harlan: But is there a level of trust behind that agreement?

Mr. Dao: Trust is something you cannot build overnight.

Gary Harlan: Right. But sometimes I wonder if the SRV feels like a pawn between the United States and China. That's the real issue, isn't it? Whether the U.S. is genuinely concerned with the interests of the Vietnamese as opposed to just the Vietnamese vis-à-vis China?

Mr. Dao: Right there is the matter of trust. There are so many instances in history when the interests of smaller countries are sacrificed for the interests of superpowers.

Bob Detty: Is there any political unrest, any political factions in Vietnam today? And if there is, how does the government deal with that?

Mr. Dao: If you look at the history of Vietnam you will see that people asked whether a multi-party system was in the best interests of the country. We also look at different models around us. For example, you had the Philippines during the Marcus era. At that time, they had so many small parties. But whether that brought about benefit for the people is a different question. As to your question, right now the ruling party is the communist party. To outsiders it might look like one party ruling, but within the party we can discuss different options. There are different opinions on how to run things. Perhaps you remember Saigon before 1975. I was born here and grew up here. I remember we had so many small parties, so many candidates from different walks of life talking about so many things, but once in power whether they could keep their promise...so I don't know if too many parties is a good thing or not.

With us right now I feel that people are happy in their lives, doing what they are doing, and they have many opportunities. They can travel abroad. There is no problem getting a visa traveling abroad as long as the host country agrees to let you in.

Mike Hastriter: What is the official name of the government?

Mr. Dao: The Socialist Republic of Vietnam. That is the direction the country wants to move into.

Mike Hastriter: What does that mean for the people?

Mr. Dao: When you think of pure capitalism that means there would be no government interference at all. There would just be the free market mechanism. Is that right? But then you have government programs that fix certain shortcomings of the market, right? In that sense, the U.S. economy also shares some socialist elements. Just look at your social security system, your anti-trust law, your efforts to create a tax system that ensures a more egalitarian distribution of wealth. You have Medicaid and Medicare, etc., right? I feel that that has a certain socialist flavor. Capitalism has evolved to include various models of equity sharing in productive means and generated wealth. You also provide free education to children attending primary and secondary public schools, among others. All in all, it's not a complete laissez-fair economic model you have in the U.S. Another aspect is the U.S. society is so developed that it bears in itself even seeds of an idealistic communism thanks to a high level of wealth accumulation and public conscience of social responsibilities. At the community level, for example, people can take care of themselves in many ways without the government's intervention. They organize their own watch groups to ensure their community safety and security. They create their own community standards as embedded in their covenants. School pupils participate in regulating the traffic for their friends to safely cross the street when coming to and leaving school, etc. Perhaps, a simplistic manifestation of the well professed communist idea of "from each according to his ability, to each according to his need" is the way we as family members treat each other while living to-gether under the same roof.

As to your question, right after 1975 all of our health and education services were free. The textbooks were free, and people can argue that having one textbook can limit your personal development. But take mathematics. I was permitted to look for other textbooks on my own. So while textbooks were provided for free, no one forced you to follow one set of text-books. You had the opportunity to look for other sources as well. The same was true for health care. Health care was free, but there was a need for choices regarding teachers, doctors, and nurses. When the market economy was introduced in 1986 when we had a reform, people started thinking about profit, and the market started to run on capitalist principles. To my understanding, what our government means by "social-ist- oriented market economy" is that Vietnam adopts the mar-ket economy model, but the government still intervenes in the market if necessary, to ensure all societal interests are taken care of. It provides people with basic needs, while letting those with means to pay more for better products and services avail-able in the market. In health care and education, everyone gets basic services. But if you want extra services, you have to pay for it. For instance, if I want my own private room with air conditioning, I have to pay extra.

Bob Detty: When we were here, we were not in the cities. We were out in the rural areas where we saw a great deal of poverty. Have things improved for those folks?

Mr. Dao: That depends on the province. Every city in Vi-etnam is surrounded by agricultural areas. In the Mekong Delta there are three harvests a year, so they stay pretty busy all year round. One trend we see nowadays is young people leaving the agricultural areas and coming to the cities looking for a happier, easier life. Before 1975 there were 3 million peo-ple living in Saigon. Today there are 13 million.

Gary Harlan: Tomorrow we will be traveling to the Quang Ngai Province where our unit operated before moving north to Quang Nam. Besides revisiting a battlefield we fought on there, we will visit the Mac Dinh Chi School which was constructed ten years ago with funds raised by a group of Marine officers. Working with the East Meets West Foundation our group raised the money for a water purification system for the school. I was told by the East Meets West representative that the students will benefit not only while they are at school but taking home water in water bottles will provide cleaner, healthier water at home. I can't help but wonder why this is so. After all, just miles away from the school there are golf courses and fancy resorts, yet there is an unmet need for clean water in the province.

Mr. Dao: You're absolutely right. And normally, those golf courses and resorts are developed by private developers. The local government provides the land in exchange for certain fees, and they use those fees for services for people in that area. It's paradoxical. Socialism is our orientation, but along the way what we are going through right now is what we call market-oriented socialism. While we are in this period of market economy, the level of distribution is not yet even.

Gene Cleaver: I read a story about the Vietnamese missing-in-action that said there are some 300,000. It said there are not enough resources to recover them. I guess what I'm asking is, is your government making an effort to locate the remains of the missing-in-action?

Mr. Dao: They have been trying to do that from day one. Because to us, when a person dies it's like a must. You have to properly bury that person or their remains. By whatever means, you need to find that person and properly bury them. Otherwise, we believe their soul will not go to heaven. They will be a wandering soul among us. So, it's not only a duty, but spiritually it's something we try our best to do. But it's not easy because you know during the war when you fight in the jungles or far from roads when you withdraw it's a long time before you come back. When you do come back the place may not even look the same. You may not even recognize exactly where you fought. I feel like we now have the cooperation of the Americans in locating the remains of our missing soldiers. Those who are searching for the remains of American service-men have also devoted their resources to assisting in locating remains of missing Vietnamese. Also, American veterans have turned over documents and relics they kept. For us it's a sa-cred thing we have to do. Family members continue to search for the remains of their lost loved ones. But it's not easy.

Gary Harlan: I've become friends with one of those veter-ans who turned over a relic. His name is Bob Frazure. You might have read the story of how he picked up the diary of a PAVN soldier, Vu Dinh Doan. Doan's son, whose name is Son, spent years traveling to Quang Ngai Province from the family home outside of Hanoi looking for the remains of his father, and was finally successful. Later, when the diary was turned over by Frazure, an effort was made to locate the family. I saw this story on PBS, of how Kyle Horst and his contacts were able to locate Doan's family in the Hai Duong Province. I con-tacted Kyle and asked him to be our guide and translator for this trip. In a week or so Kyle will take us to the cemetery where Doan's remains are buried, and we will meet Son.

Kathleen Cleaver: Has that concern been carried over to the younger generations? Do they share that same spiritual be-lief about say, finding the remains of their grandfather?

Mr. Dao: It's still a debatable matter nowadays because on the one hand, if kids were raised in a traditional family then pretty much the traditions would be passed on. But if you live in a nuclear family living far away and are busy with your work, then it's difficult for the children to follow the tradi-tions. But luckily, we Vietnamese all follow the ancestral wor-ship so no matter what, you still have to have a little alter in your home. But with the children moving around for employment, things might be different in future generations. There are different philosophies, but I'm not used to it yet.

By the way, do you speak of your experience in Vietnam with your kids and grandkids?

Ron Clay: Not so much. They don't want to hear it. I have a 12-year-old son, Tommy Lee, and sometimes we drive to Bob's [Bob Detty] and have breakfast together. And of course, we share memories of Vietnam—do you remember this, do you remember that? And Tommy Lee is sitting there, and he'll say, "Dad! How did you do that!" I'd rather not talk to him about it, but maybe when he gets older.

Doc Reyerson: I try to teach my daughters about discipline, and I tell them about things that happened to me in the service relating to discipline, and one of my daughters says under her breath, "Oh brother! Not another one!" So, I quit talking.

Gary Harlan: I married this lady in '84. When we began living together in '82 she had a 5-year-old son and a 13-year-old daughter. One day the boy hurt his eye in some way and we're cleaning it in the bathroom together and I say, "You really have to be careful. I almost lost my right eye once. He asked me how, and I said it was in the war, that a piece of metal broke my glasses and another piece was still in my cheek. I soon realized he knew absolutely nothing about the Vietnam War or even war in general. He asked me, "Were you the good guys or the bad guys?" I was really taken aback. I said, "We thought we were the good guys." His sister, who was in the other room, yelled, "You *were* the good guys!" She didn't know much about the war either, but I appreciated her saying that.

Kyle Horst: We just jumped into the wrong swimming pool at the wrong time.

Ron Clay: That's what I see now.

Kyle Horst: The ethnic Vietnamese had been marching down the southern coast of Indochina, depending on how north you are, for 450 years taking over the local governments, the local populations, violently setting up a new government, and were killing the locals, exiling the locals, and assimilating the locals. They had 400 years of practice. And we're going to jump in for ten years and do what? That's crazy. That's just crazy.

Gary Harlan: Yeah, for us it was like a movie that just started. You're pretending it just started when it had been going on forever.

Kyle Horst: One thing people don't realize is many places where there was major fighting, especially in central Vietnam, especially in the mountains, those were places no ethnic Vietnamese had never stepped foot until they came to fight the Americans. It was foreign territory to us and foreign territory to them.

Doc Reyerson: In the textbooks do they assign blame more to the French or the Americans?

Mr. Dao: Not so much blame, but there is still confusion as to why the Americans got involved, why the war happened.

Gary Harlan: Especially given the fact that the Vietnamese were allies of the Americans in World War Two. The group of Americans were called the Deer Team and they worked with Ho Chi Minh and the Viet Minh against the Japanese. Those guys were also confused as to why America got involved after the French were defeated.

Mr. Dao: I think in America there is a documentary movie, they call it something to the effect what could have been different if President Truman had read and accepted the proposal from Ho Chi Minh to recognize Vietnam's independence.

Gary Harlan: You saw that documentary?

Mr. Dao: Yes, I did. They interviewed this man...

Gary Harlan: Archimedes Patti?

Mr. Dao: Yes. That's right. He was with the former organization of the CIA.

Gary Harlan: The OSS.

Mr. Dao: Right.

Gary Harlan: I think the documentary was titled, "Was an Opportunity Missed." One of the men featured in the film was Henry Prunier who died a year after the documentary was shot. He was the youngest member of the Deer Team. Toward the end of his life he became close friends with Simon Gregory, our executive officer when we landed in Vietnam, and then became our company commander.

Mr. Dao: It's interesting to ask what could have happened. But the more important question is what can we do now? This is what happened before. How can we do things better? It goes back to what you mentioned before, trust. Always the centerpiece of any relationship.

I remember once when we had a big meeting between American veterans and Vietnamese veterans together with survivors of American bombing and Agent Orange victims. It was a big meeting in a big hall at the Reunification Palace chaired by our vice president. At one point it was so moving that veterans from both sides, they cried. And they hugged each other like brothers. We have a saying here that sometimes you become best friends with your own enemy on the battlefield. Because through the fight you know the person, you appreciate the person.

Gary Harlan: Yes! That was exactly the thought I had when I met those veterans in Quang Nam in 1994. Who knew what each of us had gone through better than the other? Not their families back home. Not our families back home. We discovered the real essence of the other on a day-to-day basis.

Mr. Dao: It was very moving to me and at some point, I could not hold back my tears too, even though I was translating at the time for the kids and the veterans.

It's really good that you've all come back to see how the country has changed, maybe for the better, maybe for the worse.

Gary Harlan: I've read about veterans who have returned and were disappointed that it wasn't the same place they remembered. I can't relate to that. I'm happy to learn that things have changed for the better.

Mr. Dao: Sometimes you have to step back and see what's going on compared to the past. Actually, we have made big strides, for the society, for the economy, in everything. All along the canal, from District One to District Eight you see businesses thriving.

Some of you have come back for the first time, right?

Gary Harlan: All of us except me.

Mr. Dao: So, what do you think about our country, our economy compared to what you had in mind before you came back?

Bob Detty: We were never in Saigon. We were up north operating in the boonies.

Gary Harlan: My wife and I were watching this movie the other night. It wasn't a war movie, but one of the characters said, "The further out you go the more intense it gets, and you have to figure out what's going on." I told my wife, "That sounds like the Nam. That's how it was for us."

Mr. Dao: During the war were you ever in a situation that you couldn't control at all?

Gary Harlan: That was pretty much life as we knew it.

Mr. Dao: So you operated by instinct?

Gary Harlan: Yes, instinct and training.

Mr. Dao: By the way, to change the topic, I'd like to ask you, nowadays I hear about a lot of people—particularly Democrats—who do not like President Trump. But when he's abroad, particularly in certain countries, he's really well admired because of his shrewdness in negotiations and the way he looks at things. He may seem unpredictable, but to me personally, he is a master of the game.

Ron Clay: A lot of people disagree with me, but that's how I see him.

Mr. Dao: A master of the game in negotiations and in hiding his ace cards until the last minute. In terms of political maneuvering in international arenas, I don't know what the phrase is for this, but it seems like he's aiming at one target, but actually he's aiming at the other target. Like you make a camouflage. For example, what happened with his meeting with Chairman Kim from North Korea. Some people said he walked away with no deal, but actually he was very successful. He achieved what he really wanted.

Gary Harlan: Which was?

Mr. Dao: Which was to get them to stop testing rockets long enough for him to concentrate his efforts on China. The trade war is only part of it. The overall panorama is larger, and in order to focus on it he had to get rid of the distractions like North Korea. If you go back and look at past history, whenever the U.S. had an issue with China, North Korea would conduct a rocket or nuclear test that would create a distraction. I don't know why, but it seems that back in the U.S. President Trump is not liked in many parts.

Gene Cleaver: Well, there's more than that aspect, of what to like or not like. Relative to Vietnam, and relative to your aspect, that might be good, and I don't disagree with that. I don't disagree with what you're saying about Korea, or China, or Vietnam. But I do disagree with other things. You know, a president or a person is not judged by only one thing. So, I can have my opinions about Trump when I think he's doing something wrong in other areas.

Mr. Dao: You can probably guess why we in Vietnam like President Trump. First and foremost is the China factor. China has invaded us and is occupying our islands in the East Sea, commonly known as the South China Sea. They are even building artificial islands over there, to name but a few. We treasure our independence and sovereignty. And that exactly was what President Trump appeared to espouse in his remarks at the 2017 APEC Summit in Danang. Living next door to a giant neighbor who has threatened and encroached on our sovereignty on many occasions, we appreciate anyone who stands up against China's chauvinism and expansionism.

Kyle Horst: I just want to say this. I've lived and worked in D.C. for 37 years. Regardless of what anyone says, we have a one-party system. I am a political atheist. I didn't vote for Trump. I don't like him. But he's the first president in decades to have a rational policy on China. The first president. And who is the main beneficiary of his rational policy outside U.S. borders? Vietnam.

Mr. Dao: All of Southeast Asia.

Kyle Horst: All of Southeast Asia generally, but Vietnam specifically because Vietnam faces a threat from China. Maritime territory. And also derives benefits from the exodus of manufacturing and investment operations from China into Vietnam.

What can you say? My mom is a JFK Democrat who is crazy against Trump.

Gary Harlan: Yeah, there are people who wake up in the morning whose first thought is, God, I hate Trump!

Kyle Horst: My mom is kind of like that. My little brother, who is not a stupid guy at all, and my father, who is also very intelligent, they are irrational screamers for Trump. Fox News is a steady drip.

Mr. Dao: I want to say one thing. I absolutely agree with you, Gene, that a president might have some policies that many agree with while others do not. That's always expected. But I feel like I have to be cautious when I see the media coverage. Nowadays whenever I turn on CNN, which is available here in Vietnam, it's all Trump-bashing. I never see anything good about Trump on CNN at all. Then they lose credibility to me. Then you have Fox News. It's all about Trump-praising. Then it's not credible either.

Gene Cleaver: I completely agree. I think the media has become a prime mover of hate in our country. People watch one or the other and we become more and more divided.

Mr. Dao: Take immigration, for example. I don't oppose migrants. But I expect them to enter my country legally. Which country would not? I would not want Vietnam to be in-fluxed by illegal immigrants.

Gene Cleaver: But you're not.

Mr. Dao: We have been though.

Kyle Horst: That's right. In the 70's and early 80's when Cambodia was collapsing, tens of thousands of Cambodians were migrating to Vietnam. Vietnam never got the credit they deserved for how they handled that.

Getting back to Trump, he's not doing this on his own. He has some good advisers. Some of these guys, like Lighthizer and Navarro, had been out in the wilderness for twenty-plus years, writing their books. They wrote this Master thesis-type paper showing how China has completely attacked, eroded, undercut, stolen all the American high-tech products over the past twenty years. This thing could have been published in 1998 or 2003 or 2008. It wasn't until 2018 that these guys who had all the facts were given a place at the table by President Trump. They had been totally sidelined by Obama who would rely on his 38-year-old Ph.D. pals. Part of Trump's genius is getting out of the way and letting the shooters do the shooting.

I confess I'm not proud to tell this story, but in a moment of temporary emotional weakness I considered registering to vote for Trump. It was the day he held a press conference with Kathleen Willey, Juanita Broaddrick, and Paula Jones. We watched these women being slagged, abused, silenced, humiliated by the press under Hillary's watch for decades. Now there's Me-too, right? Yet these women have never been rehabilitated by the press.

Mr. Dao: Before I leave, I would like to say it's been a pleasure meeting all of you.

Gary Harlan: On behalf of all of us, thank you sir for sharing your afternoon with us. It has been most informative.

Mister Dao

Lima 3/1 Officers staff in Okinawa. L to r: Lt. Steve Crowley, Lt. Gene Cleaver, Lt. Simon Gregory, Captain James Sehulster, Lt. Dan Walsh, Lt. Ben DeLaRosa.

CHAPTER 3

Lima 3/1

No one would have a clue the home of Jim and Gail Sehulster, located in the university area of uptown New Orleans, was once devastated by disaster. Gail had a brass plate attached to the wall just beyond the front door with an inscription reading, *August 29, 2005*. That was the day Hurricane Katrina struck. Gail positioned the plate at the highest level of the flooding, three feet above the floor. With the house built three feet from ground level, there was over six feet of flooding in the street.

The storm displaced over a million people in the Gulf Coast region. The Sehulsters refusal to leave, their determination to return their lives and their property back to normal, was sparked by two factors: the first of which was their two grown daughters would be coming home for Thanksgiving, just ninety days after the disaster; the second was that Jim and Gail Sehulster were both Marines. Quitting was not an option.

In 1963 Captain Sehulster's path as an infantry officer was interrupted when he was assigned duty on the USS Skagit in the capacity of Marine cargo officer. After two years at sea, Jim returned to what he regarded as the "real" Marine Corps.

"I came back to the States in April 1965. Waved my Overseas Control Date to get back into the Marine Corps and was accepted and went up to Camp Pendleton where I was assigned the commanding officer of Lima Company, 3rd Battalion 1st Marines which was just forming up."

Historically, the 3rd Battalion, 1st Marine Regiment was activated on 1 March 1941 and assigned to the First Marine Division. The battalion distinguished itself in numerous WWII campaigns including Guadalcanal, Peleliu, and Okinawa. During the Korean War, under the regimental command of the legendary Chesty Puller, they fought in the Battle of Inchon and the Battle of the Chosin Reservoir.

The formation of Lima 3/1 in the spring of 1965 is to be understood in the context of the "transplacement" system. This was basically a thirteen-month rotation cycle of infantry battalions between the West Coast and the Western Pacific (WESTPAC). The system ended that September. From then on, Marines were rotated on an individual basis. Thus 3/1 was one of the last transplacement battalions deployed as a fully staffed unit. Before that was possible, however, they had to await the arrival of the 1st Battalion, 9th Marines which would then be re-designated 3/1. The members of 1/9 were given a choice: remain in the States for a year with a new outfit or waive their Overseas Control Date and join 3/1 for another overseas tour.

"The remnants of old 1/9," recalls Sehulster, "took up the banner of 3/1. We were the last battalion to participate in what was called *lock-on*, where you form as a unit with all deployable people, go through a series of training and deploy as a unit. I would guess that half of 1/9 waved their overseas control date to stay with the newly formed battalion. So, we had a bunch of folks who had been together before and folks like myself who joined it to flesh it out."

Once formed, the battalion spent that spring and most of the summer training at Camp Pendleton. "The training," Sehulster told me, "was absolutely geared to the fact we would be deployed to Vietnam." I informed him that more than one of the original Lima Company Marines attributed our level of combat proficiency to his diligence and hard work during the training period.

"I feel very proud to have formed that company at Camp Pendleton. I was wise enough to recognize I was not there to make friends. I was there to train people to survive in an environment that was soon going to be very damned hostile. My attitude was my training made me better than my counterpart across the line. I was better than him. I would train my people to be better than his, and face to face we'd win. To this day I think that's exactly what we did."

The schedule was finally determined. In August of '65 3/1 mounted out and sailed to Okinawa. "We were at Camp Schwab," said Sehulster, "which was the northernmost full-sized camp on the island. Each of the companies was assigned a particular type of training it would be responsible for to give to the rest of the battalion. Lima Company was picked to do jungle training, and we went up to what is referred to as the northern training area, which is as far north on the island as you can get. To some degree it replicated what we would see when we got to Vietnam, lots of triple canopy and lots of undergrowth. We went through training with folks who had come back from Vietnam. Once we were trained, Lima trained the rest of the battalion on jungle warfare and all associated tactics. They would cycle platoons through at a time."

Among those who trained under Sehulster was me. I joined the unit at Camp Schwab prior to our training at the northern training area (NTA). From my point of view, the night patrols at NTA were more treacherous than the Vietnamese jungles. Granted, no one was trying to kill us in Okinawa, but there were Marines who were badly injured falling off cliffs due to the inability to see where they were going.

Lima 3/1 fought in the Vietnam War from 1966 to 1971 operating from Chu Lai up to the DMZ. Jim Sehulster was its first commanding officer when the unit boarded the USS Paul

Revere in Okinawa and sailed to the Philippines where we made a practice landing on Mindanao, one of the Philippine islands. On 28 January 1966 Lima Company was part of the Marine Corps' largest amphibious landing since Inchon, Korea. It was called Operation Double Eagle, a multi-battalion operation in Southern Quang Ngai Province that lasted 21 days.

Captain Sehulster soon discovered our landing was no secret.

"The United States always prides itself on its operational security. There was a North Vietnamese radio broadcaster by the name of Hanoi Hannah, much like Tokyo Rose during the Second World War. The code name for the operation we were going on was Double Eagle. The night before we landed Hanoi Hannah came on the radio and welcomed 3/1 and played *Under the Double Eagle*, an old Texas cowboy song."

Lima Company was part of Task Force Delta, consisting of 5,000+ Marines under the command of Brigadier General Jonas Platt. General Platt's intelligence section had estimated the enemy strength to be 6,000 regulars reinforced by another 600 guerillas.

Task Force Delta's operating area was 500 square miles, the center of which was located 20 miles south of Quang Ngai City and 10 miles west of Duc pho. The site selected for the landing was Red Beach, a thousand meters of flat sand located three and a half miles northeast of Duc Pho. General Platt had three battalion landing teams under his command: BLTs 2/3, 3/1, and 2/4.

D-Day, 28 January, was a dismal day. Light rain was falling, and visibility was poor as Lima Company and the rest of BLT 3/1 landed at 0700.

Reporting on Operation Double Eagle for *Leatherneck Magazine*, Sergeant Bob Bowen wrote:

"The rain continued to fall throughout the day and by nightfall the men were soaked to the skin. They dug their foxholes in the sandy ground and covered themselves with ponchos. The troops awoke to find the rain still falling. The water was ankle deep in the foxholes and everyone was miserable. The cold, too, added to their discomfort."

No offense to the *Leatherneck* reporter, but he had the luxury, such as it was, of hunkering down in a foxhole at night while we grunts, after humping miles during the day, carrying extra rockets, mortars, and machine gun ammo for the guys in weapons platoon, were sent out on either night patrols or all-night ambushes. There were times when I was so exhausted that when the patrol halted momentarily, I fell asleep standing up, waking up before hitting the ground.

"I can't think of a time we came back to a base camp for ages," Sehulster recalls. "We struck out and we just kept moving. There were no formed North Vietnamese Army units at that time. All we were confronting was the Viet Cong."

Twenty-one days after D-Day Lima Company got back aboard the USS *Paul Revere*. Double Eagle was over. Task Force Delta listed 312 Viet Cong killed, and 19 captured. The Marines confiscated 20 tons of rice, 6 tons of salt, and 4 tons of miscellaneous supplies including barley, copra, corn, concrete, and fertilizer. In addition, 18 weapons and 868 rounds of ammunition were captured. The cost of all this was 24 Marines killed and 156 wounded.

One of the 24 Marines was killed on 13 February. He was Sergeant James Thompson, first squad leader of Lima Company's first platoon.

Lima Company was not aboard ship for long. Two days after the completion of Double Eagle, Double Eagle II commenced south of Chu Lai. The second phase was moved north of Chu Lai. Task Force Delta remained intact except for 2/4 being replaced by 2/7.

The operating area for Double Eagle II was the same area in which Lieutenant Colonel Leon Utter's 2nd Battalion, 7th Marines had conducted Operation Harvest Moon two months earlier. As it was in Double Eagle, the Marines operated in the monsoon season. It rained every day. Viet Cong propaganda held that the Americans were soft and were not up to the task of fighting in the rain and the mud. They were proved mistaken. The USMC-ARVN operation accounted for 407 enemy killed, 33 captured. Marine casualties were 45 killed and 218 wounded. ARVN losses were 90 killed, 91 missing, and 141 wounded.

It was apparent early on in Double Eagle II that the VC were considerably less willing to engage the Marines than they had been in December. By the end of the second phase of Double Eagle, there was no sign of the principal target, the 1st VC Regiment. We only confronted isolated guerrilla bands. In the end, elements of the four Marine battalions making up Task Force Delta accounted for 125 enemy dead and 15 captured. Marine losses were 6 killed and 136 wounded.

Even though the desired results were not achieved in Double Eagle I and II, General Platt believed it was a success. He argued that the people residing in the Que Son Valley and southern Quang Ngai Province learned that it was not "the VC private backyard because U.S. Marines trampled over a huge area with little or no opposition."

General Victor "Brute" Krulak, however, saw it much differently. According to the Brute, the lessons of the Double Eagle operations were mostly negative. First of all, he argued, the operations failed primarily because the VC and NVA had been forewarned. Given Captain Sehulster's comment about Hanoi Hannah greeting 3/1 the night before the landing, that is fairly obvious. And secondly, in direct opposition to Platt's contention that the Marines showed the people that their areas were not the "VC's "private backyard," because they could come in trample all over a huge area, Krulak contended that both operations taught the people that the Marines "would come in, comb the area, and disappear; whereupon the VC would resurface and resume control." Whether they chose to fight or not to fight on any given day, it was, after all, their backyard.

Among the Lima Company casualties, one was particularly significant—namely, its company commander, Captain Sehulster. It was not inflicted by the enemy, but rather as a result of attacking the enemy. He explains what happened that day:

"We were going through this hamlet and it appeared that things had quieted down. Once it appeared it quieted, the corpsmen and the Marines went around to check the villagers to see if anyone was hurt. We stayed there several hours to see what we could do to assist the people. Our route of egress was across a river. When we started, the battalion was going back, Lima Company was to be the last company to go and the battalion would retrograde through us. Between the time we spent in the hamlet the river was ankle deep when the battalion crossed it, and when we were ready to cross, it was hip-deep, very tidally influenced.

"When I got most of the company across the river, the hamlet [where we had just spent a couple of hours trying to help the people] opened up on us big-time. So, I went forward to the edge of the river with my radio operator and forward observer and called for artillery. The marking rounds were white phosphorous which left a white plume so you could identify where the rounds hit, and the forward observer could adjust from there. We got three of those rounds and got no response. So, we maneuvered around and got closer and called for another round to be fired. It hit and it blew all the others that were in there. So, this massive white phosphorous cloud came drifting back, and that's what blew over me and got in my eyes. I didn't realize at the time I was in trouble. Made it back to the area we decided we were going to set up the entire battalion in tents, and my eyes and face blew up like a balloon. I couldn't open my eyes, and there was great fear as to whether I was ever going to see. I went to Da Nang, then to the hospital at Subic Bay. I was there a couple of days then flown to Yokosuka where I recovered. I returned to the company on my birthday, April 16th. I took the company over again and kept it until May."

From Lima Company Sehulster was sent to the battalion S-3. His last assignment in Vietnam was serving as aid to General Fields, commanding officer of the 1st Marine Division.

In 1982 Colonel Sehulster received an intense education in international politics when he was sent to Beirut where he served as senior military adviser to Ambassador Philip Habib. At their first meeting Habib explained that his goal was to evacuate the PLO and Syrians from West Bank before the Israelis or the Christians attacked them, which, Habib said, would inevitable result in a bloodbath resulting in the deaths of women, children, and bystanders.

Before saying good-bye to the Sehulsters I asked Jim what he considered the highlight of his 33-year career in the Marine Corps. I assumed it would be Beirut, but I was wrong.

"Lima 3/1 was definitely the highlight of those thirty-three years. When you are that intimately close to people and responsible for their well-being, I don't think anybody, certainly no Marine, takes that position lightly. The impact it made on my life, the friends I've made, the friends I've lost...it changes you, no question about it."

Lima Company's Executive Officer, Lieutenant Simon Gregory, took over command of Lima Company when Captain Sehulster was injured.

It was gratifying to return to the beach for some rest, but that did not last more than a couple of days when we were told to saddle up for another operation, one that would be code-named, Operation Utah.

One month after Simon married Nancy, he left for Vietnam.

CHAPTER 4

Lieutenant Simon Gregory

Holden, Massachusetts

"I wish I could have done more to prevent the loss of 10 good men and the wounding of 20 others."
Simon Gregory, 2018

In 2016 I read an article titled, "Do you still think about Vietnam?" in which the author wrote:

"A couple of years ago someone asked me if I still thought about Vietnam. I nearly laughed in their face. How do you stop thinking about it? Every day for the past forty years, I wake up with it – I go to bed with it."

This is my own response:

Yeah, I think about it. I can't stop thinking about it. I never will. But I've also learned to live with it. I'm comfortable with the memories. I've learned to stop trying to forget and learned instead to embrace it.

Considering the fact I am 74 years-old and have for the past 22 years managed to stay married to one woman, spend my days without self-medicating, I have learned to live with it. Yet for me, *it* is a complicated matter. When people think about America's involvement in Vietnam, they don't think about the early years, 1965 to 1966, when most folks assumed the government must have had a valid reason for sending boys off to die in Southeast Asia. They think of the latter years, from the Tet Offensive of 1968 to the end, when we pulled out the troops, letting the South Vietnamese handle the war on their own. They think of mass demonstrations, the Mai Lai Massacre, Walter Cronkite telling Americans that the best we could hope for is a stalemate.

I mention this in order to remind the reader that this is the story of a company of Marines who fought in the early days of the war, years before it would even occur to someone to point out that no one wants to be the last American to die in Vietnam.

On 3 March 1966 Lieutenant Simon Gregory became Lima Company Commander when Captain James Sehulster had to be medically evacuated due to damage to his eyes from a white phosphorous explosion.

Simon was born in Utica, New York to blue collar parents on 30 July 1941. They lived in a small, declining textile factory town, Chadwicks, New York until the family moved to South Hadley, Massachusetts when Simon was 11. His mother passed away when he was 8 which, he says, gave rise to his sense of independence and self-sufficiency in early life. His grandparents were major influences:

"My grandparents provided examples of how to live a life of integrity, compassion, commitment and patriotism. Their immigrant backgrounds enriched my view of humanity. My Polish born grandfather, Edward, instilled a political sense based on being an American. Edward never referred to himself as Polish, always an American."

Simon graduated from South Hadley High School in 1958 where he started to realize his budding leadership potential and was elected co-captain of the football team. He was well-respected and always known for treating everyone with respect and dignity. He championed the underdog at every juncture. After high school Simon went to UMASS, Amherst and graduated with a BS degree in 1962.

"ROTC was mandatory in those days and each man had to take two years of instruction. I was denied enrolling for the final two years and was told I'd never be officer material. My refined recalcitrance and highly polished sarcasm certainly had something to do with my rejection. Still, I wanted to serve my country as an Air Force pilot, but because I had received a concussion in my last high school football game was denied acceptance to the program in my senior year even though I had passed all the tests."

A friend, Doug Devries had gone to Marine OCS via the Platoon Leadership Course and challenged Simon to join the USMC--"if he had the balls."

"I visited the Marine recruiter on campus and said I wanted to join the Corps. The captain recruiter replied, "Who gives a shit?" Of course, I went forward to join, but had to undergo medical tests to prove my concussion would not be a deterrent to final acceptance."

Simon attended OCS at Quantico in March 1963 as a member of the 33rd Officer Candidate Course. Drill instructor Staff Sergeant John Parton started the process that would mold him into being a good Marine.

"I understood early on how important it was to accept mentoring from enlisted men."

Simon was commissioned a second lieutenant in May and graduated from The Basic School in November 1963 as an infantry officer. Certain he had "found his position in life," Simon's first assignment was with 3rd Battalion 5th Marines at Camp Pendleton.

"I was not with 3/5 for long. With the transplacement system, 3/5 became the 1st Battalion 9th Marines. I served a Far East tour with 1/9. I was a platoon commander with Charlie Company. My platoon sergeant was Staff Sergeant Joe Louis Taylor, a black man who further mentored me and helped my understanding of racism. I learned well, and eventually became a lifetime member of the NAACP."

"I returned to the Far East with my new outfit. 1/9 had become the 3rd Battalion 1st Marines. Since I had recently returned from a tour in the Far East, I had to agree to waive my 6 months minimum turnaround time in order to join the fun. Best decision I ever made because when I entered combat, I was with men I had trained with for nearly two years. A number of us signed waivers, including Sergeant Major B.C. Belvin, Jr. who had held the top enlisted billet with 3/5, 1/9, and 3/1. He enlisted in the Corps in 1942. Made the landings at Peleliu and Okinawa, was a platoon sergeant with the 5th Marines in Korea."

I mentioned that there were a number of Korean War vets in 3/1 when we landed, including Gunny Gingrich who was my platoon sergeant before his promotion to gunnery sergeant and becoming the company gunny. Gingrich served with the 5th Marines in Korea.

"He saved my life once. After I left Lima Company and went to S-2 I recommended Gunny Gingrich for the Meritorious Service Award. No one deserved it more. But back to the formation of 3/1, I was serving as the Lima Company Executive Officer when we shipped off to Okinawa where we received some valuable training all geared toward our final destination. Captain James Sehulster was the Lima Company CO. I was fortunate to have had two Company Commanders that prepared us for what was to come. The other was Captain Dan Fillmore when I was with 1/9. When we hit the beach on 28 January 1966, we were prepared."

What I wanted to get from Simon was his recollections of that first month in Vietnam, what comes to mind when he reflects on our stepping ashore for the first time in an environment unlike anything any of us had ever experienced.

"Let's face it. We were young. We had no real history behind us as Marines. We were creating it. We got history from our other Marines, but we didn't have a lot of life experience. As your life experience increases your ability to refine judgment is a lot better."

As I think about it now, I am struck by the profound implications of those two sentences he had uttered: we had no history behind us as Marines. We were creating it. For most of us, it could be said that on that day in January three decades ago, we didn't have much history behind us as people. Period. Yes, the Marine Corps training prepared us to fight. Collectively, we were prepared to a create a history, our contribution to the opening chapter of the combat history of the U.S. Marines in Vietnam. Some of us would sacrifice our lives in the process.

Our first KIA was Sergeant Thompson. It was the final day of Operation Double Eagle. For seventeen days the battalion had been operating in the mountains west of Duc Pho near the Ho Chi Minh Trail. We had covered hundreds of miles by foot. Our final objective before returning to the beach near our landing was to make a "surprise" entry into Duc Pho. Simon reminded me that no one was surprised.

"By the time we got to Duc Pho it was obvious everybody had heard about it because the civilians were leaving. Inside Duc Pho was chaos. That's where I met the brown cow which took me out of the war for a few minutes. I was the first officer to enter Duc Pho that morning. I was trying to figure out what to do because there were so many people and animals in the streets trying to go west while we were going east that the whole place was congested. The sun wasn't even up yet, but the word had gotten out. And frankly, Duc Pho was really just a garrison. It wasn't a combat outpost that I saw. The South

Vietnamese there were just garrison soldiers who didn't even patrol the surrounding area.

"So I met the brown cow. I'm standing there trying to get things moving when I feel something lick my hand. It was this little cute brown cow. She looks up at me with those big brown eyes and took me out of the war for a moment. It can't be too bad, you know. So then everybody gets through Duc Pho. We're going back to Red Beach where we'd started, and we have to cross that river we'd crossed the first day or two. And as soon as we got out, which always happened, we came under fire. Duc Pho was behind us 200 meters. All these South Vietnamese garrison soldiers were there, but the Viet Cong controlled the outskirts completely. That's when we started getting casualties. Terry O'Hara got shot in the eye. He was a real good guy. He had to push his eye back into the socket.

"I spotted a Viet Cong with a rifle. I tried to tell a M-60 machine gunner about it, but he couldn't pick it up. It was like bird watching. You know the spot where there's a bird in the bushes, but another person can't see it. So I manned the M-60 with a tripod and fired a couple of bursts and nothing happens, and then he runs out. Then I just watched the tracers eat him up. It blew him off the dike. I didn't go check him out because we were still under fire—and he was gone. It still haunts me. Was it a rifle or a farm tool?

"Then things got worse because we had to cross another rice paddy complex. That's when there were no dikes left to walk on. They were covered with water. Sergeant Thompson was with the 1st platoon up front. He got shot and me and a couple other men jumped in and pulled him out. The Corpsman came up. There was hardly any blood so we couldn't figure out where he'd been hit. Doc Reyerson was trying to find his wound, and we finally saw he'd been shot in the eye. I'd guess it was a low-speed round, probably a stolen 30 caliber carbine. It wasn't a high caliber round like a 7.62 or anything like that. It circulated around inside his skull and never came out. It destroyed his brain. There was no exit wound. But I was kneeling down next to him and that's when he died."

Sergeant James Thompson led the 3rd squad of my platoon. The Thompsons were a black family from Dillon, South Carolina who moved to Trenton, New Jersey when James was a boy. James is buried in Dillon.

"We're still coming under fire from these hummocks with Casuarina trees on them two-hundred meters away. With the elevation and all it's really hard to tell where people are shooting at you from. We had 60mm mortars which we were using against the target. In addition to that we radioed the Fire Coordination Center which is supposed to be responsible for all the fire you can use—4.2-inch mortars, artillery, everything we had. FSCC we called it. They were supposed to be coordinating all that. I gave them the coordinates and told them we needed to strike at these coordinates--where the fire was coming from that killed Sergeant Thompson. Anyway, we're still coming under fire, and we have to go. It's taking the FSCC so long that by the time they approved the mission, we were on the target. This was probably the first time they had to go through this coordination requirement on Double Eagle. Because before this, we're up in the jungle all the time, up at the feeder trails of the Ho Chi Minh Trail. So, by the time we realized we needed a strike it took them so long it was too late. In the meantime, we had to cross that rice paddy. I can remember bullets going by snipping off the tops of the rice."

"Yeah, I've been there," I said.

"Right. I couldn't get any lower or I'd be breathing under water with a straw. Finally, we reached the Song Tra Cau River which we have to cross. Most of the battalion is on the eastern side of the river when one of the Marines has a bullet zip through the side of his helmet. The bullet circles around his helmet between the steel and the webbing. The helmet collapsed on his head, but he didn't get hurt.

"So, the remainder of battalion has to cross the river to get back to the beach to end the first phase of Double Eagle. And the fire is getting heavier. It's getting even more intense for me because I'm down to the last squad in the company, and I'm the last officer there. That's when we came under a lot more fire. So we called in for air strikes. We had already called in 155mm artillery. But it was so fouled up, we were so close to the target that they're shooting at me and my men—this is our friendly artillery and mortars. My back was to the river and rounds were hitting behind me. I said, Hey! You've got to stop this shit. The VC are about 100 to 200 meters to the west of me. I called that off until they figured out how accurate they could be.

"And then I'm told about two F-4 Phantom jets from VMFA-323 that were on station out of Da Nang. They came down and I could talk to the pilot. We used smoke grenades to mark the target. It turned out to be incredibly accurate. We went under fire for fifteen minutes or more, and I remember talking to the pilot and he told me to mark the target again with a smoke grenade. Then he came in. He did one strafing run as did his partner. Then he came back. I'm crouched behind this berm alongside the river. Actually, I'm standing behind it so I can see what's going on. So, I'm watching him come in. He's got one of those Snake Eye bombs which you can drop right under your airplane, and it will float straight down nose first with enough drag to prevent the airplane from being damaged by shrapnel. The fins act as sort of a parachute. It came right down on the target we had marked. Got 'em, just like that.

"It gets even better. Being a pilot and happy that he did what he did, he and his buddy fly north, just out of sight up the river. Then they came back down the river so low their exhausts created rooster tails. Then they shoot straight up and do barrel rolls. It was like watching an air show, and they come down and do it again. His call sign was Big Daddy. I tried for years to find out who Big Daddy was but had no luck. I could hear the troops cheering.

"So that was it. We crossed the river, made it back to the beach and waited for the LSTs to pick us up the next morning. Then we went back to Chu Lai for a very short period and then commenced Double Eagle II. We went up to Tam Ky, and the same thing happens. We get out of Tam Ky maybe a few hundred yards and come under fire. Every time it was the same scenario. The lack of command and controlled communication, and the reluctance of the South Vietnamese that we're supposedly dealing with was profound. They just didn't want to participate in our kind of activity even though they were in some cases attached to us or under our command. Army garrison town. Identical circumstances. We leave Tam Ky and a few hundred yards west we come under fire. It showed me that the Viet Cong ran the countryside, and that this South Vietnamese Army had no clue what was going on 300 yards away. Or they didn't want to know about it.

"There was another operation—you were on it—when we went to Snaggletooth [so named because of the shape of the island]. The entire company left Snaggletooth and went back to Chu Lai. And a week or so later we sent back to Snaggletooth for a surprise operation. You remember that?"

"Yes, I do."

"Well, that's how I got involved with Gunnery Sergeant Gingrich saving my life. Early in the morning the company had to march an hour or two to meet up with this South Vietnamese unit. It was also in the Chu Lai enclave somewhere. One of those pie slices belonged to the South Vietnamese Army units, and we get up there—you and the whole company—we get up there before sunrise. We get to the camp of this colonel who's supposed to be in charge of this battalion of South Vietnamese, and it was like summertime camping. The officers are all hanging around washing up. We're all fully combat loaded with grenades and everything, just like we always were, and these guys are all out there like, "What's happening?"

"Just kickin' back," I offered.

"(Laughing) Yeah, just kickin' back. Some of them are still laying on their hammocks between palm trees. So it was my job to talk to this colonel, and I tell him we're ready. He's says, "Oh, we've got to have breakfast." So he had a little mess hall there. It was good. I remember having water buffalo steaks, so I was told. He recommended that special treat. By that time, it's 0930 or so, and the war is over."

"Yeah, just the way they liked it," I said.

"By the time we got to where we were supposed to be fighting the Viet Cong, at some village, all there was left were the sick, lame, old people, women and kids. It turned into one of those county fair operations. No Viet Cong were seen, nobody got shot. Then we go back to Chu Lai.

"Next morning, we have to go back to Snaggletooth by Amtracs. And that was when I decided we were not going to use the same Amtrac path used previously because chances are it would be mined. Therefore, I told the Amtrac driver to go to the left or the right through this sweet potato field. That's when this Sergeant Loi went totally, hysterically berserk and threatened to kill me. He was a very interesting guy. He was my interpreter there. He was very protective of the civilians, and he did have an enlightened understanding of how to do things. He also felt bad that we were going to destroy a few hundred yards of this guy's field. I assured him the farmer was going to be compensated, that I had the authority to get that done. So, for ten bushels of sweet potatoes I was not going to jeopardize the Amtracs and the Marines aboard them. Well, he goes totally crazy. He pulls out his .38 pistol and aims it at me from about a yard away."

"He was lucky he didn't get killed," I said.

"Yeah, he had two hands on it he was shaking so much. That's when Gunny Gingrich reached around and took his pistol with one rapid move. I called up the Colonel and said, 'You have to get this maniac out of here.' I sent him back to the battalion as soon as I could.

"Later, they sent him to Mike Company to be their interpreter. Mike Company was on a barrier island east of Snaggletooth. We knew the Viet Cong were on this little barrier island. Mike Company went in there on an operation. By this time, I had been transferred to S-2, and they called me up when this operation was being mopped up. I went down there immediately. They had these hand-dug wells laid up with stone. And the Cong had made the bunker connection entrance in this well—in the wall of the well that you couldn't see. You'd go down on this bucket and then access the tunnel that connected to their bunker. What happened was some kid and his mother had been beaten up by one of the Viet Cong. He went and told Sergeant Loi where they were. Mike Company had five or six of the Cong in that bunker red-handed. Captain St. Clair has them place shape charges above the bunker that would have blown a hole the size of a tank. Well, Sergeant Loi tells them to wait, that he wants to go talk to the Viet Cong, and persuade them to surrender. Since his Marines are no longer in danger, St. Clair says, OK. He told Loi to go down and tell them if they put down their guns and come out, they wouldn't be killed. Then Sergeant Loi goes down there and they shoot him.

I arrived shortly thereafter, and I see the dead bodies of the Viet Cong. I hadn't been told about Loi yet, but he had a set of boots we had given him that seemed too big. He was five foot two and was given boots for a full-sized Marine. As I'm walking toward the dead bodies, I see the boots and I knew it was him before anybody told me. So that's what happened. He thought he could talk his way out and felt like he was defending the downtrodden and all that stuff and that was it for Sergeant Loi. He was a good man at heart even though he tried to kill me. Can't take it personally, right?"

"Wow!" I said. "I never heard about that. But Gunny Gingrich was never one to toot his own horn. I'm glad you added that. It's a pretty interesting story."

"They're all interesting. The stupid shit the war does to you, huh? That was just a typical day for us when you think about it."

"A lot of stupid shit happened," I said.

"Yeah."

On the same day Gregory assumed command of Lima Company, General Platt was informed that the 2nd ARVN Division had obtained intelligence that the 21st NVA Regiment had recently moved into a region seven miles northwest of Quang Ngai City. The objective area consisted of hamlets of the Chau Nhai village complex. Each hamlet was designated on the map with a number in parenthesis—from (1) to (5).

Like Double Eagle phases one and two, Operation Utah would be a multi-battalion operation: 2/4, which 3/1 fought with on Double Eagle, and 2/7, that participated on Double Eagle II. The planning period for Operation Utah was amazingly brief. The plan, designed the night of 3 March, called for an ARVN battalion and a battalion of Marines--Lt. Colonel Leon Utter's 2nd Battalion 7th Marines--to be helilifted the next day to an area near Chau Nhai (5). As it turned out, however, 2/7 was seriously shorthanded. One of its rifle companies had been ordered to protect an artillery battery. In his book *Utter's Battalion* Lt. Colonel Alex Lee discusses the ramifications of this shortsighted decision on the part of the brass:

"The action would begin, as it always seemed to do, with 2/7 short one rifle company. That sort of assignment came down to the battalion from above, cast in stone. An appeal was useless; no protest was lodged with either regiment or Task Force Delta regarding this fateful reduction of combat power."

On the morning of 4 March, Marine jets bombed and strafed the objective area in preparation of the helicopter landings. Despite this bombardment the helicopters carrying the first element of ARVN troops came under heavy enemy fire. All four of the accompanying Hueys were hit. One of them was downed. One of the F-4 jets was shot down while making a napalm run. Nevertheless, the helicopters continued landing. Ten of the twenty CH-34s in the first lift were hit by enemy fire.

By 1030 the first ARVN Airborne Battalion, consisting of 400 men, had been successfully dropped off. Colonel William Johnson, commanding officer of MAG-36, expressed the opinion that "The North Vietnamese did not think we would continue the lift in the face of that automatic weapons fire. We did continue the lift and we kept the automatic weapons under almost constant attack by fixed-wing aircraft while we were going in there. And this enabled us to get in." The ARVN Airborne battalion received little resistance as it attacked toward its objective, Hill 50.

The MAG-36 helicopters returned to Chu Lai to bring the 2/7 Marines to their objective area, designated LZ Alfa. By 1040 the lift was underway. The first wave, the 1st platoon of Company F, landed under heavy fire. The 1st platoon was on the ground at 1100. One of the helicopters had been shot down and three of the remaining seven reported being hit. It took nearly an hour longer for the remaining troops to arrive, during which time the 1st platoon was not only under heavy fire, but undermanned because a contingent of the platoon was assigned security for the downed helicopter. They were fortunate to have survived. As Alex Lee puts it, "For nearly an hour Company F was forced to remain tied to the LZ with far less than half its combat power available. It was a miracle that the enemy commander failed to react to the precarious situation of Company F and failed to destroy that small force while he had the opportunity."

The last company to reach LZ Alfa was Company H. Their lift resulted in intense fire at the CH-34 helicopters, with one down and several more damaged. The primary weapon used against our aircraft—both helicopters and jets—was the dual-purpose 12.7mm antiaircraft machine gun. According to Alex Lee, "The 12.7 machine gun was devastating when used against the thin-skinned helicopters, and it was feared by everyone, air or ground, who had ever heard it thumping away in the jungle." The next morning, we Lima Company Marines would hear its deadly sound on Hill 50. I also witnessed its destructive power heading to our landing zone the night before. Looking down from the CH-34 I was in, I spotted one of the helicopters that had been shot down earlier in the day. That was my first clue that this was not going to be the third phase of Double Eagle.

As previously stated, Operation Utah was to be a combined operation using a battalion of Marines, 2/7, and a battalion of ARVN, the 1st Vietnamese Airborne Battalion. Once they were both on the ground, the plan called for the two battalions to move in a southeasterly direction on opposite sides of Highway 527, a dirt road. They were to continue on that road until 527 joined up with Route 1, approximately 6 miles north of Quang Ngai City. Initially, the plan of attack was moving smoothly for the Marines. Shortly after 1300, the battalion secured hills 97 and 85, receiving light resistance from snipers. It was a different story for the Vietnamese to the northeast who ran into heavy opposition in the area of Chau Nhai (5) and Hill 50. Unwilling to attack on their own, the ARVN commander radioed Colonel Utter for help. Utter reversed his column and headed north to support the Vietnamese.

Learning that the paratroopers' commander was going to move his battalion to the northwest side of Hill 50, Utter placed his Company F on the left to tie in with the ARVN's right. Company G would attack up the center while Company H held the exposed right flank. "We got off to a good start," Utter recalled later. "It was fairly even ground, we had a nice even line with good contact, there was enough excitement to keep everyone on his toes, air was on station and artillery was within range and in position. I wasn't even too concerned about being minus one company and short a platoon from each of the others."

Then from well-concealed positions the NVA pounded the Marines with a barrage of heavy fire from two full battalions of the 21st Regiment. The enemy commander had wisely waited until the Marines were practically on top of their positions before opening fire, thus preventing them from calling in air and artillery support. Utter had no choice but continue the frontal assault. Company G went up the center. Company H was on the right, making some headway toward cutting through the enemy's front line of defense when they were suddenly attacked on their right flank by an NVA company.

On the left flank was Company F's CO, Captain Jerry Lindauer, had just joined the unit shortly before the operation. More than a dozen of his men went down when the enemy launched its assault. Lindauer rushed forward to make contact with his two lead platoons that were pinned down. His arm was shattered by an enemy round. Ignoring the pain, he reached his 2nd platoon, and learned that his 1st platoon had been cut off. Lindauer's left flank was supposed to have been tied physically with the ARVN. But the truth was, the ARVN had not moved a step in any direction. Utter radioed the ARVN to close the gap.

The ARVN adviser was U.S. Army Captain Pete Dawkins. As a subtle way of expressing his disdain for Dawkins, Alex Lee never identifies the man by name—only by his call sign, Red Hat One.

"As 2/7 advanced to the east, the left flank of Company F was supposed to be tied, by physical contact, with a unit of ARVN rangers. Their adviser, Red Hat One, was a graduate of the Military Academy of West Point who gained national prominence as an end on the Academy's football team. He was, supposedly, to be available to 2/7, by radio, at all times for coordination of movement of the two commands. Of course, realistic coordination of movement was impossible because the communication link was as illusory as the physical contact that never was maintained by the ranger force."

The greatest danger to the 2/7 Marines was the growing gap between their left flank and the ARVN position. When Utter radioed the ARVN, imploring them to bridge the gap, the 2/7 CO was stunned to learn the Vietnamese commander refused to move. Utter stated, "This meant our left flank was wide open, with nothing to put there. But the PAVNs [People's Army of Vietnam] had plenty of people, so they poured through...and back to the south the enemy was going at it again with H Company. And there we were, taking it from three sides, the front, and both flanks, and an enemy that was literally hugging us so we wouldn't use our supporting arms."

Captain Lindauer was forthright in expressing the bitterness he felt toward our so-called allies: "I was not aware that the ARVN airborne battalion did anything except view our critical situation as detached observers." The next day it would be my company, Lima 3/1, facing the enemy machine guns while being casually observed by the ARVN from the comfort of their secure positions.

While it may be true that the ARVN adviser had no command authority over the Vietnamese battalion, it is also true that he had an obligation to provide their Marine counterparts with accurate information—especially information vital to the outcome of the mission. Alex Lee makes the case that Red Hat One not only failed to provide accurate information, but gave the Marines false information:

"The enemy, who were supposed to have been ousted from that hillside by the ARVN Rangers, were still in place, and from their vantage point, they were able to fire downward on the Marines of Company F. The American Ranger adviser, Red Hat One, earlier had made an official report to 2/7 that two companies of ARVN Rangers had moved forward and cleared the ridge of the enemy. That report was false, the maneuver never had taken place, otherwise there would have been no plunging fire possible from that hillside...One Marine was lying about five feet from his head which had been removed from his body by a tremendous impact on his neck. I surmised that he, too, had been hit by a 12.7mm round that had come down to kill him from the Red Hat One area of responsibility. Silently, I cursed Red Hat One."

As 2/7 pulled back to Chau Nhai (4) to establish night defensive positions and evacuate their wounded, 3/1 was being lifted to an LZ to their north. Lima Company set up a night perimeter on a hilltop overlooking Hill 50. All night we watched as jets bombed and strafed the area we would be approaching the next morning.

Being a PFC. at the time, all I knew was what I was told, which was to saddle up, make sure I had plenty of ammo and grenades, that we would be boarding choppers. After so many years, I was curious what Simon had been told about the operation by Colonel Young prior to our departure the afternoon of 4 March 1966. As it turned out, it was not much more than the rest of us knew. Simon replied, "Basically, that 2/7 was involved in a gigantic firefight and we would be supporting them."

"Simon," I asked, "according to the Marine Corps publication, *U.S. Marines in Vietnam: An Expanding War 1966*, that at 0730 on the 5th, General Platt ordered our battalion commander, Colonel Young, to advance south of the Tra Bong River to secure the northern flank of the 1st ARVN Airborne Battalion. We thought we would be assuming a blocking position with the ARVN, right?"

"That's correct. All I knew was that I was to take Lima Company up to connect with the people who had already taken Hill 50. The way I got it, the ARVN had already taken the hill. I was supposed to hook up and make sure we were part of that blocking force. Instead of hooking up with the

ARVN, we were ambushed by a battalion of the 21st NVA regiment."

"How is it," I asked Simon, "that the command group, Task Force Delta, who issued the order to Colonel Young, was not complicit in our being set up for a huge ambush?"

"Because they were acting on information that was not verified. If you look at all the stupid stuff I listened to—whether it be big news or little news—in dealing with the ARVN, you couldn't believe it if they told you the sun was coming up tomorrow. We're bright eyed and bushy tailed, all prepared to go out and do what we're told to do, and all the information we received was spurious. And the Marine Corps wasn't smart enough at that time to figure it out. We don't know the politics of it—who did what and where."

"Simon, my whole experience with the ARVN in 1966 was thoroughly negative. I'll tell you something that never occurred to me before writing this book. Forget about the obvious disparity between them and the Marine Corps in terms of discipline and training. Had they at least shown the willingness to fight their enemy wherever and whenever the opportunity presented itself and demonstrated a willingness to die for their own country, I seriously doubt I would have decided to join the antiwar movement after my enlistment. Privately, I still would have questioned our government's decision to intervene in a civil war 10,000 miles away. But had the South Vietnamese demonstrated the same level of commitment as their enemy, I sure as hell wouldn't have taken to the streets to protest the war. I just couldn't accept our willingness to sacrifice our lives when it appeared that the only Vietnamese who acted like they had a cause worth dying for were the ones we were fighting."

"A few days after Utah," Simon replied, "Captain Latting (Mike Company's CO) and I had lunch with General Krulak. You're talking to Krulak. You don't want to say much, but he got us talking. He says, 'OK, lieutenant, stop the BS, just tell me the truth here.'"

"'About Utah?' I asked, and he said, 'About everything'. He asked me what I thought about the South Vietnamese Army. I didn't want to say anything bad, you know, and he says, 'Tell me the truth, Lieutenant!' I said, 'They're completely useless, and he said, 'You're right! And don't ever forget it!'"

"The thing about Hill 50," Simon added, "if they were in a bad position and they knew...but of course they didn't want to know...And I don't know why the North Vietnamese were left there. Maybe the North Vietnamese figured they had it worked out, because they were only a few hundred yards or less from that ARVN unit. And nothing was happening. Evidently the North Vietnamese must have figured they've got it made. The ARVN aren't going to come after us.

"On the other hand, let's say that the ARVN really wanted to secure Hill 50, and they discovered that Hill 50 was still hostile. And then they radio to Command and say, 'We need help down here.' And then we get sent down to help them. I can understand that. They say, "'OK, Colonel Young. There's a big firefight on Hill 50 and the ARVN are taking a lot of heat. You need to go help them out.' I can understand that."

"Yeah," I agreed, "that would make sense."

"Yeah, that would make sense. But that's not what happened. The opposite took place. These guys are standing around, and a hundred yards away are a hundred NVA with AK-47s."

"Yes," I agreed. "That's what Colonel Utter said in the official literature. He said they were told to go down and help the ARVN, which they did. In doing so they ran into a buzz saw. But when they needed the ARVN to step up, they refused to move.

"I've spoken to a lot of guys who were with us that day," I said, "and there is a lot of confusion about what happened. Sgt. Boland said to me, 'You've talked to Simon Gregory. Was he informed we would be confronting the 21ˢᵗ Regiment of the NVA?' But it sounds like you didn't know any more than the rest of us."

"That's right. Young wouldn't have sent us down with the information he gave. He thought we'd be going down there and complete the encirclement of whatever is left of this unit when we met up on Hill 50. Luckily, I had the wherewithal to not just walk in single file. I remember putting two platoons up and one in reserve. That's the thing about complicated tactical math—you can count to three."

"Well, that the smart thing to do," I told him.

"Yeah, it was. I mean, we may have been stupid..."

"I think you mean we may have been ignorant, but we were not stupid."

"Yeah, we were ignorant, but not stupid. So at least we had the advantage of having two platoons up and Crowley in reserve. And then the shit hit the fan. But luckily, we were in some sort of combat-ready formation. I remember our first rounds fired back. In retrospect, I can just imagine the guys on the other side, the North Vietnamese. We just unloaded, a company of Marines. We attack you back. Can you imagine being on the wrong side of a Marine Corps company?"

"Right," I said. "But thanks to the ARVN, there were a lot of guys in 2/7 who were on the wrong side of the situation. It was horrible. It's just hard to read some of that shit in Alex Lee's book."

"Another thing," Simon replied, "it's all chaos to begin with. We're lucky we made as much sense of it as we did as far as maintaining control of ourselves. I guess that's what I was supposed to be doing, and that's what I did."

"Yeah, you did. You've got nothing to feel bad about as far as I'm concerned."

"Yeah, except for the men who were killed and seriously wounded."

"Well, it could have been a hell of a lot worse, you know that."

One month after Operation Utah Pete Dawkins was the subject of a Life Magazine cover story. The article refers to the operation:

"After a brief rest the battalion was fighting again, this time near Quang Ngai. Intelligence sources said an enemy regiment was in the area, and almost immediately a joint attack was launched by Dawkins' airborne troopers and U.S. Marines.

"'The idea was to land as close as to this suspected regimental command post as we possibly could,' says Dawkins. 'We landed right in the midst of the scoundrels.'"

"During the all-night fighting the Marines poured 1,200 rounds of artillery into the area. The enemy melted into the brush at dawn, leaving behind some 300 dead.

"'The artillery sure helped us,' Dawkins said. 'But those Vietnamese troopers were just great. When they were out of ammo and grenades they would stand up and throw rocks.'"

I believe Simon Gregory and Alex Lee would agree with me that the 98 Marines lost on Operation Utah were killed by disciplined PAVN soldiers. The only scoundrels in the area were Red Hat One and his merry band of rock throwers.

"Like the guys in India Company," Simon continued, "who were caught in a grazing crossfire for Christ sake. When you look back, the relative perception of normal contact was such that when we started having our battle, I get a call from Major Fillmore, S-3, that India Company needed us to come back because they're really in hot water. I said we can't disengage. It's too late. He had no idea what we were getting into. But India Company had a lot more casualties than we did. Then after talking to him about our situation, he knew just how bad things were for us as well."

I asked Simon to describe his encounter with an NVA soldier on Hill 50.

"I came under fire from what I think was a 12.7mm machine gun off to my far left. The sound of those high-speed rounds breaking the sound barrier are never forgotten. I jumped into a bomb/shell crater and discovered an NVA soldier was already there. At first, I thought he was dead, but he rose up with his rifle. I jumped him before he could do much else. After I grabbed the NVA soldier in the shell crater, I never gave up my grip on him with my right hand. When I started, I had him with both hands by his shirt front and I pulled so hard that he flew up and we both landed with him on top of me. We wrestled around a bit then I decided that I would kill him with my combat knife which was on my left side. When I drew the knife, he looked into my eyes and I realized that he surrendered. After that I discovered he was wounded. I took him down to our improvised aid station, but the Corpsman could not save him. "

Simon was awarded the Silver Star medal for "Conspicuous gallantry and intrepidity in action while serving as Commanding Officer of Company L, 3rd Battalion 1st Marines." It states that the enemy, occupying the objective area, "a hill covered with dense, shoulder-length underbrush, withheld their main volume of fire until Company L was 50 feet from the crest. Disregarding his own safety in the withering fire, First Lieutenant Gregory moved among his platoons, skillfully controlling their movements and encouraging his men to pursue the attack. For three hours, although continuously exposed to heavy hostile automatic weapons fire, he directed the fierce hand-to-hand fighting for the positions on the crest of the hill, at the same time ensuring that casualties were evacuated to protective areas. As a result of his daring effort, the enemy's positions were destroyed and eighty-eight of the enemy were killed. By his extraordinary professional skill, valor in the face of devastating enemy fire and unfaltering dedication to duty,

Lieutenant Gregory upheld the highest traditions of the United States Naval Service."

To no one's surprise, Simon diverts attention away from himself, saying, "My men deserve all the credit. Ten paid the ultimate price, another twenty were wounded."

Every March 5th those of us who fought on Hill 50 and are on the internet, receive an email from Simon Gregory remembering the men we lost that day in 1966. A few years ago, he included a copy of the note he received at the end of that long day from our Executive Officer, Ben De La Rosa, listing the Marines we lost on Hill 50:

Each of us has our own way of processing the experience of heavy combat. One of Simon's methods of handling it involves painting. He once painted four images titled, Four Views of a Battlefield, accompanied by this text:

Four Views of a Battlefield

On 5 March 1966 I was in command of a company of United States Marines engaged in close combat with a unit of the People's Army of Vietnam. Usually referred to as the NVA.

During the four hour battle I had 10 men killed and 20 wounded. The enemy had many, many more. They fought to the last man.

After the initial bursts of fire that morning, it was all I could to maintain a cohesive presence on the battlefield. The wounded were in need of attention, the dead had to be removed, the enemy had to be dealt with as our assault continued.

My mental state had put me past the fear stage quite early on and I essentially was comfortable with the fact that I could die at any moment. A calmness came over me that allowed me to function with effectiveness. Some have called it an "out of body experience." Needless to say, the emotions, sights, sounds and smells of that battle remain with me and rarely a day goes by that I don't recall the experience.

The four views of the battlefield still recur after all these years.

I see them screaming, but I do not hear them.

Lieutenant Simon Gregory

Gary Harlan sitting on an ammo can enjoying his C-Ration meal.

CHAPTER 5

Growing Up on Hill 50

We cannot, indeed, imagine our own death;

whenever we try to do so we find that we

survive ourselves as spectators.

Sigmund Freud

All things being equal, Freud was doubtless correct. We are spectators. In today's world we are spectators glued to our TV sets and smart phones. We watch death all the time, whether it is being simulated by actors in movies and TV shows or for real on the nightly news. But it is all filtered through TV Perception.

On the morning of 5 March 1966 all things were no longer equal. Freud was never on a hill with nowhere to hide watching bodies being torn apart by bullets. It no longer became an issue of imagining my own death. I was facing my own death.

Thirty-seven days earlier we arrived in the Nam by way of landing boats. It was the largest Marine amphibious landing since Inchon, Korea. As we approached the shore I prayed, "God, please don't let me die today." I was not being overly ambitious. I wasn't asking God to keep me alive my entire tour. I just didn't want to die before finding out what sort of man I really was and to find out what sort of place this South Vietnam was.

At the age of 19 I had been a typical boy from Springfield, Missouri, cruising around town, drinking beer, looking for girls. I had just completed six months of active duty with the Marine Reserves, attending weekend drills once a month when I read about Operation Starlite, the first significant Marine battle in Vietnam. Having nothing better to do with my life I went to the Marine recruiter with my plan of enlisting in the Regular Marines. I made two requests: that I be assigned the MOS of infantryman, and that I receive orders for duty in Vietnam. Consistent with the rationality of that decision was my underlying fear that the war would end before I got there.

The Marines complied with my request and the Viet Cong prevented a premature end to the war. Instead of being deployed directly to the combat zone, however, I was sent to Okinawa, Japan where I reported for duty with Lima Company, Third Battalion First Marines. After thirty days of grueling guerrilla warfare training, the battalion boarded the USS *Paul Revere* from which we made our amphibious landing in operation was named Double Eagle.

It turned out my prayer was unnecessary. The landing was uneventful. The first month taught us more about physical endurance than the perils of war. By the end of three weeks we had covered a 500-square mile area by foot. We were on the move all day and slept a few hours each night in the mud. We made enough contact with the VC to be reminded we were in a war, but not enough to penetrate all those years of TV glut.

I had no other way of apprehending those strange images except through the detachment of TV Perception. The difference was I was a character in this production. I was enjoying the image of myself enacting the role of a Marine grunt. Hey! That's me getting shot at; walking through that spooky village in the middle of the night; carrying a wounded Marine to a medivac chopper.

We suffered our first KIA (Killed in Action) the third week. James Thompson was a black sergeant from Trenton, New Jersey. He was liked and respected by everyone. We were pinned down in the middle of a rice paddy by rifle and mortar fire when he got shot. While he lay there, we received air support. My attention was divided between the sight of the F-4 Phantom jets striking the enemy position and this man lying 10 meters away, dying from the bullet that went through his right eye.

If at that moment someone had told me I was seeing things through TV Perception I would have been outraged. Yet it was true. I was not thinking about the inevitable suffering Sergeant Thompson's death would cause his family 10,000 miles away. We all knew that someone would inevitably be the first among us to be Killed in Action. I was not thinking, "That could be me." I was thinking, "That is not me."

Had I suddenly received orders to Stateside after the first month, I would have returned with just enough experience to tell war stories to my friends. After all, my self-image was still bound up with life in Springfield.

That social self was destroyed, and TV Perception blacked out the fifth week...on Operation Utah.

We were helilifted due south from Chu Lai to an area north of Quang Ngai City, landing on a hill dominated by tall elephant grass. We spent the afternoon marching several kilometers before bivouacking on a hill near the hamlets of Chau Nhai. That night we witnessed heavy aerial and artillery bombardment of Hill 50. The following morning, we made our assault on Hill 50, and discovered how little damage all the napalm, bombs and artillery had inflicted on the enemy position. We were up against an enemy extremely well camouflaged and shielded from sight by dense underbrush, bamboo fences and hedgerows. They were entrenched in an elaborate network of tunnel-connected bunkers and spider-traps, and protected by minefields and booby traps.

There are four platoons in a Marine rifle company--three rifle platoons and one weapons platoon, the latter consisting of men equipped with machine guns, rocket launchers, and mortars. When we were in the rear, back in the battalion area, weapons platoon lived together as a group. But whenever we went out in the bush on search-and-destroy operations or just routine patrols and ambushes, weapons platoon was evenly detached to the three rifle platoons.

As we approached Hill 50, the 2nd and 3rd platoons were ordered to move up the hill on line. The 1st platoon, my unit, was held back in reserve. But that did not last long. After the first two platoons were getting hit hard, we were ordered to get on line and join the assault. Moving up from the base of the hill my rifle jammed. Spotting a dead Marine nearby I grabbed his rifle and rejoined the Marines on line assaulting the invisible enemy position. A few meters away Sergeant David Shields, a machine gunner born in Scotland was firing his M-60 from the hip. Scotty displayed an image of confidence that was somewhat reassuring. But suddenly our assault was met not only with AK-47s but also by the deadly sound of a 12.7 mm machine gun, the enemy's equivalent of our 50-caliber.

Scotty was the first Marine in our platoon targeted by the powerful weapon. The 12.7mm projectile struck him in the forehead and exited through the back of his helmet, releasing a fountain of blood. His movement was abruptly halted by the impact. He stood motionless for a second before falling backwards. I knew he was dead before he hit the ground. More casualties followed including my squad leader who was shot and wounded.

Those whose understanding of heavy combat is limited to its depiction in movies might assume the memories of someone who has had that experience would be filled with deafening explosions of machine guns, small arms fire, rocket launchers, mortars, and hand grenades. But strangely enough, from the moment I was certain I was going to die on that hill, those sounds were muted. Only the screams of men who had been hit remain vivid in my mind.

The awareness of time also vanished. A friend once asked me how long the fighting on Hill 50 lasted. The truth was, I had no idea. And I don't remember being afraid. I guess things must be perceived as somewhat real in order to be afraid in the normal sense of the word. I just kept moving, mostly helping the wounded. Lance Corporal Gary Hester and I reached Lieutenant Gene Cleaver who commanded the third platoon. He had been shot in the chest. There was no doubt he would die if he was left untreated. We took turns, one of us providing covering fire while the other administered mouth-to-mouth resuscitation. We later learned Lieutenant Cleaver survived.

That was, at any rate, how I remembered it the five decades prior to the writing of this book. After interviewing other survivors of the battle, I have learned that besides the efforts of Hester and me, three corpsmen from three different platoons also contributed to the effort of saving Lieutenant Cleaver who, because of the severity of his wound, has no memory of what happened after he was shot.

The hill was finally taken. The wounded were picked up by medivac choppers and the dead were picked up the next day. Gathered in small groups, we were in shock, not caring what happened next.

A helicopter landed and the battalion chaplain got out. He walked around the battlefield reciting the 23rd Psalm, pausing briefly at each group. With blank eyes we observed his solemn act, his freshly starched fatigues, and his plump belly filled with mess hall chow. I never felt the intense hatred for the Viet Cong that I did for that chaplain at that moment. Though it would take fifteen years for me to fully realize my anger was misdirected, I had no way then of processing the events of that day. I only knew I was not going to allow its meaning to be covered over, buried, or disguised by any inappropriate fictions. I also knew the flimsy set of beliefs I came over with had been stripped. Back home in the Bible Belt one could enjoy warm feelings produced by religious language without ever having to stray from one's own self-interests. There was no room for lies on that hill. On Hill 50, language and action were one.

The next day we were picked up by helicopters. I sat across from the door gunner. We looked at each other and he apparently saw the insanity we had all lived through reflected in my eyes because he made a simple yet profoundly compassionate gesture. He took out a pack of Lucky Strikes and offered me one. I gratefully accepted.

Walter Gingrich, Company Gunny, Lima 3/1.

CHAPTER 6

Gunny Gingrich

Cullman, Alabama

Gunnery Sergeant Gingrich was
one of the stalwarts of the company.
Didn't say much, but when he did say
something, everybody paid attention.
His professionalism just seeped down
to everybody. A lot of people learned
from him and a lot of people lived
because of him.
Colonel James Sehulster USMC (ret.)
Commanding Officer of Lima 3/1
1965-1966

When it comes to Marine Corps lore, there is no one who
earned the title of U.S. Marine who is not familiar with the

name Dan Daly and the words he yelled to his men in a charge during the battle of Belleau Wood during the First World War: "Come on, you sons of bitches, you want to live forever?"

Less familiar is the name Lloyd W. Williams. Yet like Daly, he also distinguished himself at Belleau Wood with both his leadership and words he uttered during that battle.

As a young boy Lloyd grew up in Berryville, Virginia before the family moved to Washington, D.C. He attended Virginia Polytechnic Institute (Virginia Tech), graduating in 1907 as the captain of Alpha Company of the Virginia Tech Corps of Cadets. After graduating, just shy of his twenty-second birthday, he was commissioned a second lieutenant in the Marine Corps.

Serving under legendary Marine officers Colonel Joseph Pendleton and Major Smedley Butler, Williams saw his first combat in Nicaragua in the capture of the city of Leon.

During World War One Captain Williams was assigned command of the 51st Company of the 2nd Battalion, 5th Marine Regiment. On 1 June 1918 Williams' company was deployed to Belleau Wood to support the French army. When they arrived, however, the French were in full retreat. A French colonel ordered Williams and his men to retreat as well. Looking at the colonel with contempt, Williams replied, "Retreat Hell! We just got here."

On 11 June 1918, Captain Williams led an assault that routed the German defenders at Belleau Wood. Of the 10 officers and 250 men who started the attack, only one officer and 16 enlisted men escaped death or injury. Lying on the battlefield, having been gassed and wounded by shrapnel, Williams was reported to have told the corpsmen who approached him, "Don't bother with me. Take care of my good men."

Lloyd Williams died from the wounds he suffered that day, but his legacy lived on. The 2nd Battalion, 5th Marines adopted the motto, "Retreat, Hell!" in honor of Captain Lloyd Williams, who was posthumously promoted to major and awarded the Distinguished Service Cross.

Thirty-two years later, during the first year of the Korean War, those words surfaced once again. In November 1950 the First Marine Division, commanded by General Oliver Smith, were surrounded by 120,000 Chinese troops. What became known as the Battle of the Chosin Reservoir, General Smith directed the 70-mile march to the seaport of Hungnam. Not only did the division inflict heavy casualties on the Chinese, the march saved the division from total destruction. Upon reaching the coast the division commander, General Smith, was quoted as saying, "Retreat? Hell! We were just attacking in a different direction." Later, General Smith denied uttering those words, but pointed out that encircled Marines cannot withdraw, but must attack to break out.

On December 7, 1950, while the battle was still in progress, Warner Brothers submitted a proposal to the Defense Department to make a movie depicting the Marines' march to the coast. Even though the outcome was still in doubt, the studio explained that it wanted to make a film "based on the savage fight for life being put up presently by the U.S. Marines." In his outline the producer assured the Pentagon that the movie would not portray a defeat. "The Chinese," he wrote, "declared that they would destroy to a man the trapped American forces. Instead, Americans decimated the Chinese ranks and clawed their way out, fit and able to fight again."

The Marine Corps had no problem with the project. In fact, they permitted the studio to film the movie at Camp Pendleton, even agreeing to provide men and equipment for the production—at an estimated cost of a million dollars. Ironically, General Smith had returned from Korea to take command of Camp Pendleton. He was impressed with the way the production crew had transformed the grounds into North Korea, sprinkling gypsum over the locale to create the image of snow-covered terrain.

The only obstacle to the production of the film involved was its proposed title, Retreat, Hell! The Production Code Office refused to approve the title because it contained the word "Hell." Warner Brothers was prepared to change the title, but before they did the Defense Department and the Commandant, General Clifton Cates, intervened, managing to reverse the Code Office's decision. They pointed out that the title was based on the quote attributed to General Smith which had been received by the American public with wide acclaim.

Shortly after the release of *Retreat Hell!* the film was shown in Cullman, Alabama, the hometown of seventeen-year-old Walter Gingrich.

"I went to see it at the Saturday matinee. Then that night I came back and watched it again. Then the next day I came back and watched it during the Sunday matinee, and I returned that night and watched it for the fourth time. They didn't charge me for admission the second day. Then two days later three of us saw the Marine recruiter. We raised our right hands and the next thing you know we were on a train heading for South Carolina.

"We stopped at Yemassee. They put us on a cattle bus. A sergeant and a couple of corporals had some choice words for us as we got on. They took us over to Parris Island and dropped us off at the parade deck and we met some DI's. And that's when it got started. They herded us into the mess hall like a bunch of cattle. I tell you what. We were scared to death. Then we got outside, and they herded us around and we got down to pick up our linens. They issued me a bucket, a bar of soap, a scrub brush; I got two blankets; I got two sheets and a pillowcase. I fell back in and I heard a little commotion to my right and I cut my eyes in that direction. Corporal Howard come up. "What are you doin' lookin' around?" I thought when you were lookin' around you'd be turnin' your head, you know what I mean? Well, I made a mistake. I told him, "I wasn't lookin' around." Oh, he come undone. He come undone. But I tell you what. He came up and caught me in my ribcage there. My damned knees buckled. I had tears in my eyes. He asked my name. "Private Gingrich! And I had to yell out about a dozen times. Felt like an idiot. "Yeah, you'll be a private when you get discharged. Gingrich, I'm gonna be keepin' an eye on you." I thought, Oh my gosh!

"They put us in Quonset huts. And that's all we did was run in and out of that Quonset hut for about twenty minutes. In and out. In and out. "Platoon 84 outside!" And we'd go in and make up our bunks and they'd come in there and tear our bunks up. And we'd have to go back again. "Platoon 84, outside!" I bet we done it about 5 or 6 times. We were not to sit on our bunks. You sit on your footlocker."

"Where did they send you after boot camp?"

"They sent me to Quantico. I was supposed to go up there for mess duty for 90 days. But when I got there, I wound up in the motor pool for three months and then I went to Camp Lejeune. Weapons Company, 2nd Battalion, 2nd Marines. I went into heavy machine guns. And then I was cross-trained—heavy and light machine guns. When I got to Korea I dealt mostly with light machine guns."

"The thirty caliber?"

"Yes."

Once he turned 18, Gingrich was subject to orders for Korea. It was a different war from the one depicted in the movie he watched back home. In March 1952, the 1st Marine Division redeployed from east-central to western Korea, where they were assigned a 35-mile (56km) sector to defend on the Main Line of Resistance (MLR).

Marine Lieutenant General Bernard Trainor (Ret.) was a platoon commander in Korea. He describes the initial phase as being akin to World War Two—a war of movement. "The war I was in," he says, "was more akin to the trench warfare of World War One. It was static warfare; it was known as the Outpost War. It was a war of sergeants and lieutenants, and it was nothing bigger than a platoon because these outposts we fought over with the North Koreans and the Chinese were just squads and platoons out there. And it was a desperate war."

Gingrich was assigned to Dog Company, 2nd Battalion, 5th Marines—one of the outfits that he watched fight its way out of the Chosin Reservoir in *Retreat, Hell!* and before that Captain Lloyd Williams' battalion at Belleau Wood.

"I got to Korea in January of '53. By February, things started pickin' up with the North Koreans and the Chinese. Then we had the Battle of the Cities."

Combat outposts Carson, Reno, and Vegas, known collectively as The Nevada Cities, were each manned by elements of the 5th Marine Regiment, commanded by Colonel Lew Walt. While it is true that the Chosin Reservoir usually comes to mind when one thinks about the U.S. Marines in Korea, the battle for Outpost Vegas and the other outposts is considered some of the bloodiest, if not the bloodiest combat of the entire war.

On 26 March the Chinese army launched an attack on the Nevada Cities in an effort to gain territory. The peace talks in Panmunjon were underway and the goal of the Chinese was to improve the final solidified position of the North Koreans when the talks came to an end.

The Chinese succeeded in over-running Outpost Vegas. At 1120 the next day Dog Company launched a frontal assault on the southern slope. Casualties began mounting immediately.

"We must have lost 50 men in a matter of minutes."

By 1220 Gingrich and others from weapons platoon became part of a provisional company with H&S. The Marines now had three companies on the south slope, all pinned down by mortar and artillery fire. Gingrich's company commander, Captain John Melvin, stated that incoming rained on the troops. He reported:

"It was so intense at times you couldn't move forward or backward. It was the 120-millimeter mortars and the 122-

millimeter artillery that hurt the most. The noise was deafening. They would start walking the mortars toward us from every direction possible. You could only hope that the next round wouldn't be on target."

By 1322, Dog Company had gone over the top on the outpost's hill. Easy Company soon followed and passed through Dog Company's ranks to secure the trenches and crest of Vegas. At 1800, Fox Company was still 400-yards behind the other companies from outpost Vegas. After 10 hours of intense fighting on the 27th of March, the Marines had held the lower slopes of Outpost Vegas, Chinese soldiers held the opposite slope of outpost Vegas, but no-one held the summit.

Up until the end Marine commanders had hoped they could re-take Vegas leaving its defenses intact. That plan was scrapped on the morning of March 28th when the 1st Marine Aircraft Wing dropped 28 tons of bombs in a period of 23 minutes. Shortly after 1300 Easy Company took control of Outpost Vegas after heavy fighting. By 1500 the outpost was secured. Later that night, however, in a makeshift hospital on the Vegas slope treating 200 wounded Marines, the staff learned that an estimated battalion of Chinese were heading in their direction. Armed with as many grenades as they could carry, the wounded Marines did their best to prevent the attack.

For the next two days the Chinese attacked and counterattacked in an effort to take back Vegas. They eventually decided they could not afford to lose any more men. The Battle of Outpost Vegas was finally over.

The Division Command Diary for the month of March (primarily the last week of March) reported 169 Marines killed, 1,211 wounded, and 104 missing in action. Enemy casualties were 1,351 counted killed, with an additional estimated 1,553 killed, for an estimated 3,631 wounded, and 4 prisoners.

"When that battle ended, we came off the line for about 10 or 12 days. And whenever we went back up we were on the left of Vegas, Reno, and Carson. We were on Hill 229. Well, I had a squad leader, Sergeant Kelly, who was from my hometown. But he didn't know squat about the infantry. He'd been on embassy duty the whole time. He come up there one day and said, "Gingrich, get your gear together. You're goin' to Outpost Kate." On that outpost we had maybe 25 or 30 Marines. We'd go on watch from around dusk to daybreak. Then we'd go back to the bunkers and get some sack time. We never had any massive attacks during that time, but our lines were probed pretty regularly, and we had a lot of firefights."

"I've read that a lot of the fighting in Korea took place at night."

"Oh yeah. Chesty Puller made a comment about that. He said we needed to have more training at night."

"Did you ever see Chesty Puller?"

"Not in Korea I didn't. But he was my commanding general at Camp Lejeune. We had a CG's inspection, and I was in a platoon and I was the first man he come up to, can you believe that? I was a squad leader. I was a sergeant. I tell you what, buddy, when I seen him comin' I couldn't believe it. He had a chest on him that was somethin' else. And the ribbons, they went right above that pocket all the way up to the top of his shoulder. He came up, asked me my name, wanted to know where I was from, and then he asked me what I thought about the chow."

"What did you tell him?"

"I told him the chow was quality food."

It was standard procedure that Dog Company Marines would be sent out to the outposts for 6 days at a time and then be relieved and return to the unit. Walt Gingrich was kept out there for nearly a month. It turned out to be the last month of the war.

"The word came down that there was a truce effective 2200 on the 27th of July. We had firefights all the way up to the end."

The armistice had been signed that morning. It was the longest negotiated armistice in history, consisting of 158 meetings spread over a period of two years and seventeen days. In the context of Walt's life, the first meeting to end hostilities took place the month before he turned seventeen, when he was about to begin his junior year of high school. They ended a month before his nineteenth birthday. He was now Corporal Walter Gingrich.

"After it was over, I was sent to Charleston, South Carolina where I made sergeant. We provided security for the Naval shipyard.

"I was discharged in 1955. I came home and the co-op I wanted to work for wasn't hiring. After three days I went down to the drugstore and got me a few root beers. I decided I was going back in. I went to the recruiter and he said, "Sergeant, I have one question. On your DD-214 form does it say you were recommended for reenlistment?" and I said yes, it does. Well, I was sent to Camp Lejeune...assigned to Brig Company. I said to myself, how did I get into this? I started out as a turnkey and went up to sergeant of the guard. I made staff sergeant while I was there.

"I got married to Betty in May 1955. She was a girl I always went to see whenever I was home on leave. I got a letter from her one day. She said she wasn't going with anybody and she wanted to spend her life with me. I read that letter about 4 or 5 times. Scott, from Arizona, was standing there and he said, "Gingrich, did you get a Dear John?" I told him what it said, and he asked me what I was gonna do about it. I said I guess I'm gonna go to the PX and get a wedding band and an engagement ring and then see about getting some leave. Shortly after I put in for 10 days leave, I was told to see the warden. He was an old guy, been in for about 25 years. Never had a kind word for anyone. I reported to him and he said, "What is this, Sergeant Gingrich?" and I said it was a request for leave."

""What's your purpose for going on leave?"

"I said, Sir, I'm gonna get married. He raised his head and said, 'You're going to do WHAT?! I didn't know you were engaged.' I said, 'I'm not. But I'm fixin' to be.' I told him about that letter, and he said, 'You better take care of business, sergeant.' I said Yes, sir.'

"So, I went home to see Betty. I told her I was planning to stay in the Marines for 30 years, that I intended to make First Sergeant or Sergeant Major. She said, 'I'll be right along your side'. And we got married. She was a precious lady. I got a letter from her when I was in Vietnam one day. She told me if she could, she would be right by my side. And buddy, she would have too.

"Well, as soon as I got back, I was told the warden wanted to see me again. I thought, what in the world! Well, I reported to him and he leaned back and looked at me and said, "Well, how was it?"

"I said, everything went fine. Everything went fine, sir."

Gingrich's next assignment was at the Infantry Training Regiment at Camp Geiger where he served as a platoon commander. After a year at Geiger, he received orders for Rota, Spain.

"I had my wife and 3 boys with me to Spain. I was over there for three years. It was security duty there, too. I was assigned the second platoon. It took the first morning they fell out for me to see that this was the raggediest bunch I'd ever seen in my life. It took me about a month to get them in pretty good shape. We got 'em in shape and they turned out to be a pretty darned good platoon.

"Our CO was a lieutenant colonel who loved to compete. We had inter-league sports on the base. You got so many points for each sport—football, basketball, etc. We were a small unit. We didn't have that many Marines. But the Colonel told them we were going to participate. And we're going to win everything. And we did, too. We only got a few points for golf, but football, basketball, softball—we won all that."

"Was there boxing?"

"No, there wasn't boxing, but since you mentioned boxing, I had a lance corporal and a pfc that had been gettin' into it with each other. I took the lance corporal aside one day and asked him if he could handle the pfc. He said he could handle him. So, we took 'em out in the shed and put the gloves on. And buddy, they went at it. And when I thought they'd had enough, I stopped it. We took off their gloves and I made them shake hands. I made 'em hug one another. And when they were ready to leave that building, I told them they were to hold hands and sing the Marines' Hymn all the way back to the barracks—and I had better hear you! And they did. After that, they were like this (bringing together his index finger and middle finger).

"Like I said, that colonel would jump at any chance to compete. They had the Air Wing there, too. They had about 10 or 12 planes on the runway, and they had their own security to protect them. The captain over there wanted to see if someone could breach their security. My colonel said, "We can handle that." So he called me into his office and told me about it and asked if I could handle it. I told him I didn't know, but we'd give it a try. He asked how many men I'd be taking with me and I told him I wouldn't need but one to go with me. So, we went over to where they had the planes backed up, with their big exhausts at the rear. We went in there about 0100. We got on our hands and knees and crawled right up to the edge. We laid there and watched the sailor on sentry duty. We watched him for about 30 minutes and it was obvious he wasn't going to change his routine. So, I told my guy the second the sentry turns around you go over there and put this beer can in the exhaust of that plane. He did it and we got out of there. We went to CID headquarters and told them what we had done. The CID man asked if we can identify the plane, and we said yes, we can. So, he took my guy over there and my guy removes the beer can from the exhaust. He came back and said,

'Sergeant Gingrich, you should have seen that Chief. His eyes were this wide.' We reported what we'd done to the Colonel, and he was tickled."

"I coached a little league ball team. I learned that the Navy captain told Colonel Sullivan that his son was on a pretty good team, but they just couldn't get by the Sarge's team. The Colonel told him, 'Nobody gets by the Marines!'"

When he left Spain, Sergeant Gingrich went to Parris Island.

"Seven or eight of us staff NCOs came in. We all had orders for drill instructor school, but we would have to wait 6 or 7 weeks before the current class was over, and we could get in. So they put us out at the rifle range as primary marksman instructors. We done real well with the platoons that came through so they kept us there."

From Parris Island Staff Sergeant Walter Gingrich received orders for Camp Pendleton, to join Lima Company, 3rd Battalion, 1st Marines.

"Like I told them at a Lima Company reunion in 2014, the foundation was laid for Lima Company when it went through its formin' period under Captain Sehulster in 1965 at Camp Pendleton."

During my interview with Sehulster, the Skipper made it clear that Gingrich's feelings of admiration and respect were mutual: "Gunnery Sergeant Gingrich was one of the veteran staff NCOs I relied upon to impress the troopers with what we were going to face and to take seriously the training. He was always a stable leader."

"We went from California to Okinawa where we trained: Thirty days up in the northern training area where we were the host company for the rest of the battalion; raider training with the rubber boats; and rappelling."

"Don't forget about the PT, Gunny. Remember the 5 or 10-mile forced march in the sand with full gear?"

"That wasn't no forced march. We were joggin'."

"Yeah, I guess we were. At any rate, it kicked my butt. I think it kicked everyone's butt."

"It kicked mine. I tell you, running in that sand? It'll get you. But you know what? I think the captain enjoyed it. Captain Sehulster, he was a good man and he was in shape. And he was always leading the way. Always. Always right out front, buddy."

"Then we landed in Vietnam, beginning with Operation Double Eagle. What do you remember about the landing and the operation?"

"What I remember about the landing? I told the squad leaders to get off the beach as quickly as you can and get inland. We had to run about 40 meters to get there, and then we regrouped. And then we moved out and we began to take a little bit of sniper fire. And as we were movin' along, there was a village up there we were takin' fire from. There were some Marines in there. And Captain Sehulster told the platoon leader to get his men out of there, that he was fixin' to call in artillery on that village.

"Some days later we were walking up a trail that was pretty wide—about six or seven feet wide—it dropped off into a ravine then went up a hill. The point man, Corporal Colon, heard somebody cough on that hill and he opened up on where he heard it coming from. It turned into a firefight. They killed 8 or 10 VC.

"I tell you what. We did a lot of walkin'. Then we'd send out patrols and ambushes at night. I can remember my radio operator. I'd let him take the first watch after it got dark. Then he'd wake me up. You know, you can't sleep when you've got a radio goin' off, cause every time it goes off you're listenin' to it.

"Anyway, there was no contact on that operation against a sizable force, you know what I mean. Ten or twelve of them at the most."

"Anything else you remember about the operation? Anything that stands out in your mind?"

"Booby traps. I can't remember if it was Lima Company or Charlie Company [Charlie 1/9 his outfit in 1969] that I set up a course for. I made it about 20 yards long and about 10 yards wide. And I'd blindfold 'em. Like it was dark. And I'd give them a stick about 4 or 5 feet long. They'd go down and detect a tripwire, follow it to the grenade and disarm it. I tell you what. Those kids did a marvelous job out there."

"Tell me what you remember about Operation Utah."

"Well, that was different. If I recall, we came in from the field after 30 days or so. We were south of Chu Lai, right? We were on the beach. We set up a perimeter there and they set up a mess hall. I think we may have had steak that evenin'. Whatever it was, it was good.

"The next mornin' I was half asleep. I had my shelter-half up, keepin' the sun off me, you know? And the next thing you know these choppers are comin' in and I thought, what is goin' on? They said, 'Gunny, we're goin' back out.' So, I got my gear together and saddled up. Lieutenant Crowley had a meeting with Lieutenant Gregory and the other platoon leaders, and he briefed me on what we were doing. But nobody ever said anything to me about there being NVA in the area. All I know is that when we got to Hill 50 they had the second and third platoons online with attachments, and they started up that hill. First platoon was in reserve.

"They thought they were goin' up there to hook up with the ARVN. Let me tell you somethin'. When they opened up on those kids it was pretty much point blank—no further than from here to that door over there. That's when shit hit the fan. A lot of Marines got hit. Gunny Wagner, he caught a nasty piece of shrapnel in his face. There was that platoon sergeant from second platoon, Staff Sergeant Hultquist. His ambition was to become a sergeant major and then sergeant major of the Marine Corps. That was his vision. I tell you what. He was a durn good sergeant.

"And there was PFC. Garner. He was a runner for Lieutenant Walsh. He was killed up there. He was right in the middle of those NVA. He had to be doin' some damage up there.

"Who else we got? Fitch, from weapons platoon? Tall guy? M-60 machine gunner? He was killed too.

"At the top of that hill I walked by and saw Lieutenant Walsh. He was on the left side of me. I tell you what. Bless his heart, he had a hole that big up there on his leg. I figured two or three AK-47 rounds may have hit him. I thought he'd probably lose that leg.

"I went all the way across that hill. We were getting our wounded off. I picked up one kid, I don't know his name. But he was hit in the stomach with a piece of shrapnel. He had a gash about that big right above his navel. I picked him up and started carrying him and I had taken about 14 steps when he says, 'Gunny, you gonna have to put me down and assist me walking cause I'm about to pass out.' I said, OK, and we got to the bottom of the hill and they took him to the medivac area. And I went back and Gunder and I picked up a couple of other ones and brought them down to the base of the hill.

"The biggest thing we had a problem with was getting everybody accounted for. Sergeant McDowell came up. He was the platoon guide for the 3rd platoon. He'd been down at the evacuation area. I asked him if we know all the names of the Marines who'd been evacuated, and he said yes, and the doctor does too. He said the surgeon (Doctor Campbell) is there and he's makin' decisions about who is most critically wounded and what order they go out. So we made a round at the top of Hill 50 to make sure we told Lieutenant Gregory everybody was accounted for."

"Did you ever go up and check out those trenches?"

"Oh yeah. They were really shot up, those NVA soldiers. There was about a hundred that were killed up there, weren't there?"

"Easily. Probably more."

"When we got back some officer from battalion said something I didn't like. He said, 'Those Marines from Lima Company fought like tigers.' And I said, I beg your pardon. I said, 'Sir, with all respect, they were Marines and they fought like Marines.'"

"Good point."

"Let me tell you somethin'. When those kids were told to go up that hill, up they went."

"Tell me about it. I was one of them."

"Do you remember the machine gunner who was killed walking up that hill?"

"Yes, I do. It was Sergeant Shields. I was near him when the 12.7mm round went through his head. That was when things got unreal for me."

"Well, it was unreal for all of us really. When you go seein' things like that...let me tell you—you can't describe combat. There's no way you can describe combat. If you haven't been there, you don't know what it is.

"I can remember this other Marine who was on a machine gun. When we was checkin' the wounded and gettin' the dead, havin' everybody accounted for, gettin' them off the hill I went over to pick this Marine up and his helmet came off and up at the top of his head you know what came out? His brains. That just tore me up. That kid just 18 or 19 years old. We got him down to the bottom of the hill.

"I'm gonna tell you what. I used to know all your names. But I can't remember all of 'em like I used to. The only thing I can tell you: you were damned good Marines. You were good. How many men did we have killed on Utah, ten?"

"Yes."

"And how many wounded?"

"Twenty."

"Thirty men. That's almost a platoon."

"It is a platoon once you've been there a while. It wasn't unusual to have a squad of eight men. We went into Vietnam having experienced NCOs like you who had years in the Corps. It's amazing how in a matter of a few months we had young guys like me, 19 and 20 years-old being squad leaders."

"Yeah we had the same thing happen up there in Korea. Sure did. They moved right up."

"We had a bunch of replacements around the time Perez and I became squad leaders. Looking back on it, I find it amazing how, within a few months' time, the two of us went from being the lowest-ranking PFCs in the platoon to becoming squad leaders. I would also say that it was amazing how quickly we adapted to the responsibility, but actually there was a good reason for that. We learned from leaders like you. My squad leader, before he was wounded on Utah, was Sergeant McCauley, one of the coolest guys I ever served under. He never lost his cool. So, it wasn't surprising that when we'd receive sniper fire, these new guys could see that neither Perez nor I freaked out over it. Occasional harassing fire was just something they'd have to get used to, right?"

"That's what you do. Lead by example."

"That's what Simon Gregory said about you. Before coming here, I asked him about his recollections of Gunny Gingrich, and he sent me this email. He wrote, 'Fully respected by the troops, he led by example. Got things done in an expeditious manner without having to discuss details. He provided a sounding board as only a Gunny can do.' He also said you were always there when he was CO, and that you saved his life when you disarmed an ARVN sergeant who had drawn a weapon on Gregory to prevent him from sending an AMTRACK across a sweet potato field. Do you remember that?"

"Yes, I do."

"Is that what you did? Just take his weapon away from him?"

"Yeah, I just grabbed it, took it away from him. If he'd of shot the lieutenant..."

"He wouldn't be living much longer, would he?"

"No, he wouldn't. I'd of shot him right on the spot, and there would have been some others that would been the same way. Yeah, I told the lieutenant, get him the hell out of here. Yeah, he did not want us to go across that potato field or whatever it was. He wanted us to go the other way. And Lieutenant Gregory assumed that would be mined and he said we're not goin that way. And I agreed with him. I said you're probably right.

"You know, I never expected to become Gunnery Sergeant of Lima Company. But a few days after Utah, Lieutenant Gregory, who became CO when Captain Sehulster was almost blinded by white phosphorous, informed me I was the new Lima Company Gunny."

Gunnery Sergeant Gingrich was awarded the Navy Commendation Medal with a Combat V for "Meritorious service while serving with Company L, Third Battalion, First Marines in connection with operations against insurgent communist forces in the Republic of Vietnam from January to August 1966." The award was presented by Lieutenant General Victor Krulak.

Gunny returned to Vietnam in 1968 as a first sergeant. In January 1969 he participated in Operation Dewey Canyon, the Marines last major offensive against the NVA. He was, therefore, on the first Marine operation against the NVA and the last.

"What were you, the company first sergeant with Charlie 1/9?"

"I was the company first sergeant and I was on battalion admin. That was the biggest mess that I'd ever seen in my life. I had a captain that told me, 'First Sergeant Gingrich, over the years I've learned that first sergeants just don't know much about admin.' I said, 'I'm glad you told me that. I wasn't aware of that.'"

"Did he know you were being sarcastic?"

"I don't think he did, but it sort of pissed me off, to be honest with you. I was always wonderin' how many men we had in the field, you know what I mean? The Colonel wanted to know, and the Captain gave him this number or that. And I said, 'Captain Kelly, that is not right. That is not right. They had us down for 190 men in Charlie Company—staff NCOs, officers, and everybody.' I told him I would go back to battalion and I'll find out exactly how many men we've got in this company. He looked at me and said, 'First Sergeant, what have you got in mind?' and I told him I would go back and count the service record books, check the log book, make sure there are none checked out, and count the plates and see if the plates correspond with the record books, and if they correspond, that's how many men we've got in this company. So I went back and found out we had 170 men.

"On Operation Dewey Canyon I came back three times and picked up replacements. And each time it was about 15, 16, 17. And one day when it was really getting thick, there was a group I was bringin' out. I told them the LZ was hot, that they were takin' fire from mortars and small arms, but I told them the first hole you see, they'll probably be a Marine or two in it, but you get in that hole. They'll make room for you. Well the firing stopped in about five minutes, and a corpsman came up and brought me the dog tags of an individual that just came out, and he looked at me and said, 'First Sergeant, is this one of ours?' So I checked the list. He was one of ours. Gary, he wasn't out there but about five minutes and he got shot in the head. So he had about five days in Nam. That was pitiful."

"That's not surprising. I read that 900 names on the Wall are men who were killed their first day in-country."

"You know the old sayin'. If things start poppin' on your first day, you are a veteran. Like I said, I can't remember all their names, but I was telling my son Frank one day, those kids got the job done. And let me tell you this, on Operation Dewey Canyon we was down at the bottom of the hill and Captain Kelly called in supporting artillery fire and hit that bunker complex. It tore it up. We got up and started movin' out, and do you know what those kids started doin'? Singin' the Marines' Hymn, can you believe that? Goin' into the assault singin' the Marines' Hymn. I just shook my head. Unbelievable. I'll never forget that. I tell you what. Captain Kelly and Captain Sehulster—those were two good company commanders.

"Tell me about your tour with the 9th Marines."

"Well, my first operation with Charlie 1/9 was in November of '68. They had this company commander who was a lieutenant. He just didn't pack it. I looked around and noticed most of the troops only had 3 or 4 magazines. Had about 10 or 15 rounds in 'em and that was it. I brought that up to the lieutenant and he just shrugged it off. He said we didn't have anything to worry about since we'd be going back in the next day. I said, 'Let me tell you. One assault and we really get hit, we'd expend all that ammunition.' I told the Sergeant Major about it when I got back, and he said, 'I'll just tell you how it is. You're getting a captain coming in. Captain Jack Kelly.' When Captain Kelly reported in the sergeant major told him what went on. And later on he called me to the side and asked me about it. Well, we took care of it. We had those SKS rifles that we captured from the NVA. I guess we had about 30 or 40 of them. We were givin' them to the Army units and the Seabees, and they would give us magazines. Buddy, there was some wheelin' and dealin' goin' on. But I tell you what. We got it up to where each man had about 12 magazines."

"And bandoliers."

"That's right. They'd have 2 or 3 bandoliers strapped on. Some of them carried 4 or 5. And I always tried to get hold of white phosphorous grenades. I tell you one thing, when we used to get probed in Korea, we'd throw those out and buddy, they would scatter."

Operation Dewey Canyon ran from January until March of 1969. 130 Marines were killed in action and 932 wounded. The Marines reported 1,617 PAVN soldiers killed and the discovery of 500 tons of arms and munitions.

"Tell me about your retirement."

"When I came home after my second tour, I went to Camp Lejuene, North Carolina and they put me in Shore Party. I was their First Sergeant. Well, I guess it was about two weeks the phone rang, and my chief clerk said, 'First Sergeant, it's Headquarters Marine Corps', and I looked at him and said, 'Yeah, tell me another one.' 'Yeah, it is,' he said. So, I took the call. It was Captain Kelly my old company commander. He asked me if I'd like to go on I and I duty."

"What is I and I duty?"

"Inspector and Instructor. Working with the Reserves. He told me they had two openings. One was in Marietta, Georgia and the other in Mobile, Alabama. He said I could choose either one I wanted, and I'd have my orders within a week. I said I'd take the one in Mobile, and sure enough I got my orders three days later. Buddy, I was gone. I stayed here in Cullman for ten days on leave and then drove to Mobile. It was a reserve center for Navy and Marine Corps. When I pulled into the parking lot there was a Navy Chief outside the building. I walked up and he said, 'You're our new First Sergeant, aren't you?' and I said, 'I'm going to be, yes.' We talked about 5 or 6 minutes and I asked him, 'What kind of organization is this here at reserve unit Marines?' He looked at me and smiled and said, 'Cooks and Bakers.' I looked at him and said, 'Are you serious?' He said yes, he was. I just shook my head. I never dealt with any cooks or bakers. Always in the infantry—line company, rifle company—and now it's cooks and bakers. I said, 'Where's the closest bar?' and said he right up the road. So, I went up there and had three beers and I come back. I slept there at the reserve center, and I got up and shaved and showered, got my coffee on. The Chief came in and told me the captain would be in at 0800. He told me the captain would demand that I bring my family down. I said that's not going to work. He can forget that. He never mentioned that to me. I guess the chief told him.

"When we had a weekend drill once a month, I would stay at the reserve center. But most days I would commute from home to the reserve center. It was 140 miles. I was drivin' down one morning when I said to myself, what am I doin' runnin' up and down this Interstate when I could retire? Well, I pulled in and went into the reserve center. There was a sergeant and a staff sergeant there, and I said to the staff sergeant, "Type me up a letter of intent. I'm gonna retire.

"Fifteen minutes had elapsed, and nothing was on my desk. So, I walked down to the office and asked the chief clerk, 'Where's my letter of intent?' He leaned back in his chair and said, 'Are you serious?' and I said, 'Your damned right I'm serious and I want that letter on my desk in the next fifteen minutes.' So he typed it up and I looked it over and placed it in the captain's incoming basket. Well, shortly after that he stuck his head in my office and asked me to come into to his office. He said, 'What is this?' and I said, 'That's my letter of intent. I'm gonna retire in September.' He told me I was on the sergeant majors list. But there was a catch. To pick up sergeant major I'd have to extend my enlistment for two years, and I wasn't gonna do that. I said, 'No.' And he said, 'Yes, I know you're on the sergeant majors list. You'll be making it in December.' And I said, 'No, I won't be here. I retire in September.' He said, 'First Sergeant, will you just take off for three days and discuss this with your wife, and come back Thursday?' I said, 'Sir, with respect, will you just sign that and give it to the clerk so it can be in the mail today? And I will see you on Thursday.' And I turned around and walked out. The next thing you know I get a call from the district headquarters in Atlanta from the sergeant major wanting to know what was goin' on. He told me Major Brown up there had the impression I was retiring because of the captain. I told him the captain has nothing to do with me retiring. I said if I made sergeant major that would mean I would be extending for two years and there was no telling where they would send me. My kids are in school and I bought a house in Cullman. He wished me the best and I retired and come home to mama.

"When I got home, everybody told me I retired at the wrong time of the year, that it would be hard to find a job. I applied at the Cullman Cabinet Shop and a couple of other places. I went to Ransid Industrial and they hired me on the spot. And you know what? Those other places I applied to called me with a job offer."

"So how did it go with your new job?"

"It went just fine. They put me in quality control, and I picked it up just like that. Next, they put me over in the press department and I was the chief inspector over there. I had two inspectors under me."

"How long were you there?"

"I was there for twenty years, until they closed down."

"What did you do then?"

"I went to work at Walmart Distribution."

"How was that?"

"It was fine. The only thing with them was don't abuse your breaks and don't be late. You do those things and you'd do fine. And buddy, they took good care of me. They really did."

"And that was where you retired for good?"

"That's right."

"When was that?"

"My wife came down with cancer in 1999. And I gave that job up because I had to take care of her. She had bone marrow cancer. Bless her heart, she had a difficult time. She made it for a year."

Four years after Betty passed away Walter married Daphine, a lady with whom he shared a love of Jesus and fishing. His marriage to Daphine was a happy one, but it ended after ten years when she died suddenly from a ruptured colon.

"It would only be right to end this discussion with your thoughts about Lima Company. I think you will agree with me that we were a very tight outfit, am I right?"

"Lima Company was a damned good company. It was an honor to have served with the officers and men of Lima Company. There will always be a place in my heart for Lima Company."

"Well, I think it's safe to say that there will always be a place for you in the hearts of the Lima Marines who served alongside you. I'm proud to have served under you when you were the 1ˢᵗ Platoon Sergeant and then Company Gunny. Thank you, Gunny."

.

Dan Walsh in his Marine man cave

CHAPTER 7

Lieutenant Dan Walsh

Springfield, Massachusetts

Dan Walsh is the real Marine.

Gung-ho with the eagle, globe,

and anchor printed on his forehead.

God bless him, the Marine Corps

needs people like him.

Lieutenant Steve Crowley

After three decades since Lima Company fought on Hill 50, Simon Gregory did not expect to learn anything new about the Marines he commanded that day, least of all something involving Lima's 2nd platoon commander, Dan Walsh. What he learned was disturbing. Simon had taken it for granted that Dan had been awarded the Bronze Star Medal for his actions on Hill 50 before and after he was seriously wounded. Simon had submitted the recommendation himself shortly after the battle. From the moment he discovered the award had not been issued, Simon was determined to set things straight.

The two men live in Massachusetts, Dan in Springfield and Simon an hour away in Holden. After I arrived in Springfield to spend a couple of days at the home of Dan and Kateri Walsh, I was told we would be attending a ceremony in thirty minutes. A city park was being dedicated to Springfield native, Gunnery Sgt. Tommy Sullivan, who gave his life saving the lives of others during a terrorist attack in Chattanooga, Tennessee. Kateri, who had been reelected to the city council the day before, delivered a moving address at the dedication.

Sitting at a bar that evening, everyone and his brother stopped by to say hello to Dan including Mayor Domenic Sarno and Lieutenant Governor Karyn Polito. The next day we met with Governor Charlie Baker at the Soldiers Home in Holyoke where Dan's son Bennett is Superintendent.

Dan was politically active himself, serving on the Springfield City Council and the Park Commission. His proudest achievement as a civilian was his fifteen years as director of Veterans Services.

On the third day in Springfield we found time to talk.

OK, Dan, if you would, please share your story.

"I was born, I lived, hope to live a few more years, and be mourned by my wife and children. In between I was in the Marines and survived that. How's that?

That's a pretty good statement. What else do you need?"

"The details."

"The details, OK. I was born in Springfield, Mass in '41, eight days before Pearl Harbor. That was an auspicious beginning to say the least. Why did I join the Marine Corps? Because I got booted out of ROTC [which Dan pronounced Rotsee]. Why did I get booted out of ROTC? 'Cause I called the top cadet an asshole. He was a senior and I was a sophomore. And they didn't like that too much. I was in ROTC because the draft was on and going in as an officer was a hell of a lot better for getting meals and what not if you're an officer and not enlisted. My father told me I should do that, and I said OK. When I got thrown out I took my two roommates with me. I also took the number two senior and four other guys. We brought them all in the Marines. I told my father this guy, Lieutenant Colonel Triana, was going to commission me.

"So I went to PLC for 12 weeks—if I'd done the two 6-week elements I probably wouldn't have gone back for the second six-weeks. It was absolute terrible hell. But he did commission me and I took in the two guys and four other guys from ROTC. Instead of joining the Army they went in the Marine Corps with me. And he knew it. Smiled at me, thinking, fuck you, you little asshole. But that's the Army for you. They're lost.

"I always wanted to be a Marine ever since I was 9 years-old. My father was an officer in the U.S. Navy. He was fighter direction officer on the USS *Lexington* in World War Two. I remember him coming home after the war, walking up the steps at Union Station. So, I'm 8 or 9 years old looking at my father's cruise book. I see all these guys in white uniforms. I ask my dad who those guys in green were with knives on the end of their guns. He says, 'Well those are the Marines,' and I say, 'who are the Marines?' He said, 'Well they're part of the Navy. We take them where they go to do what they have to do.' And I say, 'What do they do?' And he tells me 'They do the dirty work.' 'What do you mean, the dirty work?' 'Well, they go in and they have to fight.' I said, 'That sounds great. I think that's what I want to do.'"

"On November 29, 1950 I turned 9. The Marines had just been surrounded at the Chosin Reservoir in Korea. I said to my father, 'Dad, what's going on? The Marines are so great and they're about to be annihilated by the Chinese.' My dad said, 'Daniel, never ever underestimate the Marines.' And sure enough. They came out smelling like roses. Got everything out. Chesty Puller had our regiment, the 1st Marines, and he got them all out. Well, you know the history of all that."

"Oh yeah."

"So, I went to Basic School and we got out of there in February '65. A month later, all the guys who got sent to the 3rd Division went to Vietnam. The 2nd Division guys went to the LeJeune, then to the Dominican Republic. I was sent to the 1st Division. Got there in March. Then they formed up the battalion. Captain Sehulster came in, then Lieutenant Gregory. We waited for Lieutenant Colonel J.R. Young to come in. When he arrived, he sent us to school for a couple of months—guerrilla warfare and what not—just some bullshit to bide our time. So, we had a great life with nothing really to do since we were forming up. So we had a great life on the coast of Southern California...Hollywood... some of the guys ended up marrying some of the girls. We just had a great time. Then all the troops came in. I got the 2nd platoon. Si Gregory had it before with 1/9 and 3/5 before that.

"Then in May we went into lock-on training for 90 days. We did nothing but hump the hills of Camp Pendleton. I don't know when you joined Lima Company, but right from the beginning we had quite a few Marines who had been Gregory's men before and ended up being mine. Pretty sure Boland was one of them, and Ferguson, and Smith. Those were my three squad leaders. Excellent guys, all of them. They were just great Marines. They took care of their men, their squads, their fire teams.

"We shoved off at the end of August from Long Beach. I remember being aboard ship looking around. There was a big thing at the time, "Ship of Fools." And I'm thinking about that. We pretty much know where we're going. Our comrades are already over there. I had friends from Basic School who had already come back pretty badly wounded. We knew what was going on. We got over there and landed in Okinawa. And we went up to the Northern Training Area which was the best thing that could have happened to Lima Company. We got all the choice assignments. With the battalion most of the time. We were in great shape. We had jungle training up there. I know you were involved in that. It was the best training we could have had.

"We went in as a full battalion. We were really lucky. We had great company commanders. We had Captain Sehulster; Latting was at Mike Company; Lecky was the CO at India. They had one guy commanding Kilo Company. We thought, what the hell is this guy doing leading a company? But they brought in Speedy Gonzales. Speedy was great.

"So again, getting kicked out of ROTC was the best thing to ever happen to me. And I get in there and we prepare for Vietnam. And we got a solid good company—and De La Rosa— what a great guy he was. He had third platoon, then he became platoon guide. Crowley had first platoon—your platoon--and Cleaver went from weapons to 3rd platoon. I had 2nd platoon. And we got some of the choice assignments. For two weeks we were the reaction platoon for General Platt's Task Force Delta. We had twelve helicopters.

Colonel Jonas M. Platt was the commanding officer of the Basic School from 1963 to 1965, the period in which all of the Lima Company platoon leaders had completed their training. In November 1965, en route to Vietnam, he was promoted to brigadier general. Arriving in Vietnam, General Walt assigned him command of Task Force Delta, a command organization that would be responsible for the planning and coordination of multi-battalion combat operations. He held this position during 3/1's first three operations—Double Eagle, Double Eagle 2, and Utah.

In 1940, before reaching his 21st birthday, Jonas M. Platt graduated from college with a degree in civil engineering and was commissioned a second lieutenant in the Marine Corps. During his 30-year career, Platt served in World War Two, Korea, and Vietnam. In World War Two Platt served with 3/1 in the battles at Peliliu and Okinawa. In a presentation he made sometime after his retirement, he spoke of his service with 3/1 and what is demanded of a Marine combat unit:

"When I think of Peliliu, I think of K Company, 3rd Battalion, 1st Marines. K Company was the left flank company in a two-regiment landing on the island of Peleliu. About 150 yards to the left of where they were to land was a point that jutted out about 25 yards into the water and had a commanding view of the entire division beach. K Company's job was to take that point. And if they didn't, the whole division's landing could be swept by Japanese fire. The point was fortified. Heavily fortified. Air and Naval gunfire didn't do the job. The company landed and assaulted the point. And they took it. They took it and held it even while they were surrounded. And at the end of 48 hours, the company that landed with 235 men had 78 left.

"The question is, what makes a unit fight like that? This unit was very well trained. They rehearsed four times what they were going to do, so each man knew what was expected of him. They had good discipline. And they were governed by a driving spirit of unshakable loyalty on the part of each Marine to his fellow Marines. In the three wars I've served in, there have been a lot of differences. We fought against different people. We fought in different countries. We fought with different weapons. But one thing I believe has been constant in all three of those wars is the basic foundation of effective combat leadership. If someone were to ask me to draw the profile of an effective combat leader, I'd say it's someone who really knows his stuff. I'd say it's someone who understands the vital importance of discipline. It's someone who understands the importance of hard, demanding training. It's someone who takes care of his men, has a sincere interest in their welfare. It's also somebody who's physically fit and leads by example. And finally, someone who's proud he's a Marine. I think that profile has been good as long as there has been a Marine Corps."

Dan and his son Bennett had dinner with General Platt in Washington, D.C. a short time before the general's passing in 2000.

"'You were in three wars,' I said to the general. 'Which was the worst?' Without hesitation he said Vietnam, and he explained why. 'You took a piece of ground and you had to come back and take it again and again and again. Civilians would size up your position so they could attack you at night. Every day you fought. Everyday someone was shooting at you. Every day you had casualties.' And he also mentioned the treatment we got when we came home. I told him I would have thought he'd say World War Two. He said, 'We picked everywhere we landed. We landed in Guadalcanal, kicked their ass, and they knew they were in trouble. We picked every battle up to Okinawa, and we were prepared to invade Japan before the atomic bombs ended it. But we would have lost many, many people and millions of theirs would have died.'

"He said, 'Everybody calls it "The Greatest Generation," but what you people did in Vietnam was probably the most significant and the hardest of what anybody did. Total guerrilla warfare.'"

Simon Gregory's efforts to secure the Bronze Star Award for Dan were successful. On 5 March 1998, exactly 32 years after the battle, an award ceremony was held in Springfield, Massachusetts. Dan's son, Captain Bennett Walsh, who led the same platoon his father did 29 years later in Somalia, pinned the Bronze Star over his dad's heart.

"What an honor it is to do this," he whispered to his dad.

"It's an honor to have you do it," Dan said to his son.

Simon Gregory was the keynote speaker.

"Thirty-two years ago today," he began, "Dan Walsh, myself, and the men of the Third Battalion 1st Marines, were engaged in combat with an enemy unit that was part of the 21st North Vietnamese Army Regiment. Within minutes, we were fully engaged with the enemy who were well dug in, heavily armed and camouflaged to perfection. The shoulder high brush offered excellent concealment for the holes and emplacements that fortified their positions. The fighting was very close in, personal, and for some of us, hand to hand. Every weapon we possessed had to be utilized, down to and including combat knives. Lieutenant Walsh never faltered. Even after he received massive wounds from a machine gun at point blank range striking him in the shin, thigh, and hip he continued to direct his platoon."

Simon ended his speech with these words:

"In addition to his personal bravery and ability to function under fire, my most enduring memory of Dan that day was his complete dedication to his men. He understood the sacred trust required to be a Marine Officer and was willing to sacrifice himself in the execution of that responsibility. Additional words are not necessary. We are fortunate to have this opportunity to honor him today. Dan Walsh has met the test and had to pay a heavy price, he is all a man can be and he is an outstanding Marine."

When Dan Walsh describes his combat experience, he does not toot his own horn. He expresses pride in the men of his platoon, in particular, his platoon sergeant, Leonard Hultquist who died on Hill 50.

"I came out of the Basic School. They gave us six months of pretty intensive training in platoon, company, and battalion tactics. It's all very intensive, just like college. When you get out, you hear so much about the platoon sergeants, how valuable they are, so you expect this great guy who's going to teach you something. Well, I get out there and I get this guy. Oh my God! I don't know why he was there. So I go to Gregory and Sehulster and I tell them, 'This guy's no good. I expected to get an E-6 who would teach me, but I'm teaching him. I mean, I'm wet behind the ears and this guy isn't cutting it, so give me another guy.' So they give me another guy. Another month after that I came back, and I said, 'Hey! I'm not a complainer, but this guy can't keep up in the field. He's great in garrison, he's got a lot of bullshit, he knows his stuff, but you got to lead from the front, and this guy can't do it. Look, I can't do this. You need to give me my platoon guide, Hultquist. He's the best Marine I got. And Boland is the next guy. They're all good, but this guy is great.' Sehulster said, 'OK, you can have him. We'll see that he's promoted to staff sergeant.'

"Staff Sergeant Hultquist. Right away we clicked. It was fantastic. The guy was just a great Marine."

Staff Sergeant Leonard A. Hultquist, killed in actin March 5, 1966.

CHAPTER 8

Staff Sergeant Leonard A. Hultquist

The invitation read:

"The Class of '54 would like to invite you to a dedication ceremony in memory of Lenny Hultquist. 10:30 a.m. June 24th 2000. Veterans Memorial, Boys Town, Nebraska."

Born in Omaha, Leonard Hultquist attended his first six school grades at Ogallala before his mother dispatched him to Boys Town where he completed grades 7 through 12. Immediately after graduating in 1954, Leonard enlisted in the Marine Corps. After his discharge in 1958 he went to work in a bakery in Ogallala where he met Nancy Blomenkamp of Keystone, Nebraska. After a brief romance the two were married.

In 1960 Leonard reentered the Marines. He was stationed at Quantico, Virginia for a short time, then four years at Kaneoke Marine Air Station in Hawaii before being transferred to Camp Pendleton where he was assigned to Lima Company 3/1. By this time Leonard and Nancy had three daughters, ages 3, 5, and 6. All three attended the memorial ceremony at Boys

Town. Sadly, Nancy passed away the year before on the 1st of October, which was Leonard's birthday.

Melody Green, the middle daughter, delivered a speech. Though she never had the opportunity to know her father, Melody had learned a great deal about him—as a Marine and a husband—by reading all the letters he wrote to Nancy along with the many letters of condolence from friends, family members and his fellow Marines.

Having served in Lima Company's first platoon, I only knew Sergeant Hultquist, platoon sergeant of the second platoon, by sight and by reputation. But thanks to Melody, who shared his letters with me, I now feel as though I know Leonard Hultquist. Specifically, I learned two essential things about the man: that he loved his family and he loved the Marine Corps—in that order. But they were not two separate things that he compartmentalized. For both Leonard and Nancy, the family and the Corps were intertwined, as we see in this letter written on 14 December 1965:

Hi Lover,

We made it! Yes, we made Staff Sgt.

He was not simply sharing the news of his own success with his spouse. He was announcing *their* success.

In August 1965, as 3/1 was about to set sail from Long Beach, Leonard wrote to Nancy promising to "write every day while aboard this tub. We are heading for Okinawa. We will stay in Okinawa for six to eight weeks and then go afloat for a month and hit the beaches in Viet Nam...but I personally don't think it [the war] will last too much longer."

In the 202 days between the battalion's departure from Long Beach and Leonard Hultquist's final day on earth, he wrote 87 letters to Nancy. What follows are excerpts from those letters:

USS Magoffin 6 September 1965

I just received the plan of the day and there is only one thing missing in that plan and that is you. I don't think I will be able to get you in my plan of the day until we are in each others arms again and it will be quite awhile before we can do that.

USS Magoffin, 10 September 1965

Well Darling, this will be my last letter aboard the USS Magoffin. We get off tomorrow morning about 0900. Heard the news that the Marines are raising hell again in Viet Nam. Did a lot of killing the last four days. I hope they keep it up. Will make it easier for us.

Camp Schwab, Okinawa 14 September 1966

Well we finally arrived in Okinawa on the 12th of September. We are going to the N.T.A. (Northern Training Area) for 30 days. Our company will be the only one there that long. Right now we are in the presence of a typhoon, condition II.

NTA 11 November 1965

Troops are getting some very good training up here at NTA. Most of it is guerrilla warfare.

NTA 12 November 1965

This plt. sgt. is something else. The troops complain that he has only been out in the field with them for three days. We have been here at the Northern Training Area for nineteen days. This guy has more ailments than Carter has pills. They all call him The Great Pretender and it fits him perfect. I sure hope I make staff sergeant next because it just isn't fair to the troops when they have to put up with something like him. And he really doesn't even know his own job.

We will leave NTA on the 24th of Nov. As soon as we get back to Schwab, we will have 3 days of raider training in rubber boats, then one week at the rifle range.

NTA 13 November 1965

Parting is always going to be bad as far as I'm concerned because you always know you are leaving your loved ones. Someday I hope it will end, but I think it will be at least 18 more years as long as I'm in the Marine Corps.

Camp Schwab Okinawa 28 November 1965

Hi Lover,

How is my wonderful wife today? Say I forgot in my last letter to wish you a happy Thanksgiving. Yes, Darling, we do have a lot to be thankful for. I'm most thankful for you being my wife for the last eight years and that you continue to be for the rest of my life. And that we together have three wonderful little girls.

Camp Schwab Okinawa 8 December 1965

I will always be alert to watch out for myself and my troops because I have too much to lose and remember that we have to always have faith and confidence and especially the wife of a Marine because the Marine wife has to be the very best, and this is one Marine that has got nothing but the <u>Best</u>.

Camp Schwab Okinawa 3 December 1965

Chu Lai is one of the hottest spots in the war so we should see a lot of action, but that is what we've been training for...It seems that the biggest problem in Viet Nam is this damned Army general, Westmoreland. Most of us Marines don't think too much of him.

I guess you're right, most people don't let this war in Viet Nam bother them because they have no personal interest in it, because they are all secure and happy in their own little world.

Camp Schwab, Okinawa 10 December 1965

Dear Lover,

Hi. I miss you very much, and I sure do love you. Do you love me? I know you do, but I just wanted to ask you. I will never stop loving you, Darling. The only thing wrong is I can't prove it to you now, but I will in a year or so, you just wait and see.

Well, Darling, I think it is about time to have a serious conversation. Now you know that there is a possibility that something might happen to me. I will do everything in my power to prevent it, but there is still that possibility. If something should, I want you to do me a favor and that is take care of the kids, and if you should get married again, Darling, pick a man that will treat you good and that will love you as I do and make sure that he will accept the girls. You will have a big responsibility in your hands if you should happen to lose me and you're going to have to be brave because of the girls. I know that you have probably thought of it many times, but I just wanted to let you know, Darling, how I feel about it. I'm just concerned for you because I want you to be very happy after I go. You know that this is probably something we should have talked about when I was home because we probably both thought that this is something that happens to others and not us. But, Darling, it could, and we both realize it, but there is nothing to get alarmed about right now. But it is something to think about. But believe me, I have a date in Denver with my wife that I intend to keep.

Sometimes I just can't get you off my mind, and just keep thinking how lucky I am having you as my wife, and how much I love you and miss you Darling. I think of the kids and how I wish I could see them. I look at the picture you sent me every day. And I really know what I have to be thankful for, that I've got all of you at home waiting for me, and I will be back some day so we can live as a family again.

You remember my platoon commander, Lt. Walsh. Today he was made a 1st Lt. When I make staff we will have a good platoon sgt. also. The lt. is going to be a fine officer.

Well Darling I will close now, and see you in Denver later. Take care of yourself and the girls, and I love all of you.

Love Always,

Len

Camp Schwab, Okinawa 26 December 1965

I really don't know when we will leave for Viet Nam, but I hope it is soon. The troops have started to get in trouble on liberty, and I'm sure it is because they are getting to the point that they don't think they will get down south.

Camp Schwab, Okinawa 28 December 1965

Well, I got some good news, love. I won't be leaving Lima Company and not only that I have become Plt. Sgt. of the 2nd Plt. The one we had was transferred today. That makes me feel awful good because the Captain kept me instead of the other SSgt. So now I will have to do a little better so I can prove to him that he made the right choice.

USS Paul Revere 12 January 1966

We are aboard ship now. We came aboard about 12 this morning and haven't done much the rest of the day. We stayed in the harbor the whole night. Tomorrow we will arrive in Subic Bay for four days of training

USS Paul Revere 22 January 1966

Tomorrow we'll make a landing on the island of Mendora, the same place we were when I was on Westpac in 1962. In fact, it will be in some of the same areas that we worked in back then. We are on our way to Viet Nam. I don't know when we'll hit the beach.

25 January 1966 USS Paul Revere

As you can guess by the way I am writing that I will be going into combat. Well, you're right, we are making a beach landing on Friday the 28th. It is supposed to be the biggest operation since the war started. Please don't talk about it to anyone. They will read of it in the paper sooner or later.

Tomorrow we go into combat. It will really be something. I wish I could tell you about it now but you know how it is. I will write and tell you all about it when it's over.

I will close for now.

I love you,

Len

27 January 1966 (D-Day minus 1) Viet Nam

Hi Love,

You know I really don't feel any different. It seems like we are going on another operation except I know this is the real thing and that I've spent 10 years of training for this and I finally get my chance to prove to myself that I'm one of the best with the help of God. I know with His help, and remembering you and the girls are all at home waiting for me to come back home I will make it, but first I have to make sure that all my troops make it, and this will be my main concern. I know that you will be set and the kids will get an education, so I'm going to make it my biggest concern that my troops will be coming back with me.

The big moment is only ten hours away, so reveille will go at two in the morning.

You keep telling me to be brave. Well, I think in this situation that we both need to be brave, and you will even have to be braver because if anything did happen, you will have to raise the family all by yourself and really you did most of the raising so far, what little I've done really won't amount to much compared to what you have done for the girls and the family as a whole. Like you said, remember that I have a beautiful and wonderful wife and three beautiful girls to come home to and believe me, Darling, I will be there.

Well, there is only two hours left and the only one I'm thinking of now is you, how much I love you and miss you and that we could spend the next two hours together before I left. Time has seemed to go by fast so far, but I'm sure it will even go faster now.

Please remember what I said before about what I would like for you to do in case something should happen. You are the only person in the whole world who means anything to me and that I want what is best for you. I love you and will always love you.

Tell the girls I love them, I miss them, and Daddy wants them to be good for you, and to help make things better while I'm gone.

All My Love,

Len

Viet Nam 30 January 1966

Our only problem when we hit the beach was getting off the ship. We had some very rough water. The Mike boat was bouncing around like a little rubber ball. Most of the men were either pulled off the nets or they fell off. One of the men fell and sprained his arm. One of my squad leaders fell in the drink between the ship and the Mike boat. I know everyone's heart was in their throats like mine, but he was a very good and strong swimmer. He swam under the Mike boat and came out the other side.

So far about the only thing that has happened to our company is getting sniped at. So far, the battalion has had 4 wounded and 2 killed in action. Mostly we have just been doing a lot of patrolling and searching villages and clearing villages. We've taken VC prisoners and VC suspects.

We had a very exciting night. Our line was being probed most of the night and fired on quite a few times. The Lt. and I managed to get a couple of hours of sleep about 0300.

Please Darling, don't worry too much about me. You take care of yourself and the girls and I will be home around September or October, and we'll have a party just the two of us. I love you Darling and miss you very much.

Sorry for the messy letter but everything is wet and sandy and I'm always in a hurry in case we have to move out.

Bye and pray for us all over here.

All My Love,

Len

Viet Nam 1 February 1966

The way the people here live is a shame, but I guess since they don't know any different. They are happy. But this country is beautiful. Another thing you really don't know is who is your friend or your enemy.

Viet Nam 2 February 1966

Before I forget, I know that we have an anniversary coming up on the 27th of Feb. I would like to wish you a very happy anniversary. You know, Darling, it seems like something always interferes with our anniversary. I don't think that we have had too many of them together, the but ones we did have were outstanding. Maybe next year we can be together. I hope we can, but in case I cannot get a card to send you, I want you to know that I love you very much and that since we have been married, I know my life has been the happiest that any one man could ask for and it is all because, Darling, I love you, and what joy you have given me, and Darling, I hope that you are happy too. That is my only desire, is to see and make you happy.

The troops are getting irritated because they want to see some action. Well, as far as I'm concerned, we will see a lot of it before we leave here, so I'm happy to have a little slack because when we get into action it will be a good one. But it is so damned hot. I think it is the biggest cause for being irritated.

My platoon still only lost two people to enemy action. That was the corpsman and one other man (I should say boy, but he was doing a man's job) then other people that were hit the same day were only attached to me.

Viet Nam 10 February 1966

What we see here the people just don't care whether they are free or not. This is the poorest way I've seen people live of any place I've been since I've been in the service. The people don't have a thing except the clothes on their backs, some run-down little hut they call a house that is made of some brick for the walls and the top made of bamboo leaves, and they don't have a thing on the inside except the four walls and dirt floor.

Well, I'm fine except I have some sore feet. We have done a lot of walking since we have been here and going through a lot of water over hills and valleys all on foot from sun up until sundown. I could use some sex and some good chow. We only have two meals a day and I need more food. The C-rations are good, but there just isn't enough of it.

Viet Nam 12 February 1966

Well Dear, another day walking over hills and valleys. We just stopped for the night and I just had myself a wonderful meal of Ham and Lima Beans and even had all kinds of company, of ants and flies. I just wonder what it will be like to have my family at the table with me. It seems like it's been a long time since I ate with all of you. I might not know how to conduct myself.

Our company captured a Chinese made machine gun today and killed two VC and wounded one more. I guess the Lord is really with us, at least my company. So far we have only had light casualties. I hope that we can continue to keep Lima Company's casualties down and bring the count of enemy casualties up.

16 FEB 1966

Viet Nam

Hi Lover,

Well Darling we're still in the combat zone. We will be pulling out of this area tomorrow heading for Chu Lai. We should be back aboard ship around 1000 on the 17th.

We came out of the mountains two days ago. We had one helluva withdrawal. First we pulled two pre-dawn raids on 4 different villages, the total casualties for the two companies was 2 KIA and 13 WIA, with the enemy around 87 KIA.

Climax of the withdrawal was the crossing of the river. There was one battalion on the opposite side of the river and was to cover our crossing. Then our company was supposed to provide cover for the last squad crossing. Just as they got into the water all hell broke loose. One man was hit and went down and it looked like another man went down. I knew we had to get them. I guess 3 others thought the same thing because by the time I had my gear off and started across the river there were the other 3 men all charging across. The four of us faced the enemy side until we just about reached our shore. The other three turned out to be my platoon commander, my company commander, and another man in my platoon. We talked

134

about it later and agreed it wasn't a very good idea to have the two of us doing something like that at the same time, but at least we know that we can count on each other when the chips are down, and anyway we received some good close air support which was both close and good.

I will close for now. Will write later.

All My Love,

Len

Viet Nam 18 February 1966

No I haven't heard from my mother. I sent her a Christmas card and wrote her once but haven't received any from any of them.

Tell Melody that her work is to be done in school and that she should always try to do her best at anything she does. But tell her I'm very proud of her.

I guess our next operation is coming up in a few days. Will let you now more about it when I find out.

Will close for now Darling. Remember I love you very deeply and my love for you grows more and more every day. Tell the girls that I will cherish their Valentine card and hope I can put this in a scrapbook someday.

Will write later Darling. Bye and take care of yourself and hope to see you in the future.

All My Love, Len

19 FEB 1966 Viet Nam

Got the word that we are moving out. I don't know anything except we are going on another operation for 10 days.

I tell you Honey we have been pushing the troops pretty hard on the last operation and we have had very little rest, and even I am beginning to feel it.

21 FEB 1966 Viet Nam

Well this is the first chance I have had to write since the second phase of Operation Double Eagle began 4 days ago. In my last letter I told you we would remain on the beach for about five days. Well we stayed the night and most of the next

135

day then moved inland about 3 miles and on the 19th started the operation. So as you can see we haven't had any slack at all. My people have had 2 hot meals and 1 shower since we got off the ship on 28 January.

Don't get alarmed but I got hit, and all it did was break the skin on the back of my neck. The Doc was checking me out when a sniper opened up on us and the doc got shot in the leg and will be out for the rest of his tour. And he was very lucky. It only got him in the ankle, but broke the bone. When I got hit I felt I got stung like a bee until I saw blood dripping off my neck and chin. I carried the doc back to a safe area and tried to find out where the fire came from and did, but I only had a .45 which wasn't any good at that distance. Then the platoon came up on line. My platoon took 5 casualties that day, none of them very serious. So I hope that is all I get for my Purple Heart. We were shot at from our rear, from the village we had just came from. So we leveled that village.

24 FEB 1966 Viet Nam

You won't believe how bad it is over here. These damn rice paddies are about to get the best of all of us. We stay wet most of the time, or either it's so damned hot, but so far we haven't lost anyone to heat stroke, but lost a couple because of feet problems.

You know Darling, you should see the troops. They might be pissed off, miserable, and everything else, but they are high in morale and spirit. If a counselor would see us now and the way we all act, he would think that we are all crazy, but that's just because he wouldn't know any better.

I guess we only got four more days of this operation. Since we landed here in Viet Nam our battalion has more firsts than any other units that have landed in Viet Nam. This was the biggest amphibious landing since Korea, and the longest operation that one unit has been committed to. We have had the least number of KIAs and we do have a few more WIA because the battalion was larger than any other unit that has landed. As far as the company goes we have the least amount of KIA and WIA in the battalion.

[Tragically for his wife and daughters, in just over a week Staff Sergeant Hultquist would participate in another first—namely, the first battle between the Marines and the NVA.]

27 FEB 1966 Viet Nam

Last night is the second time our all night ambush paid off. The third platoon got the hit. They killed two VC wounded 3, captured one M-1 rifle, one .45 sub machine gun, some ammo for the two weapons, some hand grenades and some anti-personnel mines. So we're doing pretty well as a company. We have had a lot of compliments from high ranking officers.

This is our 9th day on this phase of Operation Double Eagle, and the way it looks we are heading back towards Chu Lai, and should be there sometime tomorrow which will be a good deal because we need a couple of days of rest and get our gear squared away. Remember when I used to come home from a field problem in Hawaii and the dirty clothes I'd bring with me? If you thought those were dirty and stinky you should see the ones I wear now. You would want to burn them and I wouldn't blame you. I can't even stand myself.

Right now we are in the heart of VC territory, but we haven't found too many of them.

[Looking over the large packet of letters I received from Melody on the day it arrived, I was surprised to see the date of Hultquist's last letter to his wife—5 March 1966. That has to be a mistake, I thought. Early that morning the company was on a hilltop preparing to march down to Hill 50. But it wasn't a mistake. While most of us were trying to get some sleep between midnight and dawn, Ssgt. Hultquist was writing a letter to Nancy. The letter was found in his map case]

5 March 1966 Viet Nam

Hi Lover,

I know you won't believe this, but it's the truth. Right now I'm sitting on top a hill that is so thick with vegetation that it is almost impossible to move. My whole platoon is here. The rest of the company is about 800 meters from us, the battalion behind us, and it is almost midnight. We moved out from the beach area around 1500 today by helicopter (you see we do get to fly in them once in a while, but only to take us someplace so we can walk back) to Hill 180 which is where Battalion is and we walked about 1,200 meters to our present position. We had reports that there is or was a battalion of VC in this area. Since 2/7 was out in this area already we are being used as a blocking force again. I think if I was a VC I would quit. Just a few minutes ago we had our close air support at work for about 30 minutes. Then artillery took over, then the 81 mortars are firing now and about the only weapons that they have is a rifle for about every four men and if some of them are lucky they might have a 57 recoilless or a 60mm mortar and a few rounds. But what is that compared to what I just mentioned? Really Honey the VC should just quit and go home. Oh sure, they get a couple of lucky punches in once in a while and when they do it is usually with the South Vietnamese—and we lose a few men but it is nothing compared to what they lose. Another reason we came out here was because yesterday we lost a helicopter and came to get it back which we will do in the morning.

I'm sitting on radio watch—well in fact I've been on for about three hours to let some of the troops get a little sleep and I sure am glad I'm on our side, because you should hear and see noise and destruction of what our air power and artillery and 81s can do.

I'm writing this letter by moonlight and the light of flares when they go off. One is going on now like the light of a million candles.

I'm sorry that I didn't get your allotment today, but the company office wasn't set up before we pulled out. I still might be able to get it to you by the first of next month.

Sounds like M Company is having a good firefight. I don't think we have any trouble in the position where we're at, because it would take them too long to get up here and they would make too much noise.

You know I haven't written to your mom yet. Tell her I'm sorry and that I will get a letter off to her as soon as I get back to the beach area, and would you send me my Mother's address? I will try again and see if I can get an answer.

Sure is a nice cool night, nice moon, the kind we should have at home.

Our zip code has changed so make sure you notice it, because that way it will come directly to Viet Nam instead of going to Okinawa.

Well my Darling I Love You dearly and I wish I could show you but as usual it will have to wait. I do love you with all my heart and body.

Don't forget about the goodies.

I Love you Dear.

All My Love,

Len

Doc Robert Ingraham was a corpsman with H&S Company during Double Eagle I and II. The week before Lima Company boarded helicopters for Operation Utah he was transferred to Lima Company. Ingraham shared his recollections of 5 March:

"I spent every day in Vietnam praying that nothing horrible would happen. Then, of course, it did happen. It was traumatic, let me tell you. The wounds I saw on Hill 50 were unbelievable. And I don't know if I saved any lives that day. I probably didn't. They probably would have lived without treatment, at least for a while. It's pretty hard to talk about. I did what I knew I should do. I managed to control bleeding to some extent with battle dressings. There was a sergeant who was shot in the chest. I put a bandage over that. He probably survived."

Had he been with Lima Company from the beginning, he would have known that the sergeant he treated was the second platoon commander, Leonard Hultquist. Even after getting shot in the chest, Hultquist was alert and protecting the troops.

"I was called to help one of our sergeants. He was lying on his back with a pumping chest wound. I was just getting ready to apply a compress to it when he twisted away and yelled, "Grenade!" I looked up to see a grenade flipping through the air right over our heads. It landed eight or 10 feet away, and I hit the deck just as it exploded. Amazingly, nobody was hurt. It was apparently a Chinese grenade: they were powerful and could certainly kill you, but if you were some distance from them, they were not nearly as dangerous as American ones. If it had been one of our grenades, both the sergeant and I and a few other nearby Marines might have been killed. I went back to work on the sergeant and the same thing happened again. That second grenade injured a Marine next to me, who got a piece of shrapnel right through his buttocks and was out of the fight. I bandaged the sergeant as well as I could, and tried to patch up Lieutenant Cleaver, whose shoulder was mangled. For all I knew it could have been be a fatal wound. Then someone said there was a wounded Marine further up the hill. So I grabbed my Unit One medical bag and went looking for him, running through those winding trails."

Lieutenant Cleaver's wound was not fatal, but Staff Sergeant Hultquist's was. When Hill 50 was secured, helicopters arrived to pick up the wounded. Hultquist died at the battalion aid station later that afternoon.

The day before we boarded the choppers for Operation Utah, Nancy Hultquist received a telegram from General Wallace M. Greene, Jr., Commandant of the Marine Corps, informing her that Leonard had been "injured on 20 February 1966 in the vicinity of Quang Tin Republic of Vietnam. He sustained a fragmentation wound in the back of his neck while participating in an operation against hostile forces. He was treated in the field and returned to duty."

It was Monday night, the 7th of March 1966 in Keystone, Nebraska, which made it Tuesday morning in Quang Ngai Province where Leonard Hultqust had been killed three days earlier. But Nancy Hultquist was unaware of that when she wrote to her beloved husband.

"In the letter I got from you today you said you had gotten back to Chu Lai. But from the sound of the news your reprieve didn't last long did it? Of course I've been sitting on pins and needles since Saturday morning wondering if you're okay. I suppose you are still at Quang Ngai. NBC showed 15 minutes of film from those battles in the news tonight. The General [General Platt] pointed out where I, M, and L companies of 3 Batt 1st Mar. were located. They also interviewed several guys from M Co. One Pfc. was asked if the VC were good fighters. He said "Hell no, the Marines are the very best outfit!" The news also said M Co couldn't even recover seven of their dead until I Co came and covered for them. Also sounded like you were short of ammo and water. However, you have made the headlines all over the Nation and apparently all the Communists that were killed was a big surprise and it's the biggest victory of the war. The General also gave high praise to the ARVN—he said they fought as good as any outfit could have.

"So—is a newscast like this hogwash? Or is it the truth? Anyway the whole battle looked mighty rough. I only wish I knew if you were okay. Guess your Batt. had the bad deal of getting stationed in the bloodiest part of Viet Nam didn't you? By the way, have you had your fill of combat by now?"

The next night, now four days since her husband was killed, Nancy Hultquist wrote another letter to Len.

"I'm afraid this letter won't be much tonight—my nerves are just about shot but I am trying to get myself pulled together. NBC news reported tonight that all that was left of L Co, 3rd Batt, 1st Mar was the dead and seriously wounded. They

141

said the whole company was almost all wiped out. Ok, I pray to God that you're all right. I called Burton Bracken in Ogallala to see if the Red Cross could find any quick word as to your condition. But Mr. Bracken was in Lincoln so I talked to his wife and she said he was to call her tonight and that she would give him the message and he would wire Washington. Actually, I didn't really want him to do that. I mainly wanted to know about how long it takes before word would come in case something happened to you. But I guess that he'll send the wire anyway and it will go through all the channels and to Viet Nam, so if you are okay, I apologize for being a worried wife.

"I'll get a package of fudge and brownies and cookies in the mail soon probably in three or four days.

"Well Love I'll close for now. I'm going to take two sleeping pills and to bed. I'm praying for all you guys over there and particularly you Len.

"I Love you.

"All My Love,

"Nancy"

Apparently, Mr. Bracken's query made its way to Viet Nam because Keith County (Nebraska) News called the Associated Press in Omaha on 10 March asking why the family had not been notified of Hultquist's death. They received the following letter:

"WASHINGTON D.C. (AP)--The pentagon acknowledged today (March 10) that because of a slip-up, it announced the death of a Nebraska Marine sergeant before the next of kin were notified.

"The name of Sgt. Leonard A. Hultquist, husband of Nancy M. Hultquist of Keystone, Neb., appeared on Wednesday's official list of men killed as a result of Community action in Viet Nam."

Such public announcements normally are made only after Pentagon authorities have received confirmation that next-of-

kin have been notified. A spokesman said there had been a slip-up in the case of Sgt. Hultquist.

The Pentagon spokesman said a non-commissioned officer in the Marine Casualty Branch, checking before the public announcement, had mis-read a notification to the family that Sgt. Hultquist had been wounded and interpreted this as notification that the sergeant had died.

The spokesman said that after the error was called to the attention of the Pentagon, steps were taken Thursday morning to get in touch immediately with Sgt. Hultquist's family.

But it was not immediately. Immediately would have been that day, the 10th, but it was not until the next day, almost a week after Leonard was killed on Hill 50, that Nancy received a telegram from General Wallace Greene, Jr.:

"I DEEPLY REGRET TO CONFIRM THAT YOUR HUSBAND SERGEANT LEONARD A HULTQUIST USMC DIED 5 MARCH IN THE VICINITY OF QUANG NGAI PROVINCE REPUBLIC OF VIETNAM. HE SUSTAINED A GUNSHOT WOUND IN THE CHEST WHILE ENGAGED IN AN OPERATION AGAINST HOSTILE FORCES."

No officers were sent to her home to personally convey the tragic news as was customary at the time. No apology for the "slip-up." Just a cold telegram from Headquarters Marine Corps. Back in the Nam, would we survivors of Operation Utah been surprised by that? Of course not. There was a reason why grunts like me referred to the USMC as "the Crotch." Out in the bush we could count on one another to live up to our motto, Semper Fidelis. But from the brass, not so much.

However, when it comes to cold condolence letters from generals, it's hard to beat the form letter Nancy, along with the next-of-kin of the other 97 Marines killed on Utah, received from Army General William Westmoreland, whom Leonard had referred to as "the biggest problem in Viet Nam," informing her that he was "deeply distressed to learn of the death of her husband," and that he "always has a feeling of close personal loss when informed of the death of members of this command who have died while serving their country here in Vietnam." It's hard to imagine how he dealt with, or for that matter had the time to deal with, the approximately 30,000 instances of distress and feelings of loss he experienced during his command from '64 to '68.

Moving from cold to downright bizarre, there was the letter Nancy received from the Right Reverend Nicholas H. Wegner of Boys Town in which he began his letter expressing his hope "that the Good Lord was merciful to his soul and placed it among the elect in paradise," thus leaving open the possibility that Leonard might not have been so lucky, that he might have had the misfortune of landing in hell. But that said, the Right Reverend assured Nancy that "All the boys and I will remember his precious spirit in our prayers asking God's mercy upon it **just in case it might be detained in the cleansing fires of Purgatory on its flight into heaven.**" Somehow, I can't imagine Father Flanagan, the founder of Boys Town, writing those words to the grieving widow of one of his Boys.

Aside from all that nonsense, Leonard Hultquist was the real deal—as a Marine, as a man, as a husband and father—and there were plenty of condolence letters from folks who were aware of who he was. For instance, Nancy's sister Ginny wrote:

"I remember the last visit here, just a year ago at Easter time. Him taking your kids, and Snoopy on a leash, for walks in the snow – that first snow was such a treat after none for years. He had such love and patience with your girls – a most unusual father – something for you to always remember and be proud of. My big kids sensed this love and dignity he had for children and had the highest regard for him. He and Pat standing out in that ice cold garage for so long while Leonard taught him how to spit shine everyone's shoes for Easter – both of them so serious about the shoes being perfect."

Simon Gregory, acting CO of Lima Company on Operation Utah, wrote the kind of straightforward letter Nancy could appreciate:

"Len as you know, was Platoon Sergeant of the Second Platoon. On the morning of 5 March 1966 while participating in an operation against hostile forces, Len led his platoon in an assault against an entrenched position. It was during this assault that he was mortally wounded. First Aid was administered by the Navy Corpsman attached to the company and Len was immediately evacuated by helicopter to a nearby hospital. Everything possible was done for him, but he failed to rally and died of a gunshot wound in the chest at 3:30PM after receiving the last rites of his faith."

"Len's cheerful disposition, uprightness, and devotion to duty was for him the respect of all who knew him. Although I realize that words can do little to console you, I do hope the knowledge that your husband is keenly missed and that we share your sorrow will in some measure alleviate the suffering caused you by your great loss."

Sergeant Joseph "Jay" McDowell, 3rd platoon guide, was probably Hultquist's best friend in the outfit. Jay wrote to Nancy telling her he thought of Leonard as the brother he never had. "When the word was confirmed of his death I will admit I broke into tears. I lost many men in my own platoon, but none had as great effect on me as Leonard. You lost a great husband Nancy and I know if he could tell you he would say lift your head high and look into the future. Whatever you do don't give up living."

Gunnery Sergeant Richard Gunder, our company gunny, sent Nancy a five-page handwritten letter that was, in my opinion, the most consoling condolence letter she could have received. Not because it was particularly eloquent. In fact, the gunny tells her, "I haven't had much schooling and am not very good at writing letters." Gunny Gunder's letter stands out because it was written in the spirit of Len's letters insofar as it

145

included her in what was happening 10,000 miles away. Nancy Hultquist had more than an investment in her marriage. She had a personal investment in the Marines in general and Lima Company in particular.

First, Gunder summarizes our action on hill 50. "I was on Operation Utah along with all the men in this company and I must tell you that all our hard training we went through in Okinawa aided this company in completing its mission." Then he brings her up to date on what Lima Company was doing after the operation. "We have now been moved to an island just off the coast of Chu Lai. We are providing security and running patrols for a missile unit here.

"We are still trying to survey some of our equipment that we have in a large pile next to our supply tent. We found Len's map case in some of the equipment and it was brought to me here at the office. When going through it I found this letter he had addressed to you, 2 pictures, and some cards I thought I would send to you right away. I looked at the pictures and believe me, you can tell your daughters they can always be proud of their father. He was a hard worker and one of the better Staff in the Battalion and he was looking out for his men when this terrible thing happened."

Because of the extensive care and rehabilitation required to treat his massive wounds on Hill 50, Lt. Dan Walsh was unable to write to Nancy right away. When he was finally able, he told her what an outstanding Marine her husband was. Walsh wrote that whenever they had a personal conversation "the main topic was his wife and three little girls. In Viet Nam, I saw and knew a man whose whole life was wrapped up in his family.

"Mrs. Hultquist, he was a man at peace with himself and his creator and I'm sure he died in that same state of peace. He is in heaven today, I'm sure."

The following are excerpts of Nancy's reply to Dan Walsh:
I'm pleased that you had such a high regard for Leonard.

Of course, his death was a terrible blow, but I haven't felt any bitterness or rebellion over it. I have felt very proud of him and glad that he died doing what he wanted. I think that many people live a long and uneventful life and finally pass away without even being dedicated to one particular purpose or goal in life. So I cannot feel that Leonard's life was wasted as I think that it's very necessary for us to be in Viet Nam.

I came to love the Marine Corps as much as Leonard did and I always tried to be a good Marine Corps wife so I feel that I truly understood this compelling desire of his to be in Viet Nam.

Leonard and I knew each other only three months before we were married and we had our eighth anniversary seven days before he was killed so actually our time together was very brief. But I know I'm a much better person today from having known him and I'd like to think I helped him in the same way. I guess I'm trying to say that I'm thankful we both grew up before his death separated us. If this had happened two years before, I don't think I could have accepted it as well or had the faith that anything will be okay again.

The children have pulled through all of this like little troopers. Even after eight months they still talk about all the happy times we had together and what a good Daddy he was. It's really wonderful to see their complete trust and faith. Their main concern through all of this hasn't been for their own loss, but instead telling me how happy they are that Daddy is in heaven and doesn't have to be shot at again.

Nancy Hultquist was 26 when Leonard died. She never remarried.

Steve Crowley in Okinawa

CHAPTER 9

Lieutenant Steve Crowley

Mechanicsville, Virginia

The first stop of my Lima 3/1 road trip took me to the heart of the Confederacy, Mechanicsville, Virginia, just outside Richmond, to reunite with my platoon commander, Steve Crowley. I'm thankful for the timing. Steve passed away less than a year after our visit.

Steve was born and raised in New York City, in Jackson Heights in Queens.

"I did the basic Irish Catholic routine of Catholic elementary school, St. Joan of Arc, then onto La Salle Academy High School with the Christian Brothers, then off to Mobile, Alabama where Spring Hill College and the Jesuits took me in."

"How is it a New York boy chose a college in Alabama?" I asked.

"Well, graduating from high school I thought I was going to stay in New York. I could have gone to a local college like Iona up in New Rochelle where I could have commuted every day, or Fordham or St. John's. But my two next older brothers—Ed, who was at the Naval Academy and George who had gone to Fordham—both said I should get the hell out of New York to go to college. I had relatives from Laurel, Mississippi. They had a son who, even though he was Protestant, went to Spring Hill College. So, I looked into Spring Hill College and spoke to my high school counselor who had never heard of it. So, I got a brochure from there, and had to educate him on it. Lo and behold, two of my classmates got hold of that brochure and they went to Spring Hill College with me."

"What was it like there?"

"Spring Hill was an interesting place. When I was down there from '59 to '63, it was the only integrated educational institution in the state of Alabama. So, it was kind of rough. A year or so before I got there the KKK had a march in Mobile, and some of them came out to the campus with the intention of burning a cross. Fortunately, there were a number of kids who didn't like that—kids from New York, Milwaukee, Chicago, and Detroit, and they came out and started to get into a fight with the KKK and the Klan took off like holy hell."

"Did you have any experiences like that?"

"No, it was fairly peaceful when I was there. Of course, there was culture shock, but the odd thing about it, when we wanted to leave campus and go down to the local bar to get half a load on, we'd have to hitchhike. It was the black people that generally picked us up. You might have to climb in the back of a truck bed and share it with a bunch of vegetables, but he'd take you down there and drop you off. You would hope the whites whippin' by wouldn't throw stuff at you. But for the most part it was a peaceful existence and the education I got was excellent. It was a very diverse student body and that was good. We had some students from Central and South America even. Living with kids from all over with different social-ethnic backgrounds was an education unto itself.

"Obviously the South has changed drastically. When I first went down to Spring Hill I flew to New Orleans with my mother. We were picked up by a chauffeur named Borie who was taking us up to Laurel, Mississippi to visit our relatives. Borie was a fifty some-odd year-old black man who chauffeured for our hostess's mother. The mother had passed away. Before her death she "gave" Borie to her daughter. When we got to Laurel, I asked the lady what Borie's last name was, that I felt uncomfortable addressing an older man by his first name. 'No, you just call him Borie, she said.' It sounded like a reprimand. This was in 1959. There may not have been slavery, but it sure was an indentured kind of environment.

"Well, Borie drove my mom and me down to Mobile from Laurel. When we got to the hotel—the Admiral Simms Hotel—we asked Borie if he would be coming in and he said, 'Oh no, I'm going to be staying with some friends on the other side of town.' The next morning, he picked us up and drove us to the Dobbs House for breakfast. We invited him to have breakfast with us. He said he'd already had breakfast. So my mother and I were sitting in a booth waiting for our order to be served and I happened to look over at the counter. And I noticed that behind the counter there was an opening through which you could see into the kitchen. Past the kitchen I could see an open square in the wall. And there was Borie getting a cup of coffee. Then it occurred to me—holy shit. This is it. He's an inferior human being and he's not allowed in the Admiral Simms, and I don't know if he has friends over on the other side of town. And he wasn't allowed in the Dobbs House. And by golly if he wanted a cup of coffee, he had to go back to the black man's window. I guess that's when I start realizing what a systemic impact it had on me 'cause I must have turned white or something because my mother looked at me, and this was an Irish Catholic mother, and when you took food, you ate it. You could have all you want, but you had to eat all you took. She said, 'You don't look well. If you don't want to eat that, don't eat it.' I don't remember if I ate it or not, but that really had an impact on me. Here was this nice guy, Borie, who was a good human being, but was not treated like one.

"I wouldn't call myself a liberal. I don't go on marches or anything like that, but I guess I got my bearings straight when I saw Borie through that back window. Growing up in New York I took integration for granted. Our basketball team, our track team, everything was integrated. You didn't think of blacks as low-class or inferior.

"Next to the Marine Corps, Spring Hill was the next major event in my life. It formed a lot of my opinions and attitudes for life. Then came the Marine Corps. I spent a little time this morning looking at the cruise book. I saw this one black fellow; he was a husky guy. I couldn't remember his name. It was Carradine. Do you remember him?"

"Sure. We joined the outfit in Okinawa on the same day."

[After surviving combat in Vietnam, Corporal Carradine was shot and killed in the streets of his hometown, Compton, California.]

"I mean, there was no difference between him and Rapp, and Lucere, and you, and Gunny Gingrich. They're just people. But getting back to Spring Hill, they had been integrated for some while, and the reason for that was they had a nursing school that was integrated. In fact, if you had a black nurse in an Alabama hospital, most likely she was a graduate of the Spring Hill nursing program. They had a very good reputation. The Jesuits were active in the community. As a matter of fact, in Martin Luther King's 'Letter from Birmingham Jail,' he expresses his disappointment in the clergy who accompanied him until the stuff hit the fan. When it really got rough, he said these gray beards and holy men all took off except the Jesuits from Spring Hill. They stuck with him. There was one professor there, Father Foley. Knowing you had people like that around you, it made a difference."

[Steve's passing reference to Father Foley spurred an interest in learning more about the man. In the mid-Fifties Foley had publicly criticized the church for not taking a stand on segregation and racism. In 1956 he authored two model ordinances for Mobile, one of which would ban the police from membership in the KKK (which he called "the dunce cap and bedsheets brigade") and the other would ban "intimidation by exhibit"--that is, cross-burning.]

"So how is it you chose the Marine Corps after Spring Hill?"

"After college I was going to go into the Navy, trying to get into aviation, but my eyes weren't good enough according to them, and I sort of hung in the wind for a while. Then I got a Greetings from Uncle Sam letter. So I went to the Marine Corps and they took care of it. I got into the OCS program in '65. Went through OCS and Basic School at Quantico. After graduation, I received orders for the 1st Marine Division in California. When I got out there the place was basically empty. They were on what was called lock-on, and the company was out in the field. So, I was the lone wolf around there with a couple of company clerks. When they got back, I was assigned to the first platoon. Dan Walsh had the second platoon, Ben De La Rosa, the third, and Gene Cleaver, who was one of my classmates at Basic School, had weapons platoon.

"We shipped out in August. Went to Okinawa aboard the USS Magoffin where we were based at Camp Schwab in the northern part of the island. But we went further north to the Northern Training Area, NTA. That was interesting insofar as they gave us the training we would need for jungle warfare. The people who ran the place were an interesting crew. At the time, Staff Sergeant Jimmie Howard was one of the instructors. The following spring, he received the Medal of Honor in Vietnam.[1]

Major George, who ran the camp, was up there because he was being punished. He's the one who was using teargas in these tunnels to drive people out and they thought that was inhumane. Of course, the Marines turned around and starting using hand grenades, which wasn't too nice either.

"Served with 3/1 right from Okinawa onto Vietnam. We landed in Chu Lai. My company commander was Jim Sehulster and the executive officer was Simon Gregory. I guess for the most part we provided security for around the Chu Lai airbase.

The big event of our lives was called Operation Utah on Hill 50. We went up that hill with Dan Walsh out front. Gene Cleaver had taken over the third platoon and he was ahead of me. I was in the back with my guys, and I hear all hell break loose. When we went up I found Gene Cleaver lying head down and sort of turning blue. I couldn't tell where he'd been hit initially, but I picked him up, turned him around so the blood wasn't rushing to his head. I believe that's when you, Gary, and I think Lance Corporal Hester, my grenadier, came up. Then Doc Reyerson came up. Anyway, Gene seemed to be taken care of so I went up to see where all the stuff was hitting the fan and my folks got all spread out. Actually, I spread them out. Had some go up a little higher than where I was.

"One of them was Sergeant Rapp on my right front. He said he couldn't tell who the good guys and the bad guys were. I guess that's because the North Vietnamese had tied in with the ARVN and, I hate to say they all looked alike, but that was the problem at that point, so I said if they don't have round eyes, go ahead and shoot them. And that's what he proceeded to do.

"By the time I got up there, for the most part everything was done. There might have been some North Vietnamese still there, but by the time I got to the trench-line it was mostly dead bodies. I don't know if anybody tried to escape and had to be slowed down.

"Anyway, one thing I remember about that was I heard some of our people had been killed. I asked who and they mentioned the scout from Dan's platoon named Garner. So I asked, 'So where is he? Did anybody find his body?' and somebody said, 'It's right there,' and I looked down and saw the remains of somebody there. Didn't particularly notice it when I was coming up. So I took a poncho and scooped him up and got him down to the evacuation area and told them who it was, and got back up to where I belonged.

"I went up to the other side of the hill, and that's when I saw Lieutenant Simon Gregory having a little conversation with who I later found out was Pete Dawkins who was an Army adviser to the ARVN unit who tied in with the North Vietnamese. He was down there with Ben De La Rosa. Simon was reading him the riot act.

"Simon Gregory had taken over command of the company after Captain Sehulster's medical evacuation on Double Eagle 2. Ben De La Rosa became the executive officer and Gene Cleaver had taken charge of DeLaRosa's 3rd platoon.

"The last thing I remember is the survivors carrying the dead and wounded down the hill."

"Where were you sent after Lima 3/1?"

"The rest of my time in Vietnam was spent with 2/5 and 2/7. After that I went to Camp Lejeune as a military police officer. I had gotten married after getting back from Vietnam. I married a Washington girl. We lived in Jacksonville. I decided to get out of the Marine Corps. I got out, interviewed, and got a job with IBM. I stayed with them a couple of years as a systems engineer. During this period of time we had a daughter, Jennifer.

"From IBM I went to XEROX. Worked for them until 1980 when I decided to open my own business—total bookkeeping, accounting, and tax practice here in Mechanicsville. I did that up until my retirement in 2015. I've been enjoying the kind of freedom retirement has allowed me to have, like catching up on some of my reading. Right now, I'm reading *Uncle Tom's Cabin* which I probably should have read in high school. But I'm a little slow.

"By the way, speaking of 2/7 I have a somewhat amusing story to share with you. One of my memorable experiences in OCS was one morning when we were pleasantly aroused by our instructors, brought out onto the grinder and doing side straddle hops, squats, push-ups and so forth when the window of my squad bay opened and I hear, "Crowley!" I thought, Oh God! I go runnin' in there and lo and behold my wall locker was open and my rifle was in there. One of our instructors was there—Sergeant Bobby Lee Mullins from West Virginia—and he had me doing push-ups. He put my rifle across my hands as I'm doing push-ups and put his foot on it, pushing down. Just getting my attention, I guess. So, he did this for a while, then took the rifle and put it back in the wall locker. While he's doing that, I noticed my footlocker was unlocked. So, with one hand I reached over and locked it. And I got away with it—so I thought. When I came back in from my warming up exercises, I opened my footlocker and found the entire top tray covered in shaving cream. I took it out and discovered the bottom was covered in shaving cream. So the bastard had caught me. He not only caught me but put it back like he hadn't caught me.

"Well, lo and behold one day in Vietnam I'm a company commander with 2/7. I look at my table of operations and who do I see as my forward observer but Staff Sergeant Bobby Lee Mullins. So I thought, that son-of-a-gun, I'm gonna get him. So I'm sitting there waiting for him and waiting for him when the flap of my tent opens and I hear, "Crowley!" and I jump up and say, "Yes sir!" I thought, Dammit! I'm not supposed to do that. He's supposed to do that to me. So we chit-chatted for a while and he said, "I knew I'd run into one of you guys one of these days."

"I'm curious to know something. When we landed, were you of the opinion that we were there for all the right reasons?"

"I don't know if I ever felt that way."

"How did you feel?"

"I was probably ambivalent. How's that for an evasive answer?"

"I wouldn't call it evasive. Look, the reason I ask is, unlike me, a dumb-ass 19-year-old PFC. with a high school education, you were not only a college graduate, but someone educated by the Jesuits."

"Well, I really thought I'd rather be home dating Pat McCauley, but I was facing the draft, and I figured if I was going to go to war, I was going to go in first-class. And I knew I had to go in. It was sort of like, I don't want to be here, but I'm going to be here, so I'm going to make the most of it. I know I've heard many of you guys say 'I was never in this for God and Country and Motherhood,' and I never said that, but I guess it was part of how I felt. But when I took over a platoon, I really felt like, hey! I better take care of these goddam guys because their mothers want them home. And she doesn't want half of them home. Or a babbling idiot home. I'd better do as good a job as I can. I was blessed with having Gunny Gingrich as my platoon sergeant. He was sort of a Marine's Marine. He helped me out more than anyone else. And I guess the closest type person I could name who was like him was Sergeant Rapp. He reminded me of a Gunny Gingrich type guy. You'd say he was not a garrison Marine; he was a field Marine. That was those two guys. Their covers may have been on crooked or they needed a shave or something like that, or they looked like yesterday's clothes they had on today, but dammit, when you got out in the field, these guys were going to bring you back.

"But was I against the war? I think I'm against all wars, and always have been. There was this senior at Spring Hill when I was a freshman. I was the president of the New York Club and he was a New Yorker, and his name was Colman McCarthy. You may have heard of him; he was an editorial writer with the *Washington Post*. I was editor of the student newspaper. He was the sports editor. He wrote an editorial every week, "Rub of the Green." He was a great golfer. He would go out with a seven iron and play some of the car dealers and he'd beat them every time, using just a seven iron. And that's how he made his money. He put together an anthology at his graduation. I can remember one thing he wrote that has stuck with me all these years. He wrote, 'If wars were effective, all our problems would have been solved in the days of Caesar.' But I guess war is just a part of human nature, and back in those days I knew I couldn't do much about human nature, so I just went about my business."

"I think we all did."

"Yeah, but I think there were roots—I don't know how deep they were—but there were roots with you that this was wrong."

"Well, it was a gradual process. Look, you were from New York City. I grew up in the Ozarks. I wasn't college educated like you when I went over. These are relevant differences. I just took the government's word for things when I was a kid. I figured if they're sending us here to fight Communism, they had a good reason for doing so. My change of heart was really gradual in the making."

"Well, now you realize—I think we all realize—that the boys in the Beltway do so much damage. I mean, I read these articles and see things on television, everybody's given up on the Senate. I mean, why have a Senate? They could be on vacation for the next year and no one would know it. They could close the chamber doors and have you believe they're in there working and it could be empty. And you wouldn't know because there's nothing to report. Whether it has to do with Dreamers, or health care or taxes, or immigration, what have you, they're just not stepping up to the plate. And these are the same people who sent you and me over there. Maybe different suits, maybe some of them wear skirts, but it's a terrible thing the power these people have."

"No argument there."

"One thing that cuts through politics, something we all share, is pride in having served in the Marine Corps. The Marine Corps has always been in good hands. I've always been impressed with anything I see that's Marine Corps. It just seems to be first-class. And it doesn't make any difference whether it's officer or enlisted.

"As far as my beliefs go, I think I came out of high school a little naive, open to the world, and Spring Hill sort of set me on the right course. The Marine Corps helped me pick up speed, get a little closer to it. Working for major corporations and then being on my own, I think in my retirement now I can sit back and say this is the Steve Crowley I always wanted to be."

"Well, that's great. That's a great thing to be able to say."

"I'm glad you're doing this. I've always been curious about what these guys did after Vietnam. I mean you--you got your college degree, you got your master's, and you've really done a good job of collecting wives."

"Gee, thanks."

"You're welcome."

"Before we end this conversation, I need to get something off my chest."

"What's that?"

"You won't remember this, but several times during our first month in-country I said to you, "Sir, when are we going to see some real action?" The day after the fighting on Hill 50 you said, "Well, Harlan, did you see enough action?" and I answered, "No sir!" You gave me a funny look. Now, nearly 52 years later, I'm here to confess: I lied."

Steve Crowley passed away on December 17, 2018. Dan Walsh recalled, "Steve's sense of humor was second to none. His unflappability was a great asset."

1]Jimmie Howard had been awarded two Silver Stars and three Purple Hearts in Korea. On the evening of 13 June 1966 he and his recon platoon, consisting of 15 Marines and 2 Navy Corpsmen, were dropped off by helicopter atop Hill 488, 25 miles west of Chu Lai. Their mission was to observe enemy activity in the valley below and call in artillery and air strikes. For two days they were highly successful—until the enemy figured out the location from which they were being observed. By the time word reached headquarters that an NVA battalion consisting of 200 to 250 soldiers were moving toward Howard's position, it was too late to extract them from the hill. Howard placed his Marines in strategic positions around the summit and instructed them to drop back in a tight circle once the enemy struck. That happened at 2200, the platoon's third night on Hill 488. Lance Corporal Ricardo Binns shot the nearest enemy soldier. L/Cpl John T. Adams emptied his rifle at the enemy and then using it as a club, killed two enemy soldiers before being shot to death. Corporal Jerrard Thompson was wounded by a grenade; he killed two NVA soldiers with a knife before he died.

For a while the hill became quiet. They had repulsed the initial assault. The enemy taunted them: "Marines you die!" To the ordinary person, the Marines reaction would be deemed incredibly bizarre if not downright crazy. They responded to the taunts with a collective "horse laugh." As Howard later stated, " They were shooting at us and when we started laughing...they stopped. There was complete silence. I think it had a chilling effect on them. They must have known we were terribly outnumbered, but here we were laughing at them."

With ammunition running low and all their grenades used to push back the initial wave, S/Sgt Howard ordered the men to throw rocks. It worked. The enemy soldiers, thinking the rocks were grenades, exposed themselves so that the Marines had clear shots.

For five hours the Marines withstood probes and full assaults. Howard had been severely wounded by a grenade and was unable to use his legs. He distributed his ammunition to the other men and maintained radio communication, calling in artillery and air strikes. By dawn five of Howard's men were dead. A sixth man would die after he was evacuated. All the rest but one had been wounded. Corpsman Billie D. Holmes cared for the wounded, though he had been badly wounded himself.

Major William Goodsell brought his helicopter ten feet off the ground when it was hit. Goodsell died of gunshot wounds. A second helicopter approached, and its crew chief was killed. On the southern slope helicopters brought in First Lieutenant Marshall Darling's Charlie Company, 5th Marines. The Marines wiped out numerous enemy positions on their climb up the hill. By the time they got there, Howard's platoon had eight rounds of ammunition left. The battle continued. Four more Marines were killed.

Jimmie Howard called his 15 Marines and 2 Navy Corpsmen his "Indians." His Indians were awarded four Navy Crosses and thirteen Silver Stars.

Breakfast buffet in Hanoi. L to r: Kristina Houser, Kathleen Cleaver, Gene Cleaver, Bob Detty

CHAPTER 10

Lieutenant Eugene Cleaver

Philadelphia, Pennsylvania

The hospital personnel were baffled. What the hell is a Schwenkfelder?

Thousands of wounded Marines had been transported from I-Corp battlefields to the hospital ship USS *Repose*. Many of them required last rites. Knowing which chaplain to bring in was simply a matter of reading the patient's dog tags. If it said Jewish, bring in a rabbi; Catholic, bring in a priest; Methodist, Presbyterian, or whatever, call in the protestant chaplain. But the dog tags of this patient, lying on the stretcher in a semi-conscious state with a gunshot wound to the chest and right arm, read "Schwenkfelder"? What the hell is a Schwenkfelder?

Fortunately, the patient, Marine 2nd Lieutenant Gene Cleaver, did not require last rites. Nevertheless, just so all the bases were covered, he received prayers from two different chaplains—the Protestant and the Catholic.

Had the internet and Google been available in 1966, the problem would have been resolved instantly, with the prayer assignment given to the Protestant chaplain. The more curious-minded would have learned that the Schwenkfelder church is a "small American Christian body rooted in the 16th

Century Christian Reformation teachings of Casper Schwenkfeld von Ossig (1489-1561)." Calling the church small is a bit of a stretch considering that nearly half the American population is Protestant and there are less than 3,000 Schwenkfelders.

Numbers aside, however, one aspect of the Schwenkfelder doctrine reveals something crucial about Gene Cleaver— namely, that they regard inner spirituality as more important than outward form.

Gene grew up in Pennsburg, Pennsylvania, a half-hour drive east of Philadelphia. There are five congregations of Schwenkfelders, all of them located within a fifty-mile radius of Philadelphia. The Cleavers attended the church located in the town of Palm, where Gene's father, a general practitioner, grew up. When the Second World War broke out, Doctor Cleaver enlisted in the Army, and was awarded the Silver Star medal. After the war, he returned home and took over the practice of a doctor who had served in the First World War.

President of his high school class and a runner on the track and field team, Gene's primary extracurricular activity was scouting, achieving the highest rank of Eagle Scout. One of his fellow Eagle Scouts was the first person in his town killed in Vietnam.

Upon graduation, Gene attended Bucknell University where he graduated in 1964. In his senior year, uncertain about his future plans—possessing a degree in political science with no particular ambitions—Gene applied for both the Peace Corps and the Marine Corps. He was informed by the Peace Corps that he would be assigned to Iran, which did not appeal to him. He preferred the Far East. The Marine Corps assured him they had lots of places in the Far East he could go. So, he proceeded to OCS and then Basic School. Upon graduation Gene applied for the infantry. He received orders for 3rd Battalion 1st Marines, a transplacement battalion at Camp Pendleton.

"Steve Crowley, who was in my Basic School class, was also assigned to 3/1. He beat me out there. I did some messing around on the way to California, stopping at Taos, New Mexico where my father was doing some missionary work. Crowley got the 1st platoon, and being the last one to report in, I got weapons platoon. I lived in San Clemente with Ben De La Rosa, 3rd platoon commander, and Dan Walsh who had the 2nd platoon. We had a house next to the beach. But we only stayed there for a couple of months before shipping off to Okinawa. You've already heard from others about our training in Okinawa and how we stopped in the Philippines on the way to Vietnam. I really don't have anything special to offer about that experience. I think we were all anxious to get to Vietnam. That's what we were trained for and I think we all considered it a trial.

"When we landed in Vietnam, I spent most of the time with company headquarters because my weapons platoon guys were farmed out to the three rifle platoons. So, my experience is different from the other platoon commanders."

The situation changed on the final day of Operation Double Eagle 2, when Captain Sehulster was medevaced and De La Rosa replaced Simon Gregory as company executive officer when Gregory took command of the company. Cleaver took over De La Rosa's assignment as 3rd platoon commander.

"So, the 3rd platoon people were all new to me and leading a rifle platoon was new to me. I felt a lot of anxiety over that. That went away once I got into the situation."

The new situation did not last more than a few days when the company came under intense enemy fire on Hill 50.

"I was told my job was to connect with the South Vietnamese. I couldn't think of any way to do that but stand up and tell people we had to get up there. It was probably a stupid thing to do, but that's what I did. And that's when I was shot. I remember it was like a sledgehammer hitting my chest and arm. Most of what I remember from then on was what people have told me. I do remember getting artificial respiration and telling myself I don't give a shit. I was just glad somebody was there helping me. From that point on, I don't remember anything until we got to B-Med. I remember them putting the test tube in because what happened was, I was shot in my chest and right arm and they were draining what's called the pnuemothorax. Blood had flooded my ribcage and collapsed my lung. From then on, I can sort of remember things.

"The next thing I remember is getting to the *Repose* and the air conditioning. I thought, "Oh crap! I'm going to be OK!" They assessed my condition and found out I had a severed brachial artery. They stopped the bleeding and sent me to the end of the line where I waited for hours. There were so many guys who were going to die if they didn't get to the operating room right away. It might have meant I was going to lose my arm, but I was going to live. I was shot in the right chest and the brachial plexus(arm pit of the right arm).When they finally took me in, they did put the artery back together and saved my arm. Something I will be eternally grateful for. They also established that my median and ulnar nerves were severed. There are three nerves in the arm that make the hand work. The radial nerve opens the hand and the median and ulnar are responsible for closing and fine hand control. I could open my hand, but I couldn't close it.

"I spent a couple of days on the *Repose*. Dan Walsh was there, too. We were flown to the Philippines, and from there to Korea then to Travis. After spending the night at Travis, they flew us to San Antonio and on to McGuire Air Force Base in New Jersey. They try to send you somewhere near your home, so I was sent to Philadelphia. After a month at the Philadelphia Naval Hospital the neurosurgeon put the nerves back together. The process was explained to me as putting a wire with a bunch of small wires together and hoping the small wires connect and make the hand work. The nerves grow back an inch a month, so it took a year to see if it worked. When all was said and done, I could close my hand, but I had a monkey hand. I couldn't do fine hand movements and I could not oppose (touch my thumb to my fingers). The orthopedic surgeons took a tendon from my third finger and wrapped it around my thumb giving pseudo-opposition. What I ended up with was a right hand that was no longer as functional. I learned to write and do all things that require fine hand control with my left hand.

"The year I spent at the hospital was a huge influence in my life. First of all, I came back and was with hundreds of Marines for support. It was still the early part of the war and there was no problem with antiwar activities against me. There was a support system among the Marines, and the doctors were fantastic. I was there so long that I ran a program that provided activities for the enlisted men.

"After a year, I was able to move my hand. I was able to grasp. They did more surgery on my fingers. I had a monkey hand before. I could not use my thumbs. The surgery corrected that, though I still had to write left-handed.

"While I was in the Naval Hospital, I applied for physical therapy school at the University of Pennsylvania. I did that because I really didn't think I was smart enough to complete medical school but thought I could achieve the same experience in life as a physical therapist as I could in medicine. So I applied to Penn and was required to take prerequisites, and I did fairly well with them. One of the advantages was I had a disability. All of the professors were required to examine my hand and determine if I was physically capable of being a physical therapist. Each time I came, I showed up in my uniform, which probably got me some brownie points. At any rate, I got in and did pretty well.

"One of my first classes was in physiology. This lady would drone on as fast as she could, and I told her I could not take notes fast enough writing left-handed. She gave me permission to record her lectures with my tape recorder. That was a

Godsend, for both me and my classmates. They would come by and listen to the recordings.

"So, I ended up graduating. The night I was to graduate I was in an auto accident. I broke my left arm and dislocated my left hip. I had to call my parents and inform them they would not be coming to my graduation, that I would be going back to the Naval Hospital. Once again, I met a great bunch of Marines. It was also where I met my wife, Kathy. She was a Navy nurse and the roommate of my nurse. When we married, Kathy had a year left in her enlistment. I was working at my first job as a physical therapist with the VA."

"You once told me you gave a sermon to your church about your combat experience. Please tell me about that."

"Yes, that happened the first time I was released from the hospital. From early childhood up to my senior year of high school I attended Sunday School. My family wasn't all that religious, but the church asked me to deliver a sermon when I was recovering from my wounds. So, I dressed up in my uniform and gave my sermon. What I said basically was that when you are in combat all the trappings that are important in the outside world—whether you're rich or poor or white or black—those barriers fade away when you're in combat. I said that nobody asks, "What's in it for me?" You're all trying to pick up the other person. You aren't concerned with what's in it for me, but with what is demanded of me to hold up my end of the bargain.

"Lately I've had to reflect on that, what with all the anti-immigrant sentiment and the divisiveness in the country right now, it's made me think about that time in my life. The platoon I was leading the day I got shot was made up of Hispanics, white and black, farm boys, one from Scotland—just a variety of people. One of the strengths of the Marine Corps, at least in Vietnam, was its diversity. And I think that's true of this country in general. Its strength lies in its diversity. Right now, there are too many people concerned only with what's in it for me.

"My spiritual thinking has also been influenced by that. I've come to regard Jesus as a non-dualistic thinker. He didn't say you're with us or against us. He said everybody is welcomed. And I think that's the way it is in the Marine Corps, too. Everybody is welcomed if you can pass the test, and if you have the determination, you can pass the test. I think that was the biggest influence the Marine Corps had on me: an organization made up of a variety of people not asking what's in it for me but motivated by the belief that we're all in this together."

"So, what did the two of you do when Kathy got out of the Navy?"

"We decided we would join VISTA, which is sort of like the Peace Corps in the United States. They were going to put her in a nursing position, and I was just going to follow her. But she really didn't want to be a nurse anymore. So we ended up looking at places in Blytheville, Arkansas. They raised cotton there and had only recently become desegregated. And we also looked at Boonville, Missouri, which was more like what I was used to. We went out there and I worked in two small hospitals, and Kathy went to graduate school at the University of Missouri in Columbia. She received her master's degree in Social Work.

"After we left there I went to the graduate school at the University of Kentucky. I got a master's degree in physical therapy. After that we went to northern Indiana, which is a big Amish and Mennonite area. I worked at a couple of different hospitals there. That was also when I switched religions. I converted to Catholicism. Kathy was raised Catholic, went to Catholic high schools and Catholic colleges. My first church was Notre Dame, a very liberal church. It was a major turning point in my spiritual life. I would say the two major influences in my life have been the Marine Corps and spirituality.

"Both of my daughters were born in Goshen, Indiana. When my oldest daughter was in the first grade we moved back to Pennsylvania. My brother did the same thing I had done four years after me—went to college, joined the Marine Corps, and became a physical therapist. He had been a physical therapist in Colorado, and then moved back to Pennsylvania. After Kathy and I moved back in 1984 my brother and I opened a practice together in Allentown. From 1984 to 2006, I mostly worked. Other than work and raise my family, I didn't do much else.

"Kathy had been on a spiritual journey this whole time, and around 2006 I sort of caught the bug. For ten years I spent my weekends at a spiritual formation class. We started going to church here in Philadelphia at a very liberal, very activist church in the inner city. I'm not sure I could be a practicing Catholic in a traditional church.

"Since moving to Philadelphia, I've been very active in a number of things. I'm an active member of *Veterans for Peace*. I'm also involved with the New Sanctuary Movement of Philadelphia. We do a lot of advocating for immigrants. Our church is very active. We have a big group that works on improving the minimum wage, school funding, and all kinds of things. So that's pretty much what I do with my extra time.

"I remember retiring in 2006 and thinking it would be pretty sad if I died and all they could say about me was that I was a good physical therapist. So, I hope in the last twelve years I've been able to change that some.

"When I think back on that time in the Marine Corps, I think of the people I met. Even though that experience only lasted a few years, the role models I had then have been much more important in my life than any role models from civilian life. The Marines I consider my role models were not only ones I served with, but also those I came to know after my service in the Corps. The ones I have the most respect for are the ones who are open-minded, the ones who know the experience they had in the Marine Corps was transformative but are open. In other words, they are not dualistic thinkers. People who do not think in terms of us and them.

"I am very grateful to have had those experiences. But I'm not sure I could join the Marine Corps now. I'm not sure I could do that. Because I'm not sure I could kill anybody now."

Bob Boland, Gene Clever, Doc Reyerson revisiting Hill 50.

CHAPTER 11

HM2 Donald "Doc" Reyerson

Dubuque, Iowa

The first phase of this project involved locating Lima Company Marines and Corpsmen I served with. Once that was complete the second phase was to visit them and listen to their recollections and inquire as to what impact those experiences had on their lives. For years I had been haunted by the thought that perhaps the only reason my service as a Marine in Vietnam was such a big deal to me was because I had accomplished nothing significant enough to allow me to move on past the Marines and Vietnam.

Had it not been for this project I might have died with that lingering thought on my mind. I was disabused of that notion early on in many conversations with the participants of the project, most notably Dr. Claude DeShazo, our battalion surgeon. Claude sent me a book titled, *Once a Marine* he had organized with Charles Latting, the CO of Mike Company 3/1. The book contains the stories of thirteen enlisted Marines and Corpsmen, all Vietnam veterans, who went on to establish a variety of successful careers, and all of whom exemplify the saying, "Once a Marine, always a Marine."

The most amazing story came from Dr. DeShazo himself in which he tells of playing golf with a friend one day when the friend asked him, "What achievement in your life are you the proudest of?" Claude didn't have a ready answer, but thought about it as he walked:

"I thought about my having six kids, my career as a general surgeon, some of the work I had done with starting a hospice, starting a support group for cancer patients, leading a large group of physicians in a business venture...I kept walking along. It was a question I had never processed before. Then, in a moment, the words just popped out of my mouth, "I guess the one thing I am proudest of in my whole life is being a Marine...That moment of unanticipated clarity surprised me about as much as it did my friend."

I wondered about Doc Reyerson. Did he still think about our time together serving in the 1st platoon considering he entered medical school after his Navy enlistment and had become a pediatrician in his home state of Iowa? But it only required getting his email address to know our mutual experience in 1966 was still important to him. It was "l311"--standing for Company L, 3rd Battalion, 1st Marines, 1st Platoon.

My Lima Company project brought me together with two of those fellows who join the Navy but end up as Marines—perhaps not according to the Department of the Navy, but certainly in their own minds and the minds of the Marines they served with. I am referring, of course, to the corpsmen.

U.S. Navy hospital corpsmen, the Navy's version of Army medics, are often assigned to U.S. Marine Corps units. That's because the Marine Corps, responsible for conducting amphibious operations with the United States Navy, doesn't have its own medical division and relies on Navy doctors, nurses, and corpsmen.

The first time I laid eyes on Doc Reyerson he was laying eyes on my penis. There was nothing sordid about it. It's what the corpsmen call a "short-arm inspection." and what we

Marines called a "pecker check." It was my first week with Lima Company after arriving at Camp Schwab in Okinawa. One morning immediately after reveille, Sergeant Hudson ordered us to stand in front of our racks, something I hadn't experienced since boot camp at Parris Island. Of course, the Drill Instructors never inspected our penises since there was no liberty call in boot camp and no nearby whorehouses available to recruits. But there sure as hell were whores galore in Henoko, the small village on the outskirts of Camp Schwab. And where there are whores and Marines there will be cases of gonorrhea. And it was Doc Reyerson's job to see that no diseased penis was left untreated. After instructing me to milk it a couple of times, satisfied that no pus oozed out, Doc moved on to the next Marine.

Two months later, Doc Reyerson was no longer concerned with STDs. He had his hands full treating gunshot and shrapnel wounds on a regular basis. He arrived at my hotel room carrying a reminder of how close he had come to becoming a casualty himself. What he brought was the entrenching tool that was attached to his backpack on Hill 50. He kept it as a souvenir, a reminder of how extraordinarily fortunate he was to be alive. The steel blade of that e-tool blocked three AK-47 rounds from shattering his spine and doubtless ending his life in the process. Doc didn't realize what had happened until that evening when he opened his pack to get some chow. After piercing his e-tool blade the bullets lodged in the two C-ration cans in his pack, ham and lima beans and beefsteak and potatoes. Saved by an e-tool and a couple of cans of C-rats, Doc Reyerson was mostly upset about the beefsteak and potatoes he was looking forward to. Apparently, Doc is quite the chow hound. Until he reminded me, it had slipped my mind that we were served steak and eggs aboard ship before climbing down the nets to the landing boats 37 days before Hill 50.

Doc recalls the first few months of his Vietnam tour:

"I joined Lima Co. in the summer of 1965 at Camp Pendleton when 3/1 was based at Camp San Mateo. I didn't get to know many of the Marines in the company until we shipped over to Okinawa in August on the USS Magoffin. On Okinawa we spent days and days training together, either in the field, in war games, at the firing range, on night maneuvers, in jungle warfare training at NTA, or in Raider training.

"Shortly after Christmas we boarded ship again to head south to Vietnam, stopping to practice amphibious landings in the Philippines on Mindoro island. In late January we were off the coast of Quang Ngai province. On the way down to Vietnam we readied for our landing, which seemed like it would be like another routine practice landing. However, the night before we were to land, we were all issued live ammunition (a box of 0.45 rounds for my sidearm) and a box of 50 morphine syrettes for me as a corpsman. I realized then that possibly this landing might be different. The night before we had checked and prepared our weapons and packs. The morning of the landing we all rolled out of the rack at 0430 and were fed steak and eggs by the Navy. Little did I realize that it would be my last hot chow for more than a month. At around 0700 hrs. we boarded our landing crafts by climbing down the cargo nets hung over the side of the ship. The landing crafts pulled away around the bow and we circled in the open ocean until our wave of boats was complete. I heard the Gunny say "We're going in—lock and load.

"In a few minutes we were at the beach, the landing ramp dropped, and we hustled out into the surf. My heart was pounding, not knowing what to expect. We were greeted by a half dozen news cameras and crews——thankfully, an unopposed landing. On the beach we started to dig in to create defensive positions. Soon, we were told to saddle up and board Amtracs as another unit was in trouble with a VC encounter farther up the beach. We raced to their position as fast as the vehicles would go, but part way to the unit we were pulled back.

"I remember staying on the beach our first night in country, and next day we moved inland. The country and villages were beautiful, although we saw very few people at first. We set in for the night in an open sandy area, and dug in for the night, but as we dug in, we received some sporadic sniper fire from the tree line. That night Lt. Crowley led a patrol that left around 2300-2400 hrs. It was pitch black, and we went out in a big loop—my guess is that we were 4-5 clicks from our base area when we began to head back toward the start point. We were in wooded terrain, with scattered huts and villes along the way when we suddenly came to a halt. The word was passed back the line to get down, as the point man had heard something in the bush ahead. We sat silently in position for 30-40 minutes while flares were dropped by planes and helicopters. I was trying to figure how I was going to find and treat casualties in the dark if a firefight was going to happen. After a long wait, we got up and moved on without any trouble. We got back to our base camp just as dawn was breaking. Later we were told that the guy on point had heard what he felt was a rifle or machine gun bolt slamming home. The guys up front felt that as the flares died out, they could hear movement in the bush, moving away from our position. I guess the thought was that we were about to walk into an ambush, but luck was with us. That is how my first two days in Vietnam began.

"For the next 30 days we humped our weapons and gear over a good part of I Corps, probably getting close to Laos and the Ho Chi Minh Trail. I learned later that we covered about 500 miles in that month, most of it on foot and eating nothing but C-rats and a few goodies the choppers brought on supply runs. During the 32 days after our landing, we made little contact with the VC except for sniper fire now and then, and on a few ambushes, we did surprise a few VC. However, on the next to last day as we were heading in to Chu Lai we were crossing a large area of rice paddies when a lot of small weapons fire erupted from a tree line on our left and from a ville across the paddies to our front. Capt. Sehulster sent a squad to assault the ville, but they immediately had several casualties. Another squad with me as corpsman went into the paddies to give help. Before that I was hunkered down in the paddy water behind a dike with Sgt. James Thompson sitting a few feet to my left. When I left to go out into the paddy, Jim moved over to my position and quickly was hit. With all the gunfire and commotion, I could not find his wound, but we did get him on a chopper, but he did not make it. As far as I know, he was the first one from Lima killed in Vietnam. We did have some other wounded before that, but mostly from mines and booby traps. The next morning as we were just a short way from the Chu Lai perimeter, and while we were wading across a wide but shallow river we were ambushed again from behind and to our left. Several guys were hit, one of them was Ranshaw, a rifleman from 1st platoon.

"Once in the safety of the base at Chu Lai we were allowed to relax on the beach for 5 days with swimming, hot chow, cold beer and warm showers. After being in the field for 32 days straight, I wanted only three things——a warm shower, an ice-cold Pepsi, and a real toilet to sit on. I could have stayed there on the beach for the rest of my tour, but a few days later we told to saddle up with our gear—we were going back out for what turned out to be Operation Utah. Choppers flew us to a hilltop LZ south of Quang Ngai. We headed to another hill a few clicks away and dug in for the night. We could see Hill 50 across a valley, and the artillery and air support (jets with bombs and napalm, Hueys with rockets, Skyraiders with bombs) blasted the hell out of that place for what seemed to be forever.

"Next morning (Saturday) we humped it over to Hill 50. We got to the hill around noon, and everything seemed real quiet. I don't recall any gunfire as we walked around the base of the hill. I did walk right by an intact unexploded canister of napalm and gave it a wide berth. I think our company was asked to go up on the hill from a couple directions, and as we did that, AK-47 fire broke out around us, and right away a dozen or more Marines were hit around where I was, on the side of the hill. Guys below me on the hill got hit, and some above me were hit. To this day I don't know how I was so lucky.

"Years later I read a book written by former VC who said that in battle their priority was to first take out officers, machine gunners, and radio men —-in that order. And that Saturday, they did exactly that, where I was on the hill. Shields and Fitch were our platoon guys with the M-60 and they both were killed right away. Lt. Cleaver the 3rd platoon commander, and Rick Bartlett (radioman) were hit quickly also. I guess corpsmen (as non-combatants) didn't rate as high to the VC and NVA. I thought the afternoon on Hill 50 would never end. The noise at times was deafening with the AK-47 and M-14 fire, and the platoon leaders shouting to coordinate the fire teams. If there was a lull in the noise, I could hear Marines calling for a corpsman.

"As far as I know I was the only corpsman on top of the hill that day. I can't remember all the guys I treated except for ones named Garner, Bartlett, Lt. Cleaver, and Dave Ubersox (weapons plt. corpsman). There were three times that afternoon I nearly was hit, and many times heard the buzz and hum of rounds going by my ears. Sometime in the exchanges of gunfire my e-tool stopped a couple rounds from an AK-47. The rounds broke up and penetrated my pack, ruining my C-rats. I was allowed to keep my damaged e-tool, and today it hangs on my workshop wall as a reminder of March 5th, 1966. When all the NVA had been routed from their spider holes and neutralized, we cleared the hill of our dead and wounded, and moved away to set in for the night. Again, we dug in, with one man in each hole to be awake all night. I really expected we may be hit during the night, or at least we would get some mortars incoming. The night was quiet, and in the morning (Sunday) the chaplain had a worship service for us. We made an altar for him with ammo crates, heard a short devotional, sang a hymn, and went back to our positions. I do believe it was the most memorable worship service I have ever attended. I don't remember the number of casualties we took that Saturday. I have read varying numbers, but I know it was a tough fight, and that Lima Company paid a high price.

"The rest of my tour in Vietnam was never as crazy as it was those first 5-6 weeks. I left Lima Company in July to become senior corpsman of Mike Company. Over the past 50 plus years, I have read 45-50 books on the Vietnam war. I still don't understand it but do have a deep sense of pride for having served with so many great Marines. After leaving the military I attended college and medical school during the campus protest years. All I could do was keep quiet and think back of what we went through in 1966 and what was still happening in Vietnam those years. For me, it was very difficult to be laughing and joking with guys in basecamp, and then learn days later those same guys didn't make it back from a patrol. Vietnam to me was a paradox—-an incredibly beautiful country with many gentle people, so how could a war be going on with so many young men getting maimed and killed?"

On the first of June 2018, our Lima Company CO, Jim Sehulster, shared the Commandant's message on the occasion of the 120th birthday of the Hospital Corps. My platoon commander, Tom Eagan, who took over for Steve Crowley, wrote the following: "The Docs were my heroes throughout 'my war'. In all those years, never had a less than great guys serving us."

Jim Sehulster prefaced the Commandant's message with these words:

"We have all, at one time or another, in one manner or another, experienced the dedication of "our" Navy brethren. It is the Commandant's recognition that underscores the bond that exists. To all that I have had the honor to serve with: thank you!!"

From the Commandant:

"On behalf of all U.S. Marines, it is my great pleasure to recognize all U.S. Navy Hospital Corpsmen as you celebrate the 120th birthday of the U.S. Navy Hospital Corps.

"Since 1898, men and women of the Hospital Corps continue to provide outstanding healthcare to the Marines and their families around the world From clinics, hospitals, ships, submarines and battlefields, your service to our Nation and the Marine Corps has been of courage, loyalty and dedication. Your unwavering professionalism and commitment as you continue to answer the call of duty will forever be distinguished throughout history and battles to come. As we face the challenges of the future, we know that our Corpsmen will always be by our side ready at a moment's notice to answer the call, "Doc" or "Corpsman Up." You will be known always as a Marine's best friend.

"As you reflect upon your heritage, know that your selfless contribution to the organization will always be remembered and that Marines greatly appreciate the sacrifices you have made for our country and the Marine Corps.

"Once again, I recognize the Corpsmen on this 120th Birthday and thank you for your service.
"Semper Fidelis,

"Robert B. Neller, General, U.S. Marine Corps
Commandant of the Marine Corps"

Doc Reyerson replied to those of us who received Sehulster's email:

"Thank you all for remembering the corpsmen who have been privileged to serve with the Marine Corps. I was 1st platoon corpsman in Lima Company from August 1965 through July 1966 when I was made senior corpsman of Mike Company. I always knew when I heard "Corpsman Up!" that the

Marines around me would be giving me covering fire so I could go to work. It sounds funny to say, but I was never really afraid, knowing the guys in the platoon had my back. That Saturday on Hill 50 is still fresh in my memory. We had started around the base of the hill when I heard the first AK-47 fire, and real quick a call for a corpsman came from toward the top of the hill. I started up the hill, working my way through the scrub brush. There were several wounded nearby, and as far as I know I was the only corpsman up there. The first Marine had a real bad head wound and two Marines suddenly were by my side to move him out. The next Marine had a belly wound, and I was struggling to turn him over when Bartlett (radioman) came to help me. He had a tall whip antenna on the radio, which the NVA saw and opened fire. Bartlett was hit in the leg, and I was not, even though I was literally inches from him. Something knocked me forward over the wounded man and then Bartlett fell over me. Sometime right after Bartlett was moved out I heard another shout for a corpsman. Harlan and Hester had found Lt. Cleaver in the underbrush, with him having sustained a serious chest wound. Harlan and Hester stood over me while I worked on Lt. Cleaver, and they then moved him to the evac choppers. Down below me on the hill more Marines were dealing with the NVA in spider holes, when during a very brief lull in the shouting and gunfire, I heard Dave Ubersox (Weapons Plt. Corpsman) cry out that he had been hit. I called to him that I would work my way down to his position, and as I began to crawl down the hill, there was a burst from an AK-47 immediately to my left front. Leaves fluttered down over my helmet and I believe I felt the muzzle blast on my face, and I could smell the cordite from the blast. It also deafened my left ear for several days. I believe I was within several feet of the NVA in his spider hole. I altered my direction and was able to find Dave, but it was too damned hot to stay where we were, as grenades were being lobbed back and forth. Dave was able to crawl, and we decided to work our way up to the hilltop where there were some ARVN troops. Partway up the hill I decided to look at Dave's leg wound, when he saw that a single NVA had followed us. Dave saw him and yelled "VC! VC! VC!" I began to roll to my left while pulling my 45, knowing that it was probably hopeless. The NVA got off a burst, wounding Dave a second time, and I then heard a long burst from a M-14 AR, ending things. I don't know where that Marine came from, and I cannot remember his name, but he saved both our lives, without a doubt. I can still picture his face, and I believe he was a squad leader in Lima. During my remaining months in Vietnam there were a few other hairy situations, and Marines were always right behind me when needed. So it is obvious that the Marines looked after and protected all of the corpsmen too, and I am so proud and grateful to have served with these men.

"Doc" Reyerson, HM2, USN."

Ten months later, seven of us, including Doc Reyerson and Gene Cleaver, would revisit Hill 50 on the 53rd anniversary of the battle.

Bob Boland in Hanoi

CHAPTER 12

Master Gunnery Sergeant Robert Boland

Chandler, Arizona

"When I was young and on my
way to Vietnam, I believed that
war was simple and this war would
be very short. What did I know of
war back then? Nothing. However,
I did know just as much as 98
senators and President Johnson
who also knew nothing."
Robert Boland

So writes Bob Boland in his book, *War is a Racket II,* an up-
date of the first book by that title, written by another Marine

back in 1936. That Marine was Major General Smedley D. Butler.

Smedley Butler is my all-time favorite Marine. Not because of the two Medals of Honor he was awarded during his distinguished career, but because of his actions following his retirement, one of which was the publication of *War is a Racket*, a book about how bankers and other patriotic industrialists and speculators chiseled their way into war profits. He famously summarized his own participation in the war racket:

"I spent 33 years and four months in active military service and during that period I spent most of my time as a high-class muscle man for Big Business, for Wall Street and the bankers. In short, I was a racketeer, a gangster for capitalism. I helped make Mexico and especially Tampico safe for American oil interests in 1914. I helped make Haiti and Cuba a decent place for the National City Bank boys to collect revenues in. I helped in the raping of half a dozen Central American republics for the benefit of Wall Street. I helped purify Nicaragua for the International Banking House of Brown Brothers in 1902-1912. I brought light to the Dominican Republic for the American sugar interests in 1916. I helped make Honduras right for the American fruit companies in 1903. In China in 1927 I helped see to it that Standard Oil went on its way unmolested. Looking back on it, I might have given Al Capone a few hints. The best he could do was to operate his racket in three districts. I operated on three continents."

Another reason I admire Butler was his support of the Bonus Army—thousands of World War One vets who came to Washington, D.C. in the summer of 1932 demanding the bonuses they were promised by the federal government. In contrast to Douglas MacArthur, Smedley Butler stood up for his fellow veterans. MacArthur, disobeying direct orders from President Hoover, burned down their makeshift shacks. Talking to a group of veterans, Butler told them:

"Take it from me. This is the greatest demonstration of Americanism we've ever had. Pure Americanism. Willing to take this beating as you've taken it. Stand right steady. You keep every law. And why in the hell shouldn't you? Who in the hell has done all the bleeding for this country, for this law, and this Constitution but you fellas? But don't take a step backward. Remember that as soon as you haul down your camp flag and clear out, this thing evaporates in thin air. And all this struggle would have been no good."

In *War is a Racket II*, Boland examines just about every military action the U.S has undertaken, or in some cases, stumbled into, beginning with the Mexican American War of 1847, up to the post-9/11 war on terror. Some ventures are marginal at best (one page is devoted to the invasion of Grenada; a half-page to the invasion of Panama) while others determined the course of world history. For instance, he takes on the most popular war in American history, World War Two. Following in the steps of many others before him, Boland questions the assumption that America's entry into the war began with a surprise attack by Japan. He presents a vast amount of evidence supporting the view that the attack on Pearl Harbor was, to those in power, neither a surprise nor unwanted. Boland admits his position is controversial, acknowledging that "Some readers will want to label me a conspiracy theorist or history revisionist. I believe some readers will find the writings about Pearl Harbor disturbing. While much investigation into the role of the United States conspiring to provoke Japan into war, I present a summary of my findings and leave the rest for the readers to decide."

I won't explore each and every war Boland discusses, but departing from the "popular war," just mentioned, he also delves into a couple that are not so popular, the first of which is the one we fought in together, the Vietnam War, which Bob summarizes nicely in the opening paragraph of that chapter:

"This war between South and North Vietnam got the United States ground troops involved based on a lie called the Gulf of Tonkin Incident. Only two U.S. Senators smelled a rat and voted against the Gulf of Tonkin Resolution, which gave President Johnson authority to go to war in Vietnam. Much history, common sense and the advice of our best and most experienced generals was ignored. After about nine years, all United States forces were withdrawn with the loss of about 58,000 Americans killed and thousands crippled. By 1975, North Vietnam controlled all of Vietnam."

The second unpopular war—at least it became so once the American public woke up and began to wonder what it was all about—was the Iraq War, 2003—2010. I believe the first sentence of that chapter will suffice. Boland writes:

"If we ever needed positive proof that the President and Congress are incompetent and untrustworthy to decide to get the nation involved in a war, their decision to invade and occupy Iraq proved it beyond doubt."

"Bob, back in January 1966, when Lima 3/1 landed in Vietnam, you and I were not acquainted. You were a sergeant, a squad leader in the second platoon and I was a PFC in the first platoon. I can't recall how and when we became acquainted, but it was sometime in the late 1980s. We have corresponded and have met several times in person. I have to say, I was rather stunned to receive a copy of your book. So much so that I must ask, how in the world does a retired Marine Corps Master Gunnery Sergeant in his late 70s, who has never been known to express radical points of view, write a book like *War is a Racket II?*"

"I guess my thinking about it began in the Seventies or Eighties when my cousin, whom I regard as a perceptive person, told me Pearl Harbor was not a surprise at all, that they knew about it. How would he know that? I wondered. So I began reading about the attack on Pearl Harbor—more and more and more and more—and I became convinced it was no surprise.

"When I retired, I read a lot of history books—mostly about war—and I took a couple of college courses on the Vietnam War. And I made friends with this history professor who asked me to speak to his classes. He would buy me dinner after class, and we'd talk about different wars. One night he spoke about the Spanish-American War, about how the destruction of the USS *Maine* was blamed on an enemy mine so America could get involved in that war, even though the captain of the Maine said it was an explosion in the coal bin, not a mine that destroyed the ship and killed so many of its crew.

"Anyway, I started writing. I don't claim to be a great writer. People looked at some of the manuscripts and accused me of making this stuff up. So, I began to be more careful about citing my sources. So, I worked on it several years. Kept adding stuff and revising stuff. I kept finding more and more information about Pearl Harbor, and about the Tonkin Gulf Incident, which was not only a lie, but was part of an overall plan already in place to escalate America's involvement in Vietnam. The whole Tonkin Gulf thing was what they call a false flag operation."

Born in 1936, Bob Boland was old enough to remember the Second World War. Always impressed with all the publicity the Marines received, he was inspired to enlist in 1959. He spent his enlistment with Force Recon. When his enlistment ended in 1962, he got out. But when Vietnam was getting hot, he decided to reenlist in July 1965. Rather than return to Force Recon, Boland requested Vietnam duty with the infantry. He was assigned a squad with the 2nd platoon of Lima Company, 3rd Battalion 1st Marines, just getting formed at Camp Pendleton. On the morning of 28 January 1966, the Lima Company CO, Captain Sehulster, was certain he had suffered one casualty before the landing took place.

"I suppose you know many of us thought you were killed the morning of our landing when you were climbing down the ship's netting into the landing boat. Tell me what happened."

"That morning it was stormy. The rest of the outfit was landing on the leeward side of the ship and we were going down the stormy side. I was talking to the ship's executive officer and told him this was too dangerous and that we should wait. But he said we'd load. There were three of us climbing down the net when a big wave crashed into the ship knocking all three of us off the net. The other two Marines fell into the landing boat. I fell into the water."

"Which is why everyone, including Captain Sehulster, assumed you were crushed between the ship and the landing boat. How did you manage to survive?"

"Well, when I joined the Marine Corps the first time I couldn't swim. But when I was in Force Recon we did a lot of scuba diving and I became a proficient swimmer. So, the first thing I did was get rid of my helmet. And I swam under the landing boat. They were looking for me between the ship and the boat. But had I stayed there I would have been crushed to death. I yelled at them and they finally saw me. I was struggling with all that weight. I had held on to my rifle the whole time. With all my gear and being soaked, I was having a difficult time getting on the landing boat. I was logged with water and they couldn't lift me. I told them to throw me a rope. A sailor jumped in and tied it around my waist, and they pulled me out. I made the landing, but I was so weak it felt like I was paralyzed. So, I had to go back to the ship. I was only in sick bay for several hours before returning to the platoon."

"I know you served two tours of duty in Vietnam. What are your recollections of the first tour we served together with Lima Company?"

"Serving in Lima Company in Vietnam was the highlight of my time in the Marine Corps."

"I believe everyone participating in this project has said the same thing."

"We had a lot of skirmishes before Utah, but I don't remember most of them. One time, Lieutenant Walsh called the squad leaders together and asked how many kills we had gotten. We gave him an accurate number. He came back and told us the number wasn't high enough. We all laughed. General Westmoreland was obsessed with body counts. The lieutenant told us to go back to our squads and think about it some more. So we discussed it with our squads and guys are like, "Well, I thought I might have shot one in the bushes that time," and we go back and give the lieutenant a number two or three times larger than the original count. Anyway, you want me to talk about Utah?"

"Sure."

"Well, we were sitting on the beach and they told us to get on the choppers, we're going out. We landed on this hill, and I remember Colonel Young walked up to me with a map and said to get us to this hill which I guess was near Hill 50. I had no idea what was on Hill 50. Colonel Young didn't tell me. Anyway, we went down there. The going was pretty rough with all the tall brush. There was no human activity where we were. I remember coming across a booby-trap which the engineers disposed of. We set up a perimeter that evening and watched Hill 50 hit all night with artillery and air strikes.

"The next morning, I was on the point again. I was directed by Lieutenant Walsh to go across the rice paddy to where the South Vietnamese were. They were on our extreme right flank. So, as I was going across there, they held us up and told the company to get on line to cross the rice paddy. Well, I put my squad on line and we crossed the paddy. We went up to where the ARVN were and there were a lot of NVA bodies in front of their positions. I would say there could have been over one hundred. You had to step around them. It looked like they had tried to assault the South Vietnamese positions and were killed."

"You don't think they were killed by artillery and air strikes?"

"Well, I don't recall seeing any craters. I just saw dead NVA soldiers."

"Did you see any ARVN casualties?"

"No, if there were any they must have been evacuated. Those guys were in high spirits, almost like a party atmosphere."

"I'm wondering, why did they send your squad up to the ARVN position?"

"It was just accidental. I'm not sure anyone knew exactly where the ARVN was. I was on the point, so when we got on line I was on the extreme right flank. Moving up the hill we connected with the ARVN."

For years I tried to gain a better understanding of what took place that day on Hill 50, an objective understanding that would place my own subjective experience in a broader context. I had hoped this would be achieved by meeting with Marines and Corpsmen who were there at on 5 March and listening to their descriptions of what happened. Unfortunately, there is a disparity in viewpoints. For instance, just as we had been ordered to get on line, Sergeant Boland recalls seeing two NVA soldiers on Hill 50 gesturing for us to come on up.

"I had just gotten to the rice paddy and I saw these two people on my left front on Hill 50 where the NVA were, and they were waving us in. And then we were ordered to get on line."

"I've got to say, I replied, Simon Gregory also saw these guys waving us up, and he is certain that they were ARVN. Well, if you hadn't gotten up there yet and connected with the ARVN, what was the red flag? What made you think these weren't ARVN?"

"For one thing, they were standing on that hill that had been pounded by artillery all night. I was on the extreme right flank of the ARVN, so in my opinion, the people waving us up were too far to the left to be ARVN. I respect Gregory's opinion, but I don't see how they could have been ARVN. But that explains why Gregory was so pissed off at the ARVN that morning, if he thought those guys waving us up were ARVN."

"No, that was not the main issue. What he was pissed off about was the fact that the ARVN had reported that they had secured the ridge. Did they secure the ridge? Obviously not."

"But they did secure..."

"Secured what? Their own fucking trench? Maybe they did kill a bunch of NVA during the night, but that hill was in no way secure, and they should have informed us of that."

The lesson learned that day was basically the same lesson the Marines learned over and over during the war—namely, that we had our way of doing things and the South Vietnamese Army had their own way. After informing Simon Gregory of my conversation with Bob Boland, Simon wrote the following in an email:

"When we got the word to connect with the ARVN battalion on Hill 50, I was told that they had "secured" it. Perhaps from their point of view they had done so. However, the top of the hill is not necessarily the military crest of the hill.

"Military crest" is a term in military science that refers to, "An area on the forward or reverse slope of a hill or ridge just below the topographical crest from which maximum observation and direct fire covering the slope down to the base of the hill or ridge can be obtained.

"As Marines, when we say we have secured an objective, that means that we control it and there is no longer an enemy threat. We would have completely checked out the entire area with patrols to ensure that to be true. We would have established final defensive fire positions and also at night have set up listening posts.

It is also possible that our command did not have effective communications with the ARVN for several reasons. The language barrier and the fact that the Army adviser was not getting complete or accurate information. Also, perhaps ARVN were not as aggressive as we were. This could be because they were not as well trained or motivated to be. Also, their mindset on how to fight may have been based on big army tactics, a la, WW One and Two.

When Marines are committed to combat it is 24-7. No time outs. I have to say that the enemy we faced, both the VC and the PAVN knew what their mission was and also knew about 24-7 commitment. The 21st PAVN Regiment was hundreds of miles from home and knew it was do or die. No time outs and they did not expect anyone to come and rescue them."

As Bob continued, it was clear we had no difference of opinion regarding our casualties.

"At one point I went down the hill and I saw Sergeant Belcer. He was the 2nd platoon guide. He said the platoon sergeant, Sergeant Hultquist was dead. And Garner was dead. My grenadier, Rotowski, and I picked up Sergeant Hultquist's body. He had just one bullet through the flak jacket in the chest area. And Garner—he was awarded a Silver Star I found out years later. His body was lying near the North Vietnamese gun position. It was full of bullet holes. It was amazing to me that he got that far. And we carried his body out."

"What do you remember about Sergeant Hultquist?"

"I admired Leonard very much. He was offered a commission but turned it down. He said he didn't want to leave us. I told him he should. I knew he had a family—3 little girls and a wife back home. I remember when I talked to him at night he'd always talk about his family, his 3 girls. I met them. They told me they never got to know their dad. They were too young when he was killed."

"Where did you meet them?"

"Up in Nebraska, at Boys Town, where Leonard grew up as a boy. They were dedicating a monument in his honor. A granite monument. They had a little ceremony. Some of the guys who knew him at Boys Town spoke. Guys who played football with him. They spoke very highly of Leonard Hultquist.

"I guess I need to express my admiration and gratitude to the troops of Lima Company. They got up every day and did a difficult job—difficult days and difficult nights. But I don't remember them complaining much, do you?"

"Well, no more than usual. I mean, like they say, a bitching Marine is a happy Marine. When no one is bitching you know you've got a morale problem."

"Well, they always did what they were supposed to do."

"That's right. It's amazing just how squared away that outfit was. Because, you know, by summer us young guys started filling in the squad leader positions. The reason it worked was because there was such a solid foundation from the beginning—from people like you who had been in the Corps for a while."

"I went from 3/1 to 3/7."

"Really? When?"

"Sometime that summer. They had the Mixmaster thing going on. 3/7 had come over as a group like us, and it was time for a lot of the sergeants to rotate out. So they needed experienced NCOs. I was always amazed at the difference in the quality of the troops and the experience of the troops. I remember I had a guy from your platoon come over with me—McAllister. Remember him?"

"Sure."

"He was so different than these guys who had just come over from infantry training. He had a look in his eye like he knew what the hell he was doing. He *did* know what he was doing. Some of those guys looked like they were in shock. You'd say, "Fire your weapons!" and they would just stare out into space. Not all of them."

"You mean in a firefight?"

"Yeah."

"Oh, my God. That's pretty scary."

"Yeah. And you'd see the differences in the officers, too. They changed battalion commanders, operational people, and everybody, and it was kind of shocking to someone who'd been there quite a few months. Did you experience that when you went back with 3/27?"

"Oh, that's an entirely different story. When they activated 3/27 for the Nam at Pendleton right after the Tet Offensive of '68, most of the Vietnam vets weren't deployable, and there was a shortage of infantrymen. So, they filled the ranks with non-infantry MOS people. I was a sergeant by that time, leading a squad. I had a number of Marines with off-the-wall MOS's including a cook, a mechanic, and a water pump engineer. The Marine Corps was proud of reminding everybody that no matter what your job is, you are first and foremost a rifleman. They certainly proved that with 3/27. I remember the night we left for the Nam from El Toro. I thought, 'My God! This is a fucking suicide mission!' But you know, those guys managed to stay alive long enough to become decent grunts. So where did you go after your first Vietnam tour?"

"They put me on recruiting duty in Chicago."

"Colonel Sehulster also did some time on recruiting duty. He was very successful at it, but said he didn't consider it as part of the real Marine Corps. How did you like recruiting duty?"

"It was OK. There was some corruption I wasn't too happy about."

"What sort of corruption?"

"Well, the recruiter was responsible for making police checks on recruits. He was entrusted to eliminate the criminals and submit the police reports with the recruiting papers. Sometimes they would throw the bad police reports in the trash can, at least if they didn't involve a federal crime that would draw the attention of the FBI. In Chicago the most common crimes were curfew violations and disorderly conduct. You found very few without a curfew violation or disorderly conduct. There was cheating on the tests, but to my knowledge that was done primarily at the Armed Forces Examining Center. There was this one sergeant whose name was McNamara. He was the nephew of Robert McNamara, Secretary of Defense. He was so desperate to make his quota one time, he took the test results I submitted for a guy who had the unbelievably low score of 7 and took a felt pen and wrote a 3 in front of the 7, increasing the guy's score to 37. I guess he shipped out.

"Personally, I felt that if a recruit was mentally unstable, I didn't recruit him. But a lot of recruiters did. I had the impression that most of the stations in Chicago were doing that. I thought this would eventually blow up. It did finally blow up in 1975. And I guess it got worse.

"I began my recruiting duty in 1967 when there were inner-city riots happening around the country. It started with the Watts riot in August 1965. Within the next few years, it happened in other cities—Chicago, Detroit, Philadelphia, what have you. Anyway, shortly after I began my recruiting duty in Chicago they came up with something they called "McNamara's 100,000". They wanted more recruits for the Marine Corps and Army, of course, for Vietnam, so they lowered the minimum Armed Forces test score from 33 to, I believe, 10. I always suspected, but never had proof, that they wanted to take as many of these young men involved in the riots as they could off the streets."

Whether Boland's suspicion was true or not, one thing is abundantly clear--namely, that Project 100,000, known as McNamara's 100,000, and less charitably as McNamara's Morons, was politically motivated. The increased escalation of troops in Vietnam demanded an increase in enlistments. Solving the problem by drafting college students and deploying large numbers of National Guard and Reserve units would have been politically unpopular. Instead, they exploited a group which President Johnson privately called "second-class fellows", men who would previously have been deemed mentally unfit for military service. By the time the project ended in December 1971, 354,000 of these men had been inducted into the Army (71% of the total), Marine Corps, Navy and Air Force. The majority were sent to Vietnam.

One other aspect of the program is equally clear: it produced disastrous results. In his book, *McNamara's Folly: The Use of Low-IQ Troops in the Vietnam War; plus, the Induction of Unfit Men, Criminals, and Misfits*, Vietnam veteran Hamilton Gregory characterizes the program as "a crime against the mentally disabled." He reveals the price they paid: "A total of 5,478 low-IQ men died while in the service, most of them in combat. Their fatality rate was three times as high as that of other GIs. An estimated 20,270 were wounded, and some were permanently disabled (including an estimated 500 amputees)."

One can only imagine how many soldiers and Marines were killed or wounded as a result of serving alongside these unfit men.

"When did you get out of the Marine Corps, Gary?"

"September of '68."

"Well, you may have seen some of these guys coming in. They were different. And they probably had a lot to do with fragging in Vietnam. They kept this Category Four program up while I was a drill instructor. I saw the results of it. It was pretty horrible."

"What is Category Four?"

"Guys with extremely low IQ's, who shouldn't be in the Army or Marine Corps, actually. A lot of these guys had gang affiliations, police records, and they caused the Army and Marine Corps a lot of anguish."

"How long were you on recruiting duty?"

"Back then a recruiting tour usually ran for four years. I had only completed two years when I heard they were looking for guys in intelligence. I wanted to go back to Vietnam, and it was certain that Vietnam was where you'd be assigned. Nowadays I wonder why I wanted to return to Vietnam so badly, but that's the way I was. I volunteered for intelligence duty and was accepted. I was sent to intelligence school in Baltimore. Afterward they sent me to Vietnam. I was intelligence chief for 1st Force Recon Company."

"Where were you?"

"In the Da Nang area, but we ran patrols west of there in the jungle."

"What did you do as intelligence chief in Recon?"

"You briefed the teams before they went out and you debriefed them when they came back. What we were mostly looking for were supply trails into the Da Nang area from Laos. We eventually found them. I don't know why they didn't keep track of them before we started doing it. I mean, this was 1969 and '70 and they were just discovering these supply trails. We used a combination of things. You know, military intelligence, or combat intelligence is sort of like putting together a puzzle. You use reports from the troops in the field, of course, which are quite reliable. You use aerial photographs, reports from air observers, prisoner of war statements. Of course, you have communications intelligence also. You put all that together and you find those things."

"So you briefed the Marines going out with the knowledge you had gathered?"

"Yes. Despite going to intelligence school, the best education I received working in combat intelligence was what I learned serving with Lima Company 3/1. You walked on the ground and you've seen this stuff and when the Recon troops came in you knew what they were talking about. And when they went out you knew what they needed to stay alive. That was what I was concerned about most: keeping the troops alive. We had a very low casualty rate. And we did a lot of damage to the North Vietnamese. Most of our casualties were

199

accidental. One guy got hit in the head with a helicopter blade, another guy fell off a cliff and died, and we had a guy eaten by a tiger."

"So you were there for a 13-month tour?"

"Actually, I was there the second time for 15 months. I extended."

"So where did you go after your second Vietnam tour?"

"They sent me to El Toro."

"Doing what?"

"Intelligence. I was there for one year and I received orders for the drill field—MCRD San Diego. I wasn't too enthusiastic about that at first, but I grew to like it. It was very rewarding."

"In my opinion, it's the most important job in the Marine Corps. So, what kind of drill instructor were you?"

"Well, it's like the good cop, bad cop. You have a bad drill instructor and a good drill instructor and one somewhere in the middle. I was the senior DI. I think my assistants made me the good one. After working through 3 platoons for 12 weeks each, I became the series gunny. I was at MCRD for a total of three-and-a-half years. Like I said, it was very rewarding. You'd see the young recruits come in. Some were fat, some were skinny. They all left looking different. They were different people when they left."

"What did you do after MCRD?"

"I was sent to Iwa Kuni, Japan where I was assigned to G-2."

"Is G-2 intelligence?"

"Yeah, at the division level. The 3rd Marine Air Wing was located there.

"From there I went to Camp Pendleton. I was intelligence chief with the 7th Marines, and after that I was sent to embassy school in Virginia. After completing that my first duty station was the U.S. embassy in La Paz, Bolivia where I spent a year. Then they sent me to Caracas, Venezuela. Bolivia was the poorest country in South America, and Venezuela at that time was probably the wealthiest country in South America. Now I understand that the inhabitants there under the paradise of Socialism, have lost an average of 24 pounds each. So, if you want to lose weight, go to Venezuela."

"What did you do on embassy duty?"

"Well, the Marines are responsible for the security at the embassies. We had native national guard guys on the outside, and we were on the inside of the embassy. I was the Non-Commissioned Officer in charge of the detachment. We had between 10 and 13 Marines depending on the embassy."

"Did you have any problems?"

"I remember in Caracus we had two Communist defectors that came in. The ambassador told me he'd been in the State Department thirty years and those were the first Communist defectors he'd ever seen. And we had two of them in a row. The first one was from Poland and the second from Russia. We flew them out of the country really quick, to Puerto Rico where they would undergo extensive interrogation, and then on to the United States.

"I spent the rest of my Marine Corps career in intelligence, which isn't that interesting in peace time. From Venezuela I returned to the States. I was with regimental intelligence at Camp Lejeune—the 6th Marines. Then they sent me back to Iwa Kuni. From there I returned to the 7th Marines at Camp Pendleton where I was Intelligence Chief. After picking up Master Gunnery Sergeant I went back to El Toro. I was Intelligence Chief there from 1980 until 1987 when I retired from the Marine Corps."

"So what did you do after the Marine Corps?"

"I went to work for the California prison system."

"What was your job?"

"A common guard. I worked at the California Institution for Men at Chino. Sometimes you'd just be sitting in a tower for 8 hours. Sometimes you would be out in a compound with 100 or 200 prisoners. It was a minimum-security prison. We had a couple thousand prisoners, just walking around the compound.

I didn't stay very long there before getting married and moving to Arizona. In Arizona I worked at a maximum-security prison in Florence that housed the worst prisoners in the state. Some were a little insane, of course. We didn't associate with the prisoners. We just stuck them in a cell and pushed buttons. If we escorted them out to see their lawyers, we would handcuff them before taking them out."

"Did you ever develop any views about prison reform?"

"Not really. There were always issues about medical care, food, and so forth. And once in a while they would have a riot. It was very difficult to deal with these people. They would always tell us what goes around comes around, meaning you should respect these prisoners because they have ways of getting revenge on you. And I saw that—guards that would try to be hard on them. Those guys didn't last long. They'd have to be dismissed or transferred."

"You never had any issues like that, huh?"

"No, I never had any problems with prisoners. I knew they were at a very low point in their lives—probably had low points throughout their lives—and I treated them with respect, called them Mister, stuff like that. At least they were mostly sober and usually drug-free in prison. There was this one guy who was in charge of discharging prisoners. He would always tell them, 'Thank you very much for being with us, and we'll see you when you get back.' Which was true for a good percentage of them."

"So you basically treated them like human beings."

"Well, when you're a guard in a barracks with a hundred prisoners, you don't want to be a hard-ass. And you don't want to carry a gun or even a club, because the prisoners could take the club away from you and beat you to death with it."

"Bob it's been great visiting with you. Anything else you'd like to say?"

"Well, I guess I should express my admiration and gratitude to the troops—to the privates and corporals and sergeants and everybody in 3/1. They got up every day and did a difficult job. It was difficult nights and difficult days, but I don't remember them complaining much. They just did what they were supposed to do. I still remember the names of all the guys in my squad, and how they looked at that time."

"Your platoon commander, Dan Walsh, has expressed his gratitude and admiration to you and his other NCO's to me on several occasions."

"That's good to know."

Bob Ingraham joined the Navy thinking it would keep him out of the combat zone. Instead, he became a corpsman treating wounded Marines and getting badly wounded himself on Hill 50.

HM3 Robert "Doc" Ingraham

Vancouver, Canada

I was young and naïve when I joined

the Navy, and never dreamed I would

end up in combat with the Marines. I

didn't even know it was possible!

Bob Ingraham

Bob Ingraham is certain of one thing: he suffers symptoms of post-traumatic stress disorder (PTSD). What he is less certain of is the exact cause. It might stem from the day he was wounded while treating Marines on Hill 50, or it could be four years earlier when he was in a plane crash. Or, quite likely, a combination of the two events.

On June 2, 1962, as a *El Paso Times* correspondent, Bob was working on a feature story concerned with forest fire-fighting tactics in the Gila National Forest. At 4pm that day, Bob was granted permission to accompany a Forest Service pilot who was about to take off in order to douse a small fire in the Black

Range. There was little turbulence as they made the first three passes over the fire. Things went suddenly wrong when the pilot was preparing to make the fourth pass. "I was," Bob recalls, "occupied with something to do with my camera when I sensed that the plane had gone into a steep bank. We were, in fact, upside down. I looked "up" and saw nothing but trees — and then we hit the trees.

"I believe I was conscious for most of the time during our sudden arrival, for I remember what seemed to be a long period of violent bucking and interminable noise. I also remember thinking that I was not going to die in that way. The next thing I remember was not knowing whether I was dead or alive. Then my eyes popped open and I saw my own blood dripping from some place onto the dust. There was no sound, no dust in the air. I was hanging upside down in my seat, and when I realized this I started kicking and pawing at the restraining harness. Then I remembered the buckle assembly and released it. Out I tumbled and up the hill I scrambled, not really knowing what I was doing. I had only one shoe on, and that was half torn off. When I reached the ridge top, I stopped to try to think. Although I was a bloody mess, I thought I had only four wounds — one on my head, two minor ones on my left hand, and a bad one on my left knee."

The pilot was badly injured, and Bob did what he could for him until help arrived. Two of the Forest Service planes spotted the downed aircraft and two smoke jumpers jumped from a Twin Beechcraft to help.

"Through the night I woke about every half hour. Early in the evening one of the boys told me the rescue party, including Dr. Claran C. Cobb, was on its way in overland. I occupied my time when I was awake by listening to the night birds and watching for shooting stars.

"They finally did arrive with more blankets. I was glad for that, because it is cold at night any time of year at 8,000 feet elevation. Dr. Cobb was among the first to arrive. He worked with Wendell for about an hour, and then did a little work on me." The men worked through the night clearing a spot for a helicopter landing.

"My first helicopter ride took only about 10 minutes. We landed in front of Hillcrest General Hospital and I was carried into emergency by several men."

Bob was nineteen when he survived the plane crash. It would be years before he became aware of its psychological effects. It was not until 1980 that the American Psychiatric Association added PTSD to the third edition of its Diagnostic and Statistical Manual of Mental Disorders. Thus Bob Ingraham was left to suffer from symptoms of PTSD without the availability of a diagnosis.

With no career path in sight, Bob needed a plan for moving forward with his life. Quite unexpectedly, he received just the direction he needed one cold, rainy night in October 1962. He and his fellow pep band members were performing fight songs for the school football team, the Western New Mexico Mustangs. During a break, Bob complained to a female friend about the lack of meaning in his life. He wasn't expecting any sort of insight from the young lady. He was simply venting. But amazingly enough, his friend uttered six words that would replace the angst-filled, hapless nature of Bob's existence with genuine hope: "Bob, you should join the Navy."

My God! he thought. It made perfect sense. For one thing, he had never seen an ocean, yet Bob longed to go to sea. And didn't President Kennedy, for whom Bob had become an instant disciple, demand that he and his fellow citizens ask what they could do for their country rather than the other way around? What better way to accomplish that than follow in the President's own footsteps by serving in the United States Navy? Bob met with the Navy recruiter the next day.

The Navy recruiter, as recruiters are wont to do, made promises over which he had absolutely no authority or interest in fulfilling. In Bob's case, it was the promise that the young man would become a Navy journalist. Bob would eventually become a journalist, but he would first have to overcome an obstacle in that career path, one he had never counted on: combat duty with the U.S. Marines. I began my conversation with Doc Ingraham discussing that turning point in his life.

GH: Before we begin, Bob, I want to thank you.

BI: For what?

GH: For the photo essay you put together documenting the 37 days you spent with Lima Company in Vietnam. I can't recall how many years ago it's been—probably sometime in the 90's—but Simon Gregory sent me your writings and photos. I was so impressed. I suspect that reading your words and seeing those images made me want to learn more about the Marines and Corpsmen I served with. So thank you.

BI: You are quite welcome.

GH: I've always been fascinated with the idea of a sailor essentially being thrown into the Marine Corps. I'm sure there are some who volunteered for duty as field corpsmen, but I can't say I've met any. But I have met several who told me they joined the Navy during the Vietnam War thinking it would keep them out of combat—at least combat on the ground—only to end up in some of the most horrendous fighting of the war. What was it like being subjected to the Marine culture?

BI: Well, I've been writing for some time on these themes, exploring my reasons for joining the Navy. Tell me what you know, and I'll correct you if necessary.

GH: All right. First, you joined the Navy with the understanding that you would serve as a journalist. As it happened, that turned out to be an empty promise. Nevertheless, you described boot camp as a positive experience, right?

BI: Yes, indeed. From the standpoint of personal development, I gained a new self-confidence, and for the first time in my life I developed muscles that showed! I gained 27 pounds in boot camp, none of it fat. Also, boot camp offered an unexpected bonus for me particularly. I met the first man in my life who was a worthy father figure — Master Chief Petty Officer James Henley. He was profane. He dealt out harsh punishments that would probably land him in a court martial today, or at least a captain's mast. And I knew instinctively that he would die for me if necessary. I loved that man. I think that what I learned from him helped me get through the ordeal that I would face in Vietnam.

GH: After graduating from boot camp you were informed that your MOS would be hospital corpsman. You were sent to Hospital Corps School at the Balboa Naval Hospital in San Diego. You wrote that after your training there, you were the only corpsman in your company to have his "dream sheet" fulfilled. Your first duty station was the Naval Hospital in Yokosuka, Japan. You characterized your tour of duty in Japan as a "wonderful adventure." Your first job there was working in the delivery room and nursery, correct?

BI: That's correct. Our patients were Navy dependents. The babies, many of whom I helped deliver, opened my eyes to the incredible range of human joy and suffering. Most of the babies were normal. But some were shockingly abnormal.

I lived an idyllic life in my off-duty hours, enjoying concerts in Tokyo, teaching an English class to Japanese civilians, buying inexpensive electronics and cameras, and chasing after three very different and very attractive young Japanese women.

I caught a glimpse of my military destiny in early August 1964, when I was visiting one of the women and her family in Hamamatsu City. We were watching the evening news, in Japanese, when we heard the report that an American destroyer had been attacked by North Vietnamese gunboats. That was the beginning of the infamous Tonkin Gulf Incident, in which two destroyers were supposedly attacked on consecutive days. President Johnson used this incident as a pretext to escalate

American involvement in the war in Vietnam. My tour of duty in Japan came to an end in June 1965. On my dream sheet, I requested duty on three different types of ships--an ice-breaker, a cruiser, and a destroyer--but I was not surprised when I received orders for the Fleet Marine Force for training at the Field Medical Service School at Camp Del Mar, which was part of Camp Pendleton in Southern California.

It was obvious that the Marines were in a hurry. The course usually lasted a month. They pushed us through in three weeks. I had to wear my Navy dungarees because they didn't have enough Marine fatigues.

GH: You wrote that your first 3/1 assignment was with Mike Company.

BI: That's right.

GH: And in August, your lifelong desire to sail on an ocean was fulfilled.

BI: That's correct. I was on a real ship in the world's biggest ocean. We were on our way to Okinawa for additional train-ing, crossing the Pacific on an attack transport, USS *Magoffin*. It was no luxury liner. Our quarters were below the waterline, and our bunks were stacked three or four high. Water use was restricted, and the heads became pretty foul.

GH: How was Okinawa?

BI: As you know, the battalion spent several months train-ing at Camp Schwab, but I had been transferred to Headquar-ters Company from Mike Company because I needed to have a hernia repaired, and I stayed with Headquarters Company. The most popular off-duty activities during our time in Oki-nawa were drinking on base and frequenting bars and brothels in nearby Henoko. We treated a dozen or so Marines for gon-orrhea and one officer for syphilis.

There were some disquieting incidents. On a hike, one of the Marines shot himself in the foot. He insisted it was acci-dental. Then one of our corpsmen intentionally shot himself through his right hand. He was taken away, but I never learned what happened to him. He was probably dishonorably discharged. The most disquieting incident of all was the arrival of a group of Marines direct from combat in Vietnam, all of them aged 17. The Pentagon had ordered them taken out of combat because of their age, and they were a mess: they were angry, armed, and dangerous to themselves and to others. There were fights in their barracks, which was near sick bay. It was my first glimpse of what Vietnam could do to us, assuming we survived.

GH: Though I do not recall the details, at the end of December, a couple of weeks before we would board the ship transporting us to the combat zone, the Commanding General of the 1st Marine Division, General Fields, conducted a pre-embarkation inspection of Battalion Landing Team 3/1. Participating in the inspection was Robert H.B. Baldwin, Undersecretary of the Navy. To be honest, I have no memory of the speech Mr. Baldwin delivered to the troops that day. I only learned of his presence from the combat chronology of 3/1 provided by Simon Gregory. Online research informs me that Baldwin was a Wall Street big shot before President Johnson appointed him Undersecretary of the Navy. Then he returned to Wall Street to become an even bigger bigshot. At any rate, I was amused by your account of General Fields asking if you were ready for combat.

BI: Yes, he asked me if I was ready for Vietnam. "No, Sir!" I said. I could have said more, but the general moved on. Obviously, he didn't want to know more.

GH: Well, let me say this. Asking the same question to any of the Marines would have doubtless invoked an enthusiastic "Yes, Sir!" even though many of us were probably no more certain about the answer than you were. But as Kurt Vonnegut once wrote, "You are what you pretend to be."

BI: I appreciate your point, but I have to tell you, it took me off guard, the general asking me if I was ready. I just blurted out my response. Why I answered him that way goes back to witnessing those 17-year-old guys who had just come back from Vietnam. They were totally screwed up. The lesson I got from that was if Vietnam did that to those young guys, I don't want anything to do with it. Another reason I felt I wasn't ready was my lack of training.

GH: You did say that the course at the field med school was reduced to three weeks.

BI: That's part of it. Actually, I wasn't impressed with the training at Field Medical Service School. I felt that most of what we were doing was fairly Mickey Mouse Marine Corps public relations stuff. I got to throw a grenade once. A dummy grenade. I'm pretty sure there's a difference between throwing a dummy grenade and a live grenade. I was issued a .45 pistol and an M-14 rifle. We were required to disassemble and assemble them blindfolded. I could do that. But I was never allowed to fire the pistol and only fired one magazine with the rifle, and that wasn't even a full magazine.

GH: So, you didn't receive adequate weapons training. But let me say this: if we had to count on our corpsman to engage the enemy, we're in big trouble. Our job as Marines was to confront the enemy and kill him. Your job was to treat Marines who got wounded doing *their* job. So my question is, was the training you received at Field Med School adequate for that?

BI: Not really. I didn't really learn anything that I didn't already know.

GH: Well then, that begs the question, did you know enough from your previous training to go into combat and treat wounded Marines?

BI: Not really. I was nervous as hell about it. I just prayed that nobody under my care was so badly wounded they would die if I didn't treat them properly.

GH: I can understand the overwhelming feeling of dread you must have been experiencing. Working in the hospital, you may have witnessed some severe injuries, but the care that was provided did not sit squarely on your shoulders. You were a minor part of a team headed by doctors and various specialists working in a medical environment with state-of-the-art technology and equipment. Then you are sent to the combat zone, just you and your Unit 1 medical bag. You said General Fields didn't want to know more. The fact is, he served in WW2 and Korea. You couldn't have told him anything he didn't already know. You have acknowledged in your writings the high regard we Marines have for our corpsmen. The special place in our hearts for you is not based on some misguided notion that you perform miracles. It stems from the faith we have in your commitment, that when someone yells, "Corpsman up!" you won't hesitate to reach the wounded Marine. It's a pretty amazing deal to think that one man has that responsibility, to take care of a Marine who could be dying from a wound, and to do it while the bullets are still flying.

BI: Yes, it is.

GH: You describe one such incident on Double Eagle. You write, "A Marine was sitting in an open area only a few yards away from me. Without warning, a shot rang out and he fell over. A nearby sniper had shot him through his upper right arm, shattering his humerus and blowing out his biceps. There were bits of bone on the ground. He still had feeling in his fingers and could move them, so there hadn't been any nerve damage, and he wasn't bleeding badly, but it was nevertheless a very serious wound. We called in a chopper to evacuate him. Only later did I stop to consider the danger I had put myself in by running to help him. It wasn't heroism, just an instinctive reaction.

A worse situation occurred on Double Eagle one evening when a 19-year-old Marine who was digging his fighting hole for the night, 20 meters from my position. He stepped on a mine. I reached the Marine about the same time as another corpsman. The Marine's right leg was missing at the knee. The end of his femur was sticking right out in the air like a textbook illustration--it looked like his lower leg had just been wrenched off. His left lower leg was a bloody pulp that tapered off to nothing at what would have been his ankle. Amazingly, he was not bleeding seriously; we assumed that the explosion had cauterized his major veins and arteries. Also, amazingly, he was conscious and in good spirits. This happened just as twilight was fading, and soon it was dark. We managed to contact a Marine helicopter pilot who was flying off the coast. He managed to fly to our location and land in the dark within 10 feet of the Marine. And all we had was one weak flashlight to guide him in. We bundled the Marine into the chopper and away he went. I learned later, after I myself had been wounded and evacuated to San Diego, that he was being fitted with artificial legs."

GH: Apparently, your worst fears were realized your last day in-country.

BI: Yes, I spent every day in Vietnam praying that nothing horrible would happen. Then, of course, it did happen. It was traumatic, let me tell you. The wounds I saw on Hill 50 were unbelievable. And I don't know if I saved any lives that day. I probably didn't. They probably would have lived without treatment, at least for a while. It's pretty hard to talk about. I did what I knew I should do. I managed to control bleeding to some extent with battle dressings. There was a sergeant who was shot in the chest. I put a bandage over that. He probably survived.

GH: Well, that would contradict what you just said about not saving any lives. You said they probably would have survived without treatment for a while. But buddy, they didn't have a while to live without treatment. It would be hours before medivac choppers arrived. Why don't you start from the beginning and tell me what you remember about Operation Utah.

BI: Okay. I had been with Lima Company ten days when on the afternoon of 4 March, we were taken by helicopter to a secure landing zone. We spent the rest of the afternoon marching to a large hill overlooking Hill 50. That evening, we could hear a firefight in the distance. I actually got hit by a stray bullet that night. I was sitting on the hill talking with a friend when I suddenly felt a sharp pain on the inside of my left thigh, as if something small and fast had hit me. It had. I looked down to see a bullet lying on the ground. I picked it up and it was hot. It looked like it was from an M-14. It was scratched and had obviously gone through some brush and had come a long way. It didn't even bruise me. The damn thing had bounced off my thigh! I pocketed it as a good luck talisman. At the time of this incident, Mike Company was operating nearby and had a brief firefight with the enemy. The bullet could have come from one of their weapons. It would have made a nice souvenir, but it later went astray. Throughout most of that night, Naval artillery shells roared over our heads from ships offshore into the area beyond our bivouac, creating a memorable fireworks display. It's hard to believe, but I actually slept quite well that night.

The next morning at about 10:30 we moved right into the area that had been pounded the night before by artillery, and where that firefight had taken place. We walked maybe a half an hour or so. Signs of the artillery barrage were everywhere-- tree branches were broken and slashed, and rice paddies had craters in them. We learned that a low, green hill in the distance was our objective. We started receiving some small arms fire from the hill, and the Marines returned it. At about the same time, some soldiers wearing American-style uniforms appeared at the crest of the hill and set off a yellow smoke grenade, a signal that there were wounded, and a helicopter was needed. Our return fire had resulted in casualties. Someone passed the word to cease fire. We assumed at that point that the soldiers on the hill were ARVN, and we were correct. We further assumed that they had fired on us by mistake, but subsequent events caused us to question that assumption.

We proceeded up the hill, and within moments we were ambushed. The hill had not been secured at all, because an NVA company was well dug in on the hill between the ARVN and us. The NVA ambush was sudden and furious. The quiet morning just exploded with gunfire and explosions. Within moments of the first shot, someone yelled for a corpsman and I went flying up the trail as fast as I could, only to encounter an unexploded naval shell. It must have been three feet long and was lying right across the trail. I assumed that it came from the bombardment the night before. I was moving so fast that I couldn't have stopped short if I had wanted to, so I just leaped over it, praying it wouldn't explode beneath me. Just a few yards beyond, I found a Marine who had been shot. He seemed to be asleep, but a trickle of blood on his temple told a different story. I took his helmet off and the top of his head was gone. He was breathing but unresponsive, of course, and as good as dead. By this time, gunfire and explosions from grenades and rockets were constant. The hill was covered with thick, thorny brush that was a good 8 to 10 feet high, with trails crisscrossing in every direction. The enemy was invisible. I never did see an enemy soldier that day, but they could obviously see us. We were taking casualties every few seconds. I wasn't a Marine and had no combat training per se, but even I knew that from a tactical standpoint it was a really bad situation.

I was called to help one of our platoon sergeants. He was lying on his back with a pumping chest wound. I was just getting ready to apply a compress to it when he twisted away and yelled, "Grenade!" I looked up to see a grenade flipping through the air right over our heads. It landed eight or 10 feet away, and I hit the deck just as it exploded. Amazingly, nobody was hurt. It was apparently a Chinese grenade: they were powerful and could certainly kill you, but if you were some distance from them, they were not nearly as dangerous as American ones. If it had been one of our grenades, both the sergeant and I and a few other nearby Marines might have been killed. I went back to work on the sergeant and the same thing happened again. That second grenade injured a Marine next to me, who got a piece of shrapnel right through his buttocks and was out of the fight.

I bandaged the sergeant as well as I could, and tried to patch up Lieutenant Cleaver, whose shoulder was mangled. For all I knew it could have been be a fatal wound. Then someone said there was a wounded Marine further up the hill. So, I grabbed my Unit One medical bag and went looking for him, running through those winding trails. On the way, I found a brand-new Chinese entrenching tool. It didn't have a mark on it. It would have made a great souvenir, but I wasn't collecting souvenirs at that point. I soon found the Marine I was looking for. He was lying quietly on his right side. His abdomen had been blown open and his intestines were spilling out on the ground. At that moment, a Marine further down the hill yelled, "I'm gonna throw a grenade over you guys! I'm gonna get that sniper!" I didn't want to be killed by a Marine grenade, so I started to hit the dirt again. At that moment, I heard a gunshot to my right and in the same instant was slammed to the ground by a bullet. I had been hit on the right side of my right leg about six inches above the knee. The bullet shattered the femur, plowed on through, and just about destroyed the inner part of my thigh. It just blew it out. And I was down. Instantly. I don't remember falling--I was just knocked flat. I've been told that a rifle bullet doesn't have the power to knock a man down, and that my crash to the ground was a result of gravity taking over when my femur could no longer support my body. That may be, but my subjective feeling was that I was indeed knocked to the ground in an instant of time.

My wound frightened me immensely, partly because it reminded me of an encounter we had had a few weeks before. I was walking not too far behind our point man on a search and destroy mission. He was leading us up a ravine, and eventually climbed up out of it into a field where he surprised a young VC armed with a rifle. The VC sprinted across the field, but the Marine dropped him with one shot. The M14 bullet hit him right below his right buttock, almost tore his leg off, and burst what must have been an iliac artery. By the time I got to him, he was unresponsive, and blood was flowing out of him like a river. There is no treatment for such a wound, and within only a minute or two, he was dead. And now I too might be facing the same quick death.

Larry Skonetski, another Lima Company corpsman, had been nearby when I was shot. I had enough strength to lower my fatigue trousers to examine the wound. There was a small, blue-rimmed hole on my outer thigh, just about the diameter of a 7.62mm M14 or AK-47 round. It was scarcely bleeding. On my inner thigh was a patch of mangled flesh a couple of inches in diameter where the bullet, or what was left of it, had exited my thigh. It looked for all the world like freshly ground hamburger. A trickle of blood oozed from it. It seemed that my femoral artery had apparently escaped damage. And I could still wiggle my toes: there was no major nerve damage. In case I started bleeding heavily, I decided to use my belt as a tourniquet, but I was quickly losing strength and couldn't tighten it, which was a good thing since as it turned out I didn't need a tourniquet.

GH: Let me interrupt you for a second. Speaking of Doc Skonetski, there was one part of your photo essay that blew me away—your experience on Hill 50. While lying on the ground wounded, you hand Ski your camera and ask him to take your picture, and then you take his picture. One, when does it ever happen that in the midst of a battle, two people take each other's picture? And two, how do you explain the cheerful expression on Skonetski's face? I mean, bullets are still flying yet you'd think the guy was enjoying a day on the beach in Southern California!

BI: I agree. Let me put it into context. I don't know how long I was on that hill before they took me down to where the helicopters would land. That whole-time bullets were flying everywhere. Men were screaming. I took out my pistol and cocked it. I laid it on my chest and was determined to shoot the first Communist I saw. The hatred was still in my heart. I can tell you; I would have killed any Vietnamese I saw—man, woman, or child. Getting shot does those things to you. I didn't know Larry well when I was wounded. I knew he was nearby. He was the first person I called for. I yelled, "Larry, the bastards shot me!" He got to me quite quickly. What I remember is his incredible calmness. It was like, we're in combat, so what! Big deal! He told me he was married. I said, "Oh yeah?" He said he was married to a girl in New Mexico.

GH: He was telling you that while the fighting was still going on?

BI: Yes. I said, "Really? I'm from New Mexico." He said she was from Silver City. I said, "Really? That's where I grew up!" And he told me she had become a Wave, a corpsman.

I managed to get in touch with Larry 43 years later. I finally got a chance to tell him how important he was to me on what was arguably the worst day of my life. I learned that he received two letters in Vietnam the same day. One was from a lawyer informing him his wife was suing him for divorce, and the other was from the same lawyer informing him that because he had not replied to the first letter, the divorce had been finalized. It didn't bother him. They shouldn't have gotten married in the first place. He was an alcoholic even then. After the war his alcoholism only got worse. He literally had no idea how many children he had. He became a long-haul truck driver. He was probably drunk most of the time he was driving. He had women in practically every city he ever stopped in.

I was saddened to learn he was dying of lung cancer, probably as a result of Agent Orange. Larry died in 2009 at the age of 63.

GH: So how did you finally get to the bottom of the hill where the choppers landed?

BI: Eventually--I have no idea about the timeline here--a Marine crawled up the hill to try to help us and was shot through the shoulder. So now there were three of us lying there. The Marine with the open abdominal wound kept asking me if he was going to die. I tried to reassure him that he would be fine, but in reality, I doubted that he could survive, and I don't know to this day whether he lived. It wasn't long before I was almost completely incapacitated, not by pain as such but by extreme discomfiture, for want of a better word.

My body knew it was in danger, and was essentially locking down to preserve itself, and putting itself on high alert as well. Skonetski had treated my wound with battle dressing. When the shooting slowed down, Skonetski and three Marines put me on a poncho and half-carried, half-dragged me down the hill, crouching low because bullets were still flying around. I screamed with pain every time my butt hit a bump. I don't think Skonetski had given me any morphine. With every bump, I could feel the shattered ends of my femur grating against each other. I worried that they would cause even more damage and bleeding. I finally got to the base of the hill and a landing zone for helicopters. I talked with the Marines and began to get some idea of how bad the casualties were. One Marine was crying: his best friend had just been killed before his eyes.

GH: Before you continue with your narrative, let me point something out. When you were finally confronted with heavy combat, you did your job in a proficient manner. Your fear about a Marine dying because you didn't provide proper treatment did not happen. You did what had to be done. So, what happened after you were medevaced?

BI: After the more seriously wounded Marines were evacuated, I was flown to a nearby field hospital where corpsmen bandaged my wound more thoroughly and put my leg in a splint. I was then taken immediately by chopper out to the hospital ship USS *Repose*.

GH: What do you remember about your treatment on the hospital ship?

BI: I don't remember the arrival aboard the *Repose* or being taken below. I do recall lying on a gurney in a dark passageway for what seemed an endless period. It must have been late afternoon or early evening when I was finally taken into an operating room. My femur was badly fractured. An x-ray image that I have shows shattered pieces of bone and fragments of the bullet in the flesh. The exit wound that I first saw on my inner thigh told just part of the story. Much of the damage was hidden by intact skin, but the muscle all around the exit wound had been turned to pulp by the bullet, and it all had to be cut away. Skin and muscle around the entrance wound had to be trimmed away as well. I received two units of whole blood during the surgery. One of the procedures done during the surgery was to drill a hole through my right shin, about six inches above my knee, and literally screw a threaded pin completely through the shin so that it extended out about an inch on either side. Later it would be used as an anchor point for traction, which would stretch my thigh muscles and hold my femur at its original length while it healed. After surgery, the wound was packed with cotton and thoroughly wrapped in a bandage. Next, I was encased in plaster from my right foot all the way up to my armpits and down to my left shin. Only my lower left leg was free; I could bend that leg. I was ready to be shipped home like a parcel.

GH: Where did you go after the *Repose*?

BI: After a few days on the *Repose*, I was flown by chopper to the hospital at Da Nang and was there overnight. I remember being in bed next to a Marine I knew from my battalion.

His wound had been almost identical to mine, except his left leg had been hit. But his leg had to be amputated above the knee because the femoral artery and nerves had been destroyed, and he was getting gangrene. I was just incredibly lucky.

The next morning, I was bundled on board a C-130 Hercules and flown to Clark Air Force Base Hospital in the Philippines, where I would stay overnight. I was able to talk to my parents from the hospital. The call was patched through to a ham radio operator in my hometown. They weren't even aware that I'd been wounded. The next morning, I was taken out to the airfield and put on a C-141 Starlifter. I don't remember much about that flight; I was very ill. I no longer had much pain, but infection was raging in the wound by this time, and I was also having symptoms of a urinary infection from the catheterization on the *Repose*.

We landed at Hawaii, and a general came on board. I must have been near a hatch because I remember a blinding white light and the general coming through the door. He handed out Purple Hearts to everyone. I have no idea who he was, and I wasn't in any condition to care. I was virtually unable to communicate at that point. At last we landed at Travis Air Force Base near San Francisco and I spent the night in the hospital there. The thing I remember most about that was gas. Having been shot, having antibiotics put into me, my digestive system had just been destroyed. I thought I was going to burst from intestinal gas. The nurses were trying to help me, and I finally farted. Gary, I farted the biggest farts in the world. And the nurses clapped. Because I was in such pain. It felt wonderful. My system was finally beginning to cope with the trauma. It's amazing what a bullet can do to a body. A serious wound from a military rifle amounts to a huge physical assault that effects not just the area of the wound, but the entire body and all of its functions.

The next day they flew me to San Diego where I was taken to the orthopedic ward at Balboa Naval Hospital. I was put into traction. I was lying there with pus dripping out of the cavity in my leg, and I had a fever. My parents and fiancée, Susan Overturf, flew out from New Mexico to see me about a week after I arrived, but I don't recall much about the visit. I was a pretty sick puppy.

During the time I was in traction I lost at least fifty percent of my muscle mass in my right leg. The most significant thing that happened while I was in traction was the very deep infection I had in my leg. There were apparently several organisms in there. There was osteomyelitis—bone infection—undoubtedly carried into the wound when I was shot. Bullets are dirty, your skin is dirty, your uniform is dirty, and all that crap gets carried deep into the wound. And your leg is all mangled inside where all sorts of infections can take hold, and it did. So I was on antibiotics and the wound just kept draining and draining, and I wasn't getting any better. We had a doctor on the ward who was a reserve, a short timer. He wasn't doing his job and I was just languishing there. He finally left and a new doctor came on board, Doctor Robert Richter. He was also a reservist, but a credit to his profession, unlike the doctor he replaced. He took one look at my wound and said, "This won't do. We've got to get this fixed up." He put a drip of antibiotics directly into the wound with orders to the corpsmen to clean me up and report any changes to him. And from that day, I started getting better, and I reached the point where they thought they could safely do a skin graft. Skin was taken from my left thigh to cover both the exit and entry wounds. This was not a cosmetic procedure, but a medical one to speed healing and reduce the formation of scar tissue.

I was in traction for 111 days, but I wasn't exactly in bed all the time. I discovered that I could maneuver out of the bed and stand beside it on my left foot, with my right leg still firmly held by the traction apparatus. When the time came to get me out of traction, the corpsmen were amazed that I could stand up without feeling faint. I'm sure that standing by my bed helped a lot. Slowly but surely, my infections disappeared, although I had a flare-up more than a year after I was shot.

So after 111 days in traction they put my leg in a cast. Time passed quite quickly. I had a portable typewriter and could watch TV. For a short period, I was placed in an isolation room because of my infections, and from there I could watch Navy seaplanes and ships in San Diego Bay. Susan had graduated from university and got a summer job at Ryan Aeronautical, so she could visit me every evening and on weekends. I formally proposed to her one night on the ward and presented her with a ring which I ordered from a jeweler in Silver City, all to the great delight of the other patients and corpsmen. She accepted my proposal, and we started planning for a wedding on 27 December 1966. A few weeks after that I got out of traction into a great big cast and got my first leave. I would stay with Susan on weekends in her apartment.

GH: Were you and Susan a couple when you went overseas?

BI: No, we weren't. She was the younger sister of my best friend in high school. A friend of hers suggested she write to me when we were in Okinawa. She signed the letter, "Love, Susan," which impressed me since I knew her family quite well and was always impressed with her. I thought she was unobtainable. I never even asked her for a date. She continued writing to me the whole time I was in Vietnam. So she came out and spent the summer with me. Then she got her first teaching job in Kansas City, Kansas. So she went to Kansas City and I returned to San Diego. I was discharged on December 16 and we got married on the 27th. Around March, one year after I was wounded, the cast was removed. I limped for quite a while, but gradually improved to where I could hike and ski.

GH: I understand you finally got your shot at journalism.

BI: Yes. Susan and I moved to Columbia, Missouri where she taught school while I earned a degree from the MU School of Journalism. I graduated in August 1969—at the head of my class I might add. After that I decided to move to Ottawa to work for the Canadian Wildlife Federation. I worked for the Wildlife Federation for about a year-and-a-half. We did not get along well. The boss was a difficult man, and I grew to hate the job. I was fired after writing an article for another journal that directly contradicted my boss's stance on an issue. The next day I walked into the offices of the Canadian Press which is the Canadian version of the Associated Press. I introduced myself, told them I had a journalism degree from the University of Missouri, and they hired me on the spot.

My wife was a teacher and she really liked her teaching, and I decided I would become a teacher. And that's what happened. I got home and told my wife I was quitting my job and was going to become a teacher. I enrolled at the Simon Fraser University's teaching program. It took a year, and afterward got my first teaching job at Prince George which is about 500 miles north of Vancouver. I ended up in a brand-new school, working with colleagues I got along well with. I finally found my niche. Susan worked at the Turkish Embassy for four months before getting a teaching job. Then she got pregnant and got out of teaching. When our son Paul was old enough to have a babysitter, she went back to work teaching.

GH: So when did you become aware of PTSD?

BI: There can be no doubt that the T-34 crash threatened my life, not just once, but twice: although I survived the crash itself, I knew that I might die overnight from exposure, assuming that we weren't soon rescued. What I didn't know was that, even though my injuries were relatively minor, the crash and its immediate aftermath were sufficiently traumatic to trigger a strong stress reaction in my body. Stress hormones flooded my system, resulting in a "fight or flight" reaction characterized by hyper-alertness, increased heart rate and blood pressure, and unreasoning fear.

In the coming months, I would develop multiple symptoms of PTSD, although physicians and psychologists were only just beginning to understand the nature of such injuries, and were unaware, as I was unaware, that trauma can result in permanent changes in the areas of the brain responsible for memory and emotion. As my physical injuries healed, I tried to return to school and work. I told people that the T-34 crash had been little more than an exciting incident in my life. It would be decades before I understood how my seemingly simple decision to ask for a ride in an airplane upended my life.

I've now had three psychologists tell me that I was probably a terrible candidate for combat, in part because of the plane crash. PTSD, especially if it's untreated, colors every aspect of one's future life. I'd survived the crash, but I had become intimately aware of how very easily life can end. It was a hard lesson to learn.

One of the common symptoms of PTSD is hypervigilance, and I developed that in spades. From the time of the plane crash forward, I was hypervigilant, seeing everything, hearing everything, expecting the worst. I had trouble concentrating on anything, which meant that my grades got even worse than they had been before. I was unable to return to journalism with anything like my previous enthusiasm. In the five months following the plane crash, I had one photograph published in our local newspaper, and one story in the *El Paso Times*, not counting my final story about forest fire fighting (which doesn't mention the plane crash). By contrast, in the year prior to the plane crash, 30 of my news stories and photographs had been published.

It wasn't until 1985 that I first had an inkling of PTSD. That was when psychiatrists starting writing about it. One of my first indications was my temper. I would lose my temper and become violent. One of the first indications that there was a serious problem was one Sunday when my wife and I went snowshoeing in Ottawa at a place we were fond of going. When we got there, we found that the place had been taken over by the Ottawa snowmobile club. On the trails we used to hike with our snowshoes were snowmobiles all over the place. I had my snowshoes on my shoulder when I saw this sign saying "Project of the Ottawa Snowmobile Club. Welcome!" I swung my snowshoes like a baseball bat and destroyed the sign. My wife was aghast. "What was <u>that</u>?!" I couldn't really explain it other than I was really mad.

GH: What impact, if any, did this stress disorder have on your teaching?

BI: It had a significant impact. I was an authoritarian. I could be mean. My meanness was offset by the fact that I was a good teacher. If the kids were good, we were all right. If not, we would have problems. I once grabbed a kid who flipped me off. I pushed him back, tearing off three buttons from his jacket. For the most part, my students respected me. Many of them were probably frightened of me. It was all just self-protection, what I felt I had to do to preserve myself in that situation.

GH: You seem to describe these things in the past tense. Did you learn to identify and manage your PTSD?

BI: Yes, things began to improve once I received therapy. I had changed doctors. I complained to the new doctor about stomach pain and sleep disorder. He recommended I go to *The Haven* which is a developmental, self-help program on an island here in British Columbia. I attended a program there called "Come Alive."

I had a flashback. It was late one night, and I was talking to one of the counselors. I don't remember what we were talking about exactly, but it was about Vietnam. You have to remember that up until then, I didn't think the war had affected me. And suddenly I had a flashback of an event that happened in Vietnam that I had completely forgotten about. And it was devastating. It was the worst thing that's ever happened to me, worse than being shot.

GH: Having the flashback was worse than being shot?

BI: Yes. It involved a puppy. We were on Double Eagle 1. We'd been marching for days and days and days, crossing rice paddies endlessly. On this day we awakened, had no food, we'd run out of food. The weather was so bad that helicopters couldn't get in to resupply us. And we began marching again down this beautiful green valley. The first thing that happened was I found a propaganda leaflet on the trail, a Viet Cong propaganda leaflet accusing Americans of raping their women, spreading noxious chemicals—and warning that every step you take will lead to death. The scary thing about it was it was almost dry, and it was pouring rain. That leaflet had just been dropped. There had to be Communists all around us in that thick terrain and we just couldn't see them. The next thing that happened was we received one round of sniper fire. The Marines in that column expended hundreds of rounds of counter-fire. No one was injured, and we continued the march.

But backing up just a bit, shortly before that I had picked up a puppy, a little brown and white puppy that couldn't have been more than 6 weeks old. He was on the trail and I picked him up and put him inside my flak jacket. I love dogs. I've always loved dogs.

It was a rough day all around. After the incident with the old man we started climbing an extremely steep hill. There was an 81mm mortar team in front of me. I've never seen anybody in my life work harder than those guys did. We were all having to grab hold of grass, tree branches, anything we could get hold of to get up that hill. And those mortar tubes are heavy, and so are the base plates. Anyway, we eventually got to the top of this hill onto an open area, and it was getting late by then. Still pouring rain. The decision was made that we would set up a perimeter for the night on that hill. They still hadn't supplied us with C-rations, but I had kept a can in my pack. I had a can of chicken and noodles which I shared with some guys around me. The dog was starving so I put my finger in the chicken juice and let him have a taste. He about chewed my finger off he was so hungry.

It got dark and we couldn't talk. There were Communists everywhere. There was gunfire in the distance. Heavy rain, fog all around us. It was clear that if we made any noise, we could be killed. So we hunkered down, pulling our ponchos over us in a futile effort to keep out the rain. It was impossible to stay dry. Water kept running down my neck. At some point in the middle of the night the puppy started crying. I tried to shush him, and it didn't work. Then a sergeant told me, "Ingraham, shut that fuckin' dog up! He's gonna get us killed!" In rage, anger, I don't know what my emotion was, I stood up and grabbed that puppy and threw him down that hill as hard as I could. And I went back to sleep. And I did not think about that incident for 25 years or so. Then it suddenly came to me in a flashback. It was just devastating. That wasn't a formal diagnosis, by any means, but it was my first awareness of PTSD. I learned that wars really do affect people.

That program, "Come Alive," really did help me. I went back to my teaching with a much more positive frame of mind. I learned tricks about communicating with people that work well for me. I became a happier person as a result of that experience.

The following year I was transferred to a high school. I never thought I could teach high school, deal with those big kids. But *The Haven* gave me a new sense of confidence, and I did well teaching high school students. I actually enjoyed it.

One of my students in English class was Vietnamese. She was a boat person. Her family had survived twelve days in the South China Sea with virtually no water to drink before they were rescued. Her dad was working three jobs in Prince George. Anyway, my student, a very attractive young lady, invited me to a Vietnamese New Year party held at a local church. The first part of the program was a style show. I'm sitting in the audience with my wife watching Vietnamese people walking across the stage, the women wearing gorgeous Ao Dai dresses. And then a little man came out wearing black pajamas and a conical hat. I froze. I could not move. I couldn't look at the stage. I felt the blood drain from my extremities. My heart started pounding and I broke out into a sweat. I was absolutely immobile to the point my wife noticed. She asked me what was wrong. I couldn't even talk. I was shaking. I was never really threatened by men in black pajamas wearing conical hats, but that image was apparently ingrained in my mind. We left right after that. I offered our apologies. I'm sure my student wondered what was wrong.

I didn't have many more flashbacks after that. There was one time, however, when I was watching Hawaii Five-O. Did you ever watch that?

GH: No, I didn't.

BI: Well, the main character was a Vietnam veteran. On this one episode he's describing an experience he had. They're showing what was in his mind's eye and I swear it looked exactly like Hill 50. An ambush, low brush everywhere. Sudden. Deadly. And again, I just froze.

As life went on, my problems didn't completely go away, but I read a lot and learned more about PTSD, and I reached a point where I decided I needed help. By that time, I knew that counseling was available, so I went to the VA. They told me I had to get a proper diagnosis and set up an appointment for me with a psychiatrist. I was formally diagnosed with PTSD. I filled out the paperwork and in no time, I received a letter informing me that my disability rating, which had been 20% for my leg wound, would be doubled, now 40%.

GH: I began this conversation thanking you for your writing and photographs of your 37 days in Vietnam. I'll close by mentioning that I'm aware of what a positive effect it had on other Marines who have perused your web page. So, thank you again for that, and thank you for your time.

BI: Your quite welcome. I wish you the best of luck.

GH: Thanks, Doc

Doctor Claude DeShazo examines a MEDCAP (Medical Civil Affairs Program) patient.

CHAPTER 14

Helping the Vietnamese

Growing up in Oxford, Mississippi, Claude DeShazo was seven years old when he became aware of his calling. He arrived at that understanding while spending six months in bed, having been diagnosed with rheumatic fever. "There was," he recalls, "loneliness and pain, but out of that time our family doctor, Eugene Bramlett, MD, became my role model. From that time onward I knew I wanted to be a physician."

A second momentous event occurred in the boy's life about five a.m. January 10, 1952, three months before his twelfth birthday, when he awoke to what felt like a thump under his bed:

"Moments passed as I, unperturbed, tried to drift off to sleep again. Then I became aware of another sound, my mother crying out to someone, her voice a spewing, choked wail, a mixture of fear and exasperation. I got up, guided by her voice to the landing at the top of the stairs to our basement. The desperation in her voice was gradually filling me with apprehension. My daddy had taken his Browning shotgun to the basement and blown off the back of his head. I didn't go down to see. I remained on the landing, too afraid to descend, listening to mother's sobs of 'Why? How could you leave me alone?' break the silence."

From that point on, Claude DeShazo was in a hurry to get to where he was going. He graduated from high school in three years, and then completed the necessary coursework required for admission into medical school in three years. At 18 he married his high school sweetheart and had two daughters and a son by the time he completed a year of internship at Minnesota. With the draft being an issue, he and several classmates joined the Navy reserves in 1961. In early 1965, Claude received a notice informing him that he was being called to active duty. He did not want to be separated from his family and mentioned something to that effect to the Navy chief corpsman conducting Claude's physical. "There is another way," the chief told him. "You can request the Marines. The First Marine Division hasn't left California in fifteen years." Claude took the man's advice. It wasn't long before he was driving his young family to California. The first step in his new adventure was Field Medical Service School Class 1965-A1.

Upon completion of Field Med School, Claude was assigned to the 3rd Battalion, 1st Marines as battalion surgeon. In August 1965, the battalion set sail for Okinawa.

"Eventually we arrived on Okinawa for additional training. En route, some of the Marine officers in the battalion let me know that my Navy uniform and insignia were out of place. 'You're a Marine now, Doc,' one of the company commanders told me. So, I changed the way I dressed. I substituted Marine insignia for everything except the oak leaf emblem of the Medical Corps, and in other ways began to learn what was expected of me. Changing clothing and insignia is one thing, understanding what all those traditions mean and matching Marine Corps expectations was another."

I never met Dr. DeShazo during his time with 3/1, which was fortunate for me, considering the circumstances. But having acquainted myself with the man since then, from what he revealed about himself in *Once a Marine*, from our conversations, and from the high praise he received from the Lima

Company officers I spoke with, there is no doubt in my mind that Claude DeShazo has, both then and now, met the expectations of what it is to be a Marine.

As we sat down for a conversation on the patio of his home in California, my first question was about the MEDCAP program in which our doctors and corpsmen treated a wide range of ailments from the civilian population. I was surprised to learn that when we landed on Operation Double Eagle there was no formal MEDCAP program in place. According to Claude, it evolved from identifying a need for medical care.

"After landing on Operation Double Eagle, we started treating people immediately. By the way, when we landed, the battalion had 70 corpsmen which was nearly twice the number normally prescribed for a battalion. We discovered that all these people living simple lives near the beach had never met anyone professing to know anything about medicine. So before long they were bringing in people who had been injured or sick. The people we encountered in the villages were simple people, Third World people who could speak their language but could not read or write, no knowledge of hygiene, living in a constant state of fear. I'm saying something very simple here, but as a physician or a corpsman you go in and see someone with an immediate medical need you know what you're supposed to do. You don't need to consult a book when you find someone who has been gored in the thigh by a water buffalo. You just treat the wound. My whole point in saying all this is I don't think there was a formalized MEDCAP program when we started. If for no other reason than the fact that there had not been anyone around before we got there to do something like that."

"You're saying there had never been any talk beforehand about you providing medical care for the people?"

"No, not a word. No one ever said anything like, 'Now when you get to Vietnam, we want you to work with the people.' It just started when these people, once they understood we weren't there to harm them, became curious and started wandering up to the beach—a mother with a sick child, someone with an obvious wound or infection and they were doing things that were really contraindicated, like rubbing water buffalo dung on a leg wound because they didn't know any better. So that's how it all got started. These people didn't know what a bar of soap was. They would take a bite out of it thinking it was candy. There was no precedent for what we started with 3/1. What made it work was, I enjoyed being there, but the real secret was getting other people to multiply your abilities, to have ten or twenty corpsmen along. When it began to grow, we would have hundreds of people, and it's not an overstatement to say that this got into the thousands of people. [Footnote: According to records maintained by Assistant Battalion Surgeon Kiefer Campbell, 12,663 Vietnamese civilians were treated by the battalion MEDCAP teams during 3/1's first five months in-country. Dr. Campbell also stated in his report that 18 corpsmen were wounded, and one killed while administering aid to wounded Marines.] It was not an occasional person wandering in. The word spread. And I would also say to show how primitive this all was, when we first got there, we were dipping into our medical supplies which was sort of tolerated. But there were a lot of things that weren't there that I wanted. And I, coming out of an academic background, wrote to any number of my teachers, professors, young doctors, and asked them to send samples. Back in those days' doctors got a lot of samples to give out, and many of them just shoved them in a drawer. So, several doctors would put together large boxes of pills and injectibles and send them to me."

Following his service with the Marines, Dr. DeShazo continued to identify and serve the needs of others. "I became involved in a number of projects and in expanding services to the public. I evolved over time to having some definite opinions about the balance between the role of surgery and our ability to heal ourselves, even when we cannot be cured. Heal and cure are distinctly different terms. I started a support group for cancer patients and met with them weekly for over twenty-two years. I also helped found a hospice program and became its first medical director.

Here is how Dr. Claude DeShazo sums up his Marine Corps service:

"In those hectic, dangerous days in 1966 I had accepted that I would not survive. I joined my corpsmen in ducking down during mortar attacks, running between bullets from rifle fire and tiptoeing through mine fields to retrieve casualties. I accepted all these events as duties assigned by fate. It shaped my concept of leadership, to be out front sharing the danger, to fully participate. I made a pact with myself along the way. My desire for a life of service survived intact and had even been intensified. I decided from 1966 on I was living on extra time, enjoying an extension. Whatever good I could do would be a bonus, but I would never do anything which I didn't feel was worthwhile. Combat medicine is an extra dimension for any physician, especially surgeons, and especially with the Marine Corps. It also raises the stakes in the game of what you can do if the fear of death, and failure, and isolation, can be displaced."

****

Charles Craft, who grew up in Hickman, Nebraska, a town with less than 500 people, was a fifth grader when Claude DeShazo first stepped onto Vietnamese soil and observed the absence of medical care. In 1992, visiting some of the same villages the 3/1 Marines had seen 26 years earlier, Craft could see that health conditions had not improved.

After earning a degree in dental surgery, Craft became a commissioned officer in the U.S. Public Health Service assigned to Anchorage, Alaska, which is where he was serving when he took time off to visit Southeast Asia. Like Claude DeShazo before him, Charles Craft identified a need, and three years later he returned to Vietnam with a plan on how to fill it.

He met with Mark Conroy, country director for the Da Nang based non-profit organization East Meets West Foundation (EMW), founded in 1989 to partner with the Vietnamese people in health, education and development projects. Craft explained that he wanted to establish a dental program for poor children in central Vietnam. Conroy agreed to help him set up the program.

There was a precedent to Craft's plan, one that dated back to early days of the war. In October 1966 the civic affairs section of the Seventh Marine Regiment and the Navy's 1st Dental Company organized a program they called Operation Toothbrush, the goal of which was to provide basic dental hygiene to every child in the Binh Son school district located south of Chu Lai. In early 1967 Task Force X-Ray, the operating headquarters for the 1st Marine Division in Chu Lai, reported that more than 13,000 treatments had been performed to villagers by dental clinics in the Chu Lai area.

A fourteen-year-old boy named Binh Nguyen hung out with the Marines of the Combined Action Program (CAP) who operated near his village of Ky Khuong. Binh also spent a good deal of time at Task Force X-Ray. He earned money from the Marines shining boots and performing odd jobs. The legal officer, Lt. Colonel John Zorack, took an interest in the boy, impressed with his hard work in support of his family. One of the Marines gave Binh a dictionary. Learning English one word at a time, Binh became reasonably proficient at speaking English, so much so that Colonel Zorack brought him along as a translator when he met with village chiefs. As Jack Wells wrote in his article, "Full Circle", "A strong bond developed between the colonel and the boy. At times, Zorack provided financial help for the Nguyen family, who were facing a difficult life in wartime Vietnam. Before Zorack returned to the United States, he bought Binh a bicycle."

After returning home Zorack continued to help Binh. Desiring that Binh receive the best possible education, the colonel, with the help of his contacts, managed to secure for the boy a visa to the United States. In April 1969, Binh arrived in Springfield, Virginia where he attended junior high school and high school while living with the Zoracks. Before completing high school, however, Binh went back to Vietnam to see his mother and sister and his girlfriend, Khoa. When it came time to return to school in Virginia, Binh decided to remain in Vietnam.

With the education he had received in the U.S. and the support of the Marines, getting a job was not difficult. Binh went to work for the U.S. Defense Attaché Office in Saigon. Four years later, when the North Vietnamese were heading to Saigon, Binh helped with the evacuation of Americans and Vietnamese orphans. By this time, he and Khoa had married and she was expecting their first child. The two of them also evacuated. After stops in the Philippines and Guam they ended up in a refugee camp at, where else, Camp Pendleton, back with the Marines. Two weeks after their arrival, Khoa gave birth to a son whom they named John, after Lt. Colonel John Zorack. Jack Wells describes the subsequent events in the life of Binh Nguyen:

"Back in the United States, Binh took adult-education classes and received his high school diploma. [He would later earn an MBA from the Massachusetts Institute of Technology in 2006.] Zorack recommended Binh for a position with a rapidly growing air transportation company called Federal Express Corp. founded in 1973 by the former commanding officer of Kilo Company, 3rd Battalion, 5th Marines—Frederick W. Smith.

"By 1989 Binh had worked his way into management at Federal Express. That year, he traveled to Vietnam to apply for a petition so his mother could immigrate to the United States. At that time business with Vietnam was forbidden by a U.S. trade embargo, but Binh foresaw a possible future market for Federal Express as Vietnam slowly recovered from the long war. After listening to Binh's observations from his trip to

Vietnam, Smith started making plans for Federal Express, which he had shortened to FedEx, to expand into Southeast Asia and Vietnam when the timing was right. In February 1994 the U.S. trade embargo was lifted, and two months later FedEx opened an office in Ho Chi Minh City."

After establishing a working relationship with East Meets West, Charles Craft proceeded to acquire $250,000 worth of dental equipment and supplies donated by hospitals, clinics, and dentists in Alaska. He contacted the FedEx facility in Anchorage and asked if they would be willing to ship the equipment and supplies to the EMW office in Da Nang for a minimal fee. The manager told him it would cost $20,000.

Apparently, the word of Dr. Craft's project reached the CEO of FedEx, Frederick W. Smith, because two weeks later Craft received a phone call from the manager who said, "You're good to go. Our truck will pick up the equipment at your garage tomorrow." Over the next two years, FedEx shipped several more containers with dental supplies to Vietnam...at no cost.

The EMW dental clinic opened its doors on 25 March 1996. Staffed by Vietnamese and a few international volunteers, the clinic was housed in a building near the old Marine Marble Mountain Air Facility in Da Nang. Two years later, Charles Craft and Mark Conroy, loaded with portable dental equipment, began making trips into the rural areas of central Vietnam.

"The Vietnam War experiences of Binh, Zorack, Smith and Craft," writes Jack Wells, "came full circle during a March 2012 EMW dental outreach event at the Phan Chau Trinh junior high school in Tam Giang Commune, near Chu Lai. Construction of the school, which opened in December 1999, near where Smith had served, was funded by FedEx working through the Vietnam Children's Fund."

The 2012 event commemorated the 100,000th patient treated by the EMW dental program. Six of the original sponsors were on hand at the Chu Lai ceremony including Craft and Conroy. "Joining them," writes Wells, "were international dental volunteers, several Marines who served during the war and Binh, now FedEx's Indochina senior country manager—whose presence reflected the influence of Colonel Zorack's kindness. The transportation required to move 2 tons of dental equipment and supplies from Da Nang to Chu Lai and back was provided by the FedEx licensee in Vietnam."

Since then, FedEx has built three additional schools. The second school, opened in 2004, was dedicated to the memory of Father Vincent Capodanno, a man for whom Fred Smith holds in the highest esteem. Known as the "Grunt Padre," Father Capodanno chose to become a Navy chaplain and serve with the Marines in Vietnam. He was assigned to the 3rd Battalion 5th Marines, the unit 2nd Lt. Frederick W. Smith was assigned to in 1967. Fred was leading a platoon of 3/5 Marines on Operation Swift when, on 4 September 1967, they were ambushed by an NVA force. The Marines were seriously outnumbered. When the firefight began Father Capodanno, unarmed, left the company CP and ran toward the action, administering last rites and providing medical attention to the wounded. Capodanno was totally unconcerned with his own safety. He was awarded the Medal of Honor posthumously, the citation of which reads:

"For conspicuous gallantry and intrepidity at the risk of his life above and beyond the call of duty as Chaplain of the 3d Battalion, in connection with operations against enemy forces. In response to reports that the 2d Platoon of M Company was in danger of being overrun by a massed enemy assaulting force, Lt. Capodanno left the relative safety of the company command post and ran through an open area raked with fire, directly to the beleaguered platoon. Disregarding the intense enemy small-arms, automatic-weapons, and mortar fire, he moved about the battlefield administering last rites to the dying and giving medical aid to the wounded. When an exploding mortar round inflicted painful multiple wounds to his arms and legs, and severed a portion of his right hand, he steadfastly refused all medical aid. Instead, he directed the corpsmen to help their wounded comrades and, with calm vigor, continued to move about the battlefield as he provided encouragement by voice and example to the valiant marines. Upon encountering a wounded corpsman in the direct line of fire of an enemy machine gunner positioned approximately 15 yards away, Lt. Capodanno rushed a daring attempt to aid and assist the mortally wounded corpsman. At that instant, only inches from his goal, he was struck down by a burst of machine gun fire. By his heroic conduct on the battlefield, and his inspiring example, Lt. Capodanno upheld the finest traditions of the U.S. Naval Service. He gallantly gave his life in the cause of freedom."

The third school FedEx built was completed in 2006 and dedicated to Richard "Dick" Pershing, grandson of WWI legend, Army General John J. "Black Jack" Pershing, a close friend and classmate of Smith's at Yale University, class of '66. Dick Pershing joined the Army and became an infantry officer in Vietnam. He was killed in action near Hue in 1968.

The fourth school, completed in 2012, honors the memory of two of Smith's platoon commanders when he was company commander of Kilo 3/5, Lieutenants Joseph T. Campbell and John R. Ruggles III.

The organization Fred Smith worked with in the construction of his first school, the Vietnam Children's Fund, was the creation of Lewis Puller, Jr., son of Chesty Puller. Lew traveled to Vietnam in 1993 for the purpose of establishing a living memorial to the men, women, and children of Vietnam who lost their lives during the war. He decided on the construction of schools. Sadly, Lew took his own life shortly before the first school was built in Dong Ha. The school, dedicated in 1994, was named The Lewis Puller, Jr. School.

A decade later, a group of Marine officers from Basic School 6-67, working with the East Meets West Foundation, built a school in honor of the members of their class who were killed in action. 6-67 was the hardest hit Basic Class since the Korean War. They were ordered to report for duty in Vietnam one month from their graduation. Within ten days of their arrival some of the classmates were killed or wounded. Within the first twelve months, half of the infantry and artillery officers from the class were killed or wounded. On 22 February 2006, surviving members of 6-67 dedicated the Mac Dinh Chi Primary School to the students and families of Thang Binh District.

One of the Basic School 6-67 survivors was Lt. Colonel Jack Wells. I had read some of Jack's writing and contacted him. He informed me that a memorial wall was being constructed on the grounds of the Mac Dinh Chi School. The wall would contain 4" x 6" marble plaques which could be purchased by anyone wishing to honor a friend, comrade, or family member killed in action in Vietnam. The proceeds would go into a fund for the school. A small group of us from Lima Company 3/1, 1st platoon, purchased a plaque on which to honor a beloved member of our platoon, Charles Alexander, killed by a VC sniper round in February 1967. We also installed a plaque honoring our battalion Sergeant Major, Melvin Davis, killed in an ambush in January 1967. With Gerry Haugen, brother of Tom Haugen, and Leroy Gonzales, we purchased a plaque honoring Nate Lee, killed on Go Noi Island serving with India Company 3/27, and Tom Haugen, whose death in 1975 was a result of Tom suffering from PTSD.

The same week we made our contributions to the school, Jack Wells received an email from Dr. Charles Craft. "You probably don't know me," Craft wrote, "but I have been the dental director for the East meets West dental program in Danang for 12 years. I have been running around with Mark Conroy for a long time. Together with our staff of ten

Vietnamese dental professionals and hundreds of international volunteers, we have been able to build the program up over the years to the point where we now have three parts to our operation: a dental clinic, a dental trailer and a portable dental outreach program. These three sections combine together to provide free treatment to over 10,000 children per year." Aware of what the Basic School 6-67 survivors had accomplished, Craft informed Jack of his intention to conduct a week-long dental outreach effort at the Mac Dinh Chi School. "I am sure the children there receive no dental care now from the government and therefore our corrective and educational care would be extremely beneficial to them. We would be able to provide exams, cleanings, sealants, fluoride treatments, alloy and resin fillings, extractions and medications along with a lot of educational training on proper oral hygiene." He wondered if the members of Basic School 6-67 could help meet the cost of the project. When Jack informed us that our contributions would help defray the cost of the dental outreach at the school, we were, of course, delighted to be part of such an effort.

Ten years later our group of 3/1 Marines and Corpsmen and two spouses visited the Mac Dinh Chi School. When I contacted the East Meets West office in Da Nang, informing them of our plan to visit the school, I asked Mr. Hiep Nguyen if there was anything we could bring to the students. I was thinking in terms of books or school supplies, but Hiep had a much more ambitious idea. He told me the school could use a water purification system. Not only would the students have clean water at school, but they could bring containers of it home with them, that the school's water would be healthier than the water from their wells. We succeeded in raising the funds needed for the water purification equipment. It was installed the week before we arrived for our visit.

Hiep told me there would be a "hand-over ceremony" when we got there. I expected something simple, imagining the kids would all line up while their principal thanked us for our donation. Instead, we were entertained. Prior to the trip I thought about visiting Hill 50 and how it was unlikely that being back there would invoke any emotions. After all, I had spent decades processing that, and all my other war memories. I certainly didn't expect to be brought to tears by Vietnamese children.

The first performance was a song by a pretty six-year-old wearing a lovely yellow dress. I lack the words to adequately describe her talent. She radiated complete confidence. Had she been performing in front of the judges of American Idol, they would have been utterly stunned by the amazing performance by this child from one of the poorest provinces in Vietnam. The reaction from this audience of Marine grunts went much deeper. Walking through villages in that province on a daily basis, we encountered hundreds of poor, hungry kids begging for whatever we had to give. And here we were, half a century later, receiving the most precious gift imaginable from one of their descendants. There were eight days left in our visit, but had we departed at the end of that day, I would have returned home a very happy man.

Of course, given the endless controversy surrounding the Vietnam War, we can hardly expect everyone to accept at face-value a humanitarian gesture such as donating a water purification system to a poor Vietnamese school for what it is—namely, identifying a need and filling it. Fred Turner, for instance, writes, "Belief in one's capacity to 'help' Vietnam transformed a veteran's healing journey into a moral and salvation mission in which the long-delayed fantasy of rescuing Vietnam was finally realized." When Doctor DeShazo first stepped foot in a rural Vietnamese village, his inclination to provide medical treatment was not the enactment of some fantasy. It was about a medical doctor doing what comes naturally, providing medical treatment to those who need it. The same applied to the corpsmen. As for the Marine grunts who provided security for them, if we arrived in-country with any notion that we were there to rescue Vietnam, we were soon disabused of that notion. That "fantasy" was replaced by one and only one purpose: staying alive. As for our impressions of Vietnam today, none of us found it to be a country in need of rescue.

There are those critics who interpret the phenomenon of veterans returning to Vietnam with a mission in terms of gender politics. Take Christina Schwenkel, for instance, who describes the Vietnam vet as suffering from "the specter of an emasculating defeat and compounded victimization by the U.S. Government, the Vietnamese population, and the larger U.S. Society." Thus, humanitarian missions such as our group donating a water purification system to the Mac Dinh Chi School is simply an attempt at remasculation. I do not make a practice of voicing my objection to authors with whom I disagree, but I had to send Schwenkel the following email:

Dear Professor Schwenkel,

Do you recall the tornado that struck Joplin, Missouri in 2011? Living an hour and a half from Joplin, I decided to drive there to help with the clean-up effort. I brought my chainsaw. It was quite an experience. Hundreds of folks came to help--men, women, children--most of them without any particular skills or equipment to offer. Just there to lend a hand. Consequently, each time I'd saw a branch, someone was there to haul if off.

Did I feel a sense of personal satisfaction afterward? Yes, I did. Being a two-tour Marine Vietnam veteran, however, I guess you would see it as yet another pathetic moment in the endless remasculation project--an attempt to regain some semblance of the masculine self-image I once had before it was stripped away by 'emasculating defeat and compounded by the U.S. government, the Vietnamese population, and larger U.S. society.'

"'I make no effort to create my own historical "truth" about Vietnam's past or present,'" you write. Yeah, sure. And I suppose you want to say that you make no effort to promote one narrative and silence another, right?

"Twenty-two days from now seven of us will visit the Mac Dinh Chi School in the Quang Tin Province, about seven miles north of the site of a battle we fought with the 21st PAVN Regiment. We are donating a water purification system to the school. The school was built 12 years ago with money raised by a group of Marine officers who served in Vietnam. I asked one of them if the school had a need for anything we could provide, and he referred me to a Vietnamese gentleman working with the East Meets West Foundation who suggested the water purification system.

"Little did I know, prior to reading your book, that this act of giving is actually a case of 'reinscribing gendered, hierarchical relations of power between (re)masculinized providers and feminized recipients of aid.'

"Thank you so much for enlightening me, Professor Schwenkel."

I never received a reply from the professor.

I cannot speak for all Vietnam veterans any more than Schwenkel. What I can say is, our leaders, Generals Walt and Krulak, took civic action seriously. They were guided by the *Small Wars Manual* published in 1940, which states that "in small wars, tolerance, sympathy, and kindness should be the keynote of our relationship with the mass of population...the purpose should always be to restore normal government...and to establish peace, order, and security." Restoring normal government may have been beyond our reach, but the civic action programs, the CAP Marines in particular, carried out those instructions at the village level.

Dr. Craft writes that when he and Mark Conroy first began their outreach program, they were taken aback by the warmth and friendliness shown them by the villagers. How could this be, Craft wondered, given the massive amount of suffering endured by the people during the war? He asked the interpreter to pose that very question to a village elder. This was his response: "The rural people of Vietnam understand war. We know suffering, fear and death. For over 50 years our countryside and homes were torn apart by war from many armies; the Japanese, French, Viet Cong, American, the former Army of the South, and the Army from the North. Only the soldiers from one of these armies tried to help and not exploit us. Our lives have improved very little over all these years. It was only the Americans who came into our villages and built roads, bridges and schools and dug wells. They helped us farm the land and provided medical care for us and our children. Some of the American Marines lived side by side with us. The Americans showed us promise for a better life someday in the future. It is the memory of that brief time of hope that allows us to forget the pain of the past and smile today when we see an American."

Helping the Vietnamese

Gary Harlan with Chuck Searcy in Hanoi.

CHAPTER 15

CHUCK SEARCY: POSTWAR HERO

Personal healing was only one aspect of the Lima Company journey I had organized. We were visiting a country the United States had devastated. For Americans to return to Vietnam, be welcomed by the Vietnamese with open arms, and enjoy their culture without being cognizant of that tragic history struck me as unacceptable. As novelist Viet Thanh Nguyen wrote, "A just memory says that ethically recalling our own is not enough to work through the past." The return visit I planned would be a project of just memory. I could think of no better way to recall the suffering of the Vietnamese than by scheduling a meeting in Hanoi with Chuck Searcy.

Chuck had enlisted in the Army in 1966 but did not serve as a combatant in Vietnam. He was assigned to an intelligence unit in Saigon. "Until I came to Vietnam," Chuck told us as we sat together in a meeting room at the infamous 'Hanoi Hilton,' "I thought our government could do no wrong. My year in Vietnam really shook me to my roots because it shattered all those ideals, I grew up believing in. I realized that the U.S.

Government was not only lying to the American people about what was going on, I was part of the institutional lie."

Hanoi's Hỏa Lò Prison was built by the French in the late nineteenth century when Vietnam was part of French Indochina. Thousands of political prisoners advocating independence were subjected to subhuman conditions that included torture and execution. During the Vietnam War, American POWs were held there. They jokingly referred to it as the Hanoi Hilton. They too were subjected to torture. In the mid-90's most of the prison was demolished. A museum was established in the part that remained intact. That was where we met with Chuck on Day 10 or our visit. It was a fitting place to meet this man who has spent the last 25 years of his life working with the Vietnamese to undo some of the damage done 50 years ago during the American War on Vietnam.

After high school he was admitted to the University of Georgia but dropped out after two years. Knowing this would likely result in his being drafted, he enlisted in the Army, thinking this would improve his chances of being assigned an MOS (Military Occupation Specialty) other than the infantry. He was right. He served a tour of duty in Vietnam as an intelligence analyst in Saigon in '67 to '68. He was not traumatized by his Vietnam service, but he was severely disillusioned.

"You mentioned that you were part of the institutional lie," I said. "Can you elaborate, please?"

"We produced a lot of reports that would go out the front office and up the chain of command," he replied. "But before they were dispatched a lot of these reports were rejected by the higher-ups I worked for. We had a colonel that was in charge of the center and there was a Lieutenant Colonel, and they did the final check. They would bounce back a lot of reports for the obvious reason that it was stuff that did not align with what they were saying in Washington. Instead of saying this was what we learned in the field, or this is what we learned from various sources, we had to make the report fit the pattern. It was very dishonest."

Chuck went on to say that one of the reasons he learned about it so quickly was not only the classified documents they worked up that revealed the government's dishonesty, but also access to unclassified materials.

"I was very lucky to be assigned to the intelligence center. There was a collegial atmosphere. We talked very freely and critically about what was going on, and we learned from each other. We'd pass books and magazine articles around and we read a lot—including Ho Chi Minh's speeches, the Geneva agreement—so we had a full immersion course. It was obvious we were giving the American people a different version than what was shown in those documents. It was an eye-opening experience, and it caused me to be skeptical to this day about anything the government tells us."

After his discharge Chuck returned to the university.

"When I returned to classes I didn't know anyone and things had really changed on campus. When I left everyone was wearing blue blazers and red ties. I got back and it was longhair, beads, peace symbols and smoking dope. Anyway, I got back to a quiet pattern. There were a few people in my classes who knew I was a Vietnam veteran. They were curious about my service. They were very polite about it. Nobody ever harassed me or anything."

One day a classmate informed Chuck that they were holding a demonstration, a peace vigil with some singing and speeches the following night at the quadrangle. He asked if Chuck would be willing to speak. He agreed. "I basically told them what I just told you—that I went over believing everything Johnson said, but ended up being opposed to the war.

"After the speech nine guys came down and introduced themselves as Vietnam vets. None of us knew each other, but the next morning we got together and decided to form a chapter of *Vietnam Veterans Against the War*. We started speaking to classes, Rotary Clubs, churches, and other groups."

"I was with an antiwar group in San Diego that did the same thing," I said. "I never thought it was particularly fruitful. One day a lady walked by the table we had set up somewhere in Chula Vista, and yelled, 'Communists!' It was kind of ironic really, being called a communist when you have actually killed communists."

One night Chuck's father, a World War Two veteran who was taken prisoner at the Battle of the Bulge, saw his son on TV. "He was furious. He said, 'We don't know who you are anymore. You're not a patriot. What happened to you over there? Did they turn you into a communist?'"

They were estranged for two years. Then one day, when Chuck was living in Athens, Georgia, and his folks had moved to South Carolina, he received a phone call from his dad telling Chuck he was passing through town and would he care to meet for a cup of coffee.

"So, we met at the Waffle House, and after a long discussion about the weather, Dad said, 'Your mother and I have been talking and we decided this war is a terrible thing. It's just wrong. It's got to stop. We decided you were right, and we were wrong, and we want to welcome you back into our house.' It was a moment I'll never forget. But it was something a lot of families went through. They were tough times."

Though he was never a politician himself, Chuck helped different candidates run for office. He helped Max Cleland pass veteran's legislation and worked in the Carter Administration. He and a friend started a newspaper that ran for fifteen years.

In 1992 an old Army buddy was in town and during dinner the two of them decided to return to Vietnam together as tourists. Chuck said he was amazed at the warm welcome he received from the people who were struggling to rebuild their country. He said he returned home wishing he could help with their struggles. Three years later he got his chance.

In 1995 the *Vietnam Veterans of America Foundation* received a $1 million dollar grant from the *U.S. Agency for International Development* (USAID) to start a humanitarian project in Hanoi. VVA president Bobby Muller offered Chuck the job of project manager. The mission was to improve and expand production of orthopedic braces for children with polio, cerebral palsy, and other mobility problems. That involved rebuilding and renovating a large section of the rehab department at the Children's Hospital, installing routers, band saws, ovens, work benches, and creating sufficient ventilation. While this was all being done, Vietnamese were being trained in the fabrication of lightweight polypropylene braces designed and custom-made for disabled children.

Shortly after the workshop opened in 1996 the doctors and technicians reached full capacity. Patients came from all over the country to be examined and fitted with assistive devices. The staff began treating 30 to 40 patients a month, providing them with devices that enabled many of them to walk without assistance for the first time in their lives.

During the early years there was discussion among Chuck's Vietnamese doctor friends and medical staff about bombs and mines and the damage such explosives were causing throughout Vietnam. "We read newspaper accounts every week of accidents and casualties throughout the country," Chuck recalled. The military was given the job of cleaning up the unexploded ordinance, but they were inadequately equipped and insufficiently funded. "Many Vietnamese, including officials, seemed to accept that this problem would never go away because the challenge was overwhelming. The U.S. dropped at least 8 million tons of ordnance during the war, of which the Pentagon has said about 10 percent did not detonate. That's a massive amount of ordnance still in the ground—impossible to clean up in a generation."

From the beginning, however, Chuck was confident that Vietnam could be made safe. Rather than attempt a hit-or-miss effort covering the whole country, it was decided that Quang Tri Province, the country's most contaminated province from unexploded ordnance (UXO), would be the focus. "Quang Tri," Chuck told us, "has been the model for making the rest of the country safe."

After a good deal of lobbying by Chuck and the leadership of the *Vietnam Veterans Memorial Fund* (VVMF), the door was opened to funding from the U.S. "The Department of State's Office of *Humanitarian Demining* showed sharper interest in the possibility of U.S. cooperation with Vietnam in cleaning up UXO contamination." Other countries, including Ireland and Norway, have also provided funding. The first direct U.S. Involvement came from A Seattle-based organization, *Peace-Trees*, which had planted trees around the world in areas of former conflict, disaster, and environmental degradation. Founders Jerilyn Brusseau and Danaan Parry came to Vietnam to propose a similar project.

"I encouraged them to visit Quang Tri. The provincial government welcomed the idea but noted that any tree-planting effort would first require a very careful clearance of bombs and mines in that area. That led to the safe clearance of six hectares of land by the Vietnamese military, funded by *Peace-Trees*, and followed by the planting of more than a thousand trees."

Other groups from various countries joined in the effort. "Soon afterward a German organization, *SODI-Gerbera*, got involved, followed by the large British demining organization, *Mines Advisory Group* (MAG), *Clear Path International*, and *Golden West Humanitarian Foundation*. The situation was now ripe for the introduction of the concept that became *Project RENEW*. Chuck explained to us how it came about.

"The decision to launch *Project RENEW* depended on raising $500,000 to guarantee at least two years of adequate funds to make the project a reality. Jan Scruggs, VVMF's president, convinced Christos Cotsakos, a Vietnam veteran who had been wounded in Quang Tri, to come up with half the funding. Cotsakos had been very successful with E*Trade Online Financial Services. I approached the *Freeman Foundation*, which matched Cotsakos's donation with another $250,000. Project RENEW was underway."

Project RENEW was co-founded by Chuck and his young colleague, Hoang Nam. "We hired core staff, allocated some of our budget to bring in a technical expert, Bob Keeley from *European Landmine Solutions*, to help us structure the project and train staff, and we focused on risk education—teaching people how to be safe, to avoid accidents and injury, and to report ordnance as they found it."

Risk education was the first of the three-prong approach developed by Chuck and his team. The other two were victim assistance and bomb clearance. "We soon learned that without trained personnel to safely destroy or remove dangerous ordnance when calls for help came in, our effort was quickly losing credibility with local people. We had to intensify our efforts to raise funds to deploy Explosive Ordnance Disposal (EOD) teams to answer urgent calls for help." The funds were raised, and the EOD teams are still in place.

In 2008 *Project RENEW* partnered up with *Norwegian People's Aid* (NPA). An NPA team had come to Quang Tri looking to expand into Vietnam with its impressive global mine work. The partnership was a perfect fit. The Norwegian government provided substantial funding as well as technical support. Nowadays, the *Project RENEW* team does not simply wait for reports of UXO. The process has become highly sophisticated:

"We are now following a plan developed by NPA's country director at the time, Jonathon Guthrie, which is an evidence-based Cluster Munitions Remnants Survey (CMRS). That initiative combines surveying of UXO-contaminated areas, interviewing local residents, comparing bombing records turned over by the Department of Defense, and using that data to deploy teams that remove or destroy ordnance in those areas. As the footprints of cluster munitions strikes are reduced and eliminated, and all other ordnance in the area neutralized, this evidence-based information goes into a comprehensive database available to all who need the information."

It isn't difficult to judge the success of *Project RENEW*. In 2001, the year they established the risk education program, 89 Quang Tri residents had been killed or injured by unexploded ordinance. During our meeting on 10 March 2019, Chuck told us, "For the first time since 1975, there hasn't been a single unexploded ordinance accident in Quang Tri Province for 2 straight years."

With *Project RENEW* running smoothly, Chuck has also devoted his time to providing aid to Agent Orange victims.

In early 2020 I had a phone conversation with Chuck. I was curious about a subject that had not been discussed in our meeting at the Hanoi Hilton museum—namely, his impressions of the Vietnamese having lived there for 25 years. He began by saying, "In the 25 years I've been here, I've never encountered any animosity or bitterness from the Vietnamese people. Some people have lamented the loss of loved ones, and remembering things that happened during the war, but no blame or harsh attitudes toward us for causing it. I've really learned a lot from the Vietnamese and admire and respect their culture. I've learned a lot of life lessons from them."

"What sort of life lessons?" I asked.

"In some ways they are accepting of circumstances around them. They are very adaptable. I know they have opinions, but they are not judgmental. They don't make judgments about religion or lifestyles. They just let you do your thing as long as you are not hurting your family or anybody else. They focus on what we can share together rather than what separates us. It's a refreshing attitude."

I mentioned a couple of authors I had read who had the idea that the Vietnamese were more welcoming to former American antiwar protesters than veterans. "What do you think?", I asked.

"Well, they are welcoming to everyone, and they are always happy to meet Americans who protested the war. But they really do put veterans on a slightly higher pedestal than others. That may seem counter-intuitive, but their view is, the veterans didn't make the policy. It was a tragic mistake made by the government. 'You served your country when you were called, and we respect that. You know what we suffered through because you suffered the same thing. So we're brothers.' I've seen this happen countless times. They reach out and shake hands—guys will reach around and hug them. I've seen guys as big as linebackers with tears running down their faces because this huge burden they've carried around so long has been lifted.

"The Vietnamese say, 'It's over. That was a long time ago. We're looking to the future. We're friends.' Yes, they really do treat veterans in a special way. It's ironic, but it's true."

Gary Sooter was killed March 5, 1966 on Operation Utah.

CHAPTER 16

PFC Gary Sooter, Bravo 1/7

Halfway through the first day of Operation Utah, the thinking at Task Force Delta headquarters was now that we have this NVA regiment in our sights, the last thing we want to do is allow them the chance to escape. To prevent that, General Platt deployed Lt. Colonel Young's 3rd Battalion 1st Marines to the northern portion of the operation and Lt. Colonel P.X. Kelley's 2nd Battalion 4th Marines to the southern flank. Because Kelley had only two available companies for the mission, Bravo Company of the 1st Battalion, 7th Marines (1/7) would be attached to 2/4.

At 0830 on the morning of 5 March, as 3/1 was marching toward the Chau Nhai (3) area to commence a bloody battle with the 21st NVA Regiment, helicopters began dropping off 2/4 at their LZ 4,000 meters south near An Tuyet (1) followed by Bravo 1/7. As was the case with Lima Company's assault on Hill 50, preparations were made to secure the LZ in the form of artillery fire and air strikes throughout the previous night. And like Hill 50, those preparations made little difference in effecting the outcome. 2/4 met heavy resistance upon landing. Three helicopters were destroyed by enemy machine gun fire, one of which was repaired by a mechanic, and two that remained out of commission on the landing zone. At 1100

General Platt ordered 2/4 to move north and carry out its mission which was to hook up with 2/7 and establish a blocking position. At 1500 they reached their objective, 2,000 meters southeast of Hill 50. Meanwhile, Bravo 1/7 was ordered to remain at the LZ to protect the downed helicopter. They would soon be fighting for their lives.

The enemy could not have hoped for more favorable circumstances in which to launch an assault. As Bravo Company Commander Captain Robert Prewitt later wrote, "Bravo Company was now on its own in a remote, isolated position with no physical contact with any friendly forces. The ridge line ran from our northwest to our southeast at about 400 meters distance and provided the NVA with excellent observation of our position. A cane field grew along the base of the ridge line that gave good concealment to the enemy. It allowed them to move undetected very close to our perimeter. We were thinly spread out in a large circle in the dry rice field. The total strength of our reinforced rifle company that day was only five officers and 160 enlisted Marines, well under strength."

That afternoon Bravo 1/7 came under heavy attack from the east, west, and south by two NVA companies. Air strikes were called in by their forward air controller, Lt. Bob McCormick. The bombs and napalm dropped on the enemy reduced but did not completely halt the enemy fire. It was around this time that Bravo Company got hit with mortar strikes. About 35 NVA had been seen moving across the ridge line carrying large loads judged to be mortar rounds. At 1630 the NVA established a position on the north, thus completely surrounding Bravo Company. In the words of Prewitt, "We could not maneuver away from our position; we were tied to the downed helicopter until it was repaired or lifted out. It acted like a magnet that drew the NVA to it. They knew they had us pinned down. They were like hungry wolves circling for a tasty meal!"

The company gunny, Gunnery Sergeant Ira Riley, whom Prewitt described as "a lanky South Carolinian who continually looked out for the welfare of our men," requested an ammunition resupply over the battalion radio net. All 60mm and 81mm mortar rounds, 3.5 rocket rounds, and M-79 rounds had been expended. The ammunition was loaded into two helicopters at the Quang Ngai Airfield. At 2000 it was already dark when the lead helicopter pilot, Lt. Terril J. Richardson spotted the small strobe light from the ground directing him to the landing zone. However, the intense fire he received which included three machine guns that covered the landing zone in a crossfire, drove off the resupply choppers. When Captain Prewitt informed the pilot how desperate the situation was, that the company had less than 100 rounds of rifle ammo and the NVA was closing in, the pilot said they would get the ammunition to them somehow. And they managed to do so, taking a number of hits in the process. Lt. Richardson commented afterward that "It seemed as though the whole world was firing at us." Had those choppers failed to make the drop, Bravo Company would almost certainly been overrun. Prewitt later learned that the lead helicopter showed over forty bullet holes in his machine, including eight through the cockpit and fourteen through the troop compartment, yet miraculously, not crewman in either chopper was injured.

Around 0130 the enemy attacked Bravo Company from three sides with an estimated 100 soldiers on each side. With the help of Marine and ARVN artillery, the Marines held them off. The forward observer attached to the company brought the artillery rounds as close 50 meters from their perimeter. At 0745 on the morning of the 6th, General Platt ordered 2/4 to return to the LZ to provide relief to Bravo Company. By the time they arrived, however, the enemy had left. Prewitt's men found 38 enemy dead outside their perimeter. Twice that number were likely carried off. The Marines suffered five killed and twenty-four wounded. One of the fallen Marines was Gary E. Sooter, a nineteen-year-old Pfc. from Independence, Missouri.

On 28 December 1964, 13 days after his 18th birthday, Gary Ercil Sooter enlisted in the United States Marine Corps. Two days later he arrived at boot camp in San Diego. On 25 March 1965 he graduated from boot camp, and proceeded to the next step in the process, infantry training. On 1 July 1965, Gary was promoted to Private First Class. Two months later he was aboard the USS *General Mitchell* sailing to Okinawa for training in jungle warfare and counterinsurgency. On 12 November Gary and his unit, Alpha Company, 1st Battalion, 3rd Marines, departed Okinawa for Da Nang, South Vietnam, arriving there on 18 November. On 17 December, Gary celebrated his 19th birthday hunting VC. From 10 to 17 January 1966, Alpha 1/3 participated in Operation Mallard. On 22 January 1966, Alpha 1/3 was rotated to the 1st Battalion 7th Marine Regiment at Chu Lai, becoming Bravo Company 1/7. On 5 March 1966, on Operation Utah in the Quang Ngai Province, Pfc. Gary E. Sooter was killed instantly from a bullet wound to the head fired from an NVA machine gun.

There you have it. A neat and tidy summary of the last 432 days of a young man's life—a life abruptly ending just as it was getting started. A short life reduced to a statistic: One of 5 Bravo 1/7 Marines killed on Operation Utah; one of 6,186 Pfc's killed during the Vietnam War; one of 8,283 19 year-olds killed during the Vietnam War; one of 1,412 Missourians killed during the Vietnam War; and the one service member killed who mattered most to his mom and three sisters.

One of his sisters, Marjorie Garner, devoted years putting together a book honoring the memory of her brother, documenting the fact that Gary E. Sooter was much more than a statistic. Titled, *Tribute to a Hero*, the book is a true labor of love. Reading her book, in which she traces every detail of his life—from his early upbringing to the day he was killed in combat—it is clear that Marjorie considered her brother a hero long before he enlisted in the Marines. He demonstrated that one day when they were kids.

The family lived in a four-room farmhouse on a hilltop outside of Ulman, Missouri. At the bottom of the hill was a creek. Each day when the school bus dropped them off at the mailbox, Gary and Marjorie walked a mile and a half to their house. Marjorie recalls one day, after a hard rain, when they reached the creek and discovered "it was well beyond its banks and rolled like a pot of boiling water. We had absolutely no concept about the danger of rushing flood water, but just watching it we knew it was bad. When we saw no way to cross, fear gripped me so much that I broke into tears." She was seven and Gary was nine.

"Gary said, 'Sis, you stay here. I'm going to the house to get Dad's gum boots. I'll be back. Just stay here and don't move.' I watched him cross the water never realizing as a child how easy he could have been swept away. By the time he reached the other side, his jeans were soaked high above the knees...When Gary returned, he was wearing boots that were almost as big as him. He could hardly walk and had to throw each leg side to side just to walk forward. He finally made it across and lifted me on his back. The fear of the rushing water was gone. I felt safe and we made it to the other side. He saved us...he was a hero."

Ten years later, Gary Sooter is facing a threat much greater than a flooded creek. His platoon is pinned down, outnumbered, and under attack by a company of well-armed NVA soldiers. According to the statement from Gary's squad leader, Sergeant Simon Serrano, "Our squad had the right flank. PFC Sooter and Lcpl McCann had the last position with a 30-meter gap between them and the next squad." Several times Gary had been warned to stay down, but he continually ignored the warnings. Gary could hear the enemy communicating but could not see them. He stood up again and killed three of the enemy no more than 20 meters from his position. Sergeant

Serrano stated that "it was at this time that the 30-caliber machine gun opened up from his right rear and he was mortally wounded."

PFC Gary E. Sooter was awarded the Silver Star medal posthumously.

In a *Kansas City Star* article titled, "A Horror of War," Gary's mother Lizzie recalled the day her son called to inform her he would be going to Vietnam.

"He told me, 'I'm going to Vietnam and I know I'm not coming back,' she said. I told him that all boys said that and they were usually the ones who came back. But I knew in my mind that he would not be back."

I asked Marjorie if perhaps Gary knew himself well enough to know that that was a definite possibility. Without hesitation, she agreed.

"Oh yes, if something had to be done, Gary would not hesitate to do it. Even if it meant his own death."

The cathartic effect of working through a tragic event by means of writing about it is not unheard of. But for Marge Garner, the effort produced much more than a book. It brought her into the lives of Marines Gary served with. While contacting Bravo 1/7 Marines to gather information about her brother, she and her husband Scott became honorary Marines. That's what one of them told me when I was introduced to Scott at a Bravo Company reunion held at the home of Dave Shelton in Billings, Missouri, an hour from my home and a short distance from Marge and Scott's home in the town of Republic. In 2011 he and Colonel Prewitt traveled to Republic to celebrate Thanksgiving with the Garner family. Dave felt a kinship with them, so much so that he moved to the Ozarks. In 2012 Marge and Scott hosted the first of three Bravo Company reunions.

Thanks to one of the Bravo Company Marines, my desire to meet 21st NVA Regiment survivors was realized. His name is

Bob "Ira" Frazure. As I recount in Chapter 17, Ira was instrumental in helping us meet our former enemy.

Gary Harlan with Vu Dinh Son at the tomb of Son's father, Vu Dinh Doan.

The Diary of Vu Dinh Doan

"On the 5th day of the 9th lunar month I was standing on top of a pass that was 1,500 meters high...On the 10th day of the 9th lunar month, my paternal grandmother's death anniversary, I was standing on top of a pass 1,800 meters high. I sat down at the top of the pass with Bong, Sao, Con, and Gia. I remembered my life back home."

It had been four months since Vu Dinh Doan joined the Army. That was when his unit, the 21st Regiment of the People's Army, was formed in his home province of Hai Duong, 35 miles outside Hanoi. Prior to that, Doan served as the Deputy Commander of his village militia. Those who knew him described him as happy and outgoing, and that he loved to sing and play the guitar.

Two young girls, Yen and Nhat, also served in the militia. As Doan and the others were leaving the village to fight the Americans down south, they gave Doan a photo of the two of them as a memento. Doan placed it inside a small red book which would be his diary. In it he describes his life as a soldier, how he and the others were first sent to Chi Linh for two months of training before their long, grueling march down the Ho Chi Minh Trail.

"On this march I have encountered a great deal of problems. I ate cold rice gruel made of leaves."

Doan's friend, Vu Ba Con, remembers Doan as a "straightforward and emotional man" who would write in his diary every chance he got. On one such occasion Doan reflects on his father on a special day.

"On the 13th of October, the death anniversary of my father [footnote: Those of us who entered the huts of Vietnamese civilians understand the significance of the death anniversary for every home contained a death altar] I had to climb a pass that was 2,800 meters high. The sweat was pouring off of me. It took eight hours to reach the top. When I reached the top, I could see South Viet Nam."

The 21st Regiment's first area of operations was around Da Nang in the Quang Nam Province. Then they moved south to Quang Ngai Province where they would fight U.S. Marines.

"On 9 January 1966, we marched into Quang Ngai Province. Our march took a total of 15 days. Canh was wounded on 15 January. On 19 January we stopped to rest for 10 days. We ate cold rice with fermented fish sauce at the edge of the jungle tree line in Quang Ngai. My arduous but glorious life."

Every NVA unit, from the regiment down to the company level, had two commanders: a military commander and a political commander, both of equal rank. Before every battle it was the political officer's responsibility to rally the troops—to remind them why they were fighting, the history of their struggle, and so forth. Though Doan does not identify any of his officers by name, some of his diary entries document the work of the political officer.

"On 1 February 1966 our unit passed our battle resolve. On Tuesday we held the ceremony for us to move out to fight. Our unit consists of 97 men, including an assault unit to destroy enemy tanks...When we read the Army's ten oaths, zeal filled us. The atmosphere in the meeting was boiling with enthusiasm, like a giant storm ready to shake the earth and roil the sea. We swore that we would destroy eight enemy aircraft and five tanks. At 6:00 in the evening of 1 February 1966, we marched out. I carried two pieces of the gun."

Thus began the NVA's Western Son Tinh Campaign that ran from February 1966 through early April in the northwest sector of the Quang Ngai Province. As mentioned in chapter three, the first phase of the campaign was "lighting the fuse," launching a series of attacks on ARVN troops designed for "drawing in, pinning down, and annihilating a portion of the enemy's mobile forces in order to force the enemy to send troops to conduct a large sweep operation into the western portion of the of Son Tinh District." Though the drawing in and pinning down portions of the plan succeeded, no Marine unit was annihilated. Before the Marines were drawn in, Doan experienced a joyful moment one evening when he recon-nected with an old friend.

"I was sitting around when I heard someone call for Doan. It was 7:00 at night on 9 February 1966. I ran over and saw my friend True, the husband of Aunt Ty in Quang Ngai. It is won-derful to see a friend in a difficult situation, and it turned out we were both living in the same combat area. Then we talked about the long march and the hardships of the life of a sol-dier."

The fuse had obviously been lit when Doan wrote that "twelve helicopters landed troops 200 meters from my sector. Then my unit fought all day." He is clearly referring to Opera-tion Utah for he mentions a nearby battle in which "Uncle An was killed on Hill 50 and Quang was wounded."

Based on the location of Doan's last firefight, all indications are that his unit operated on the southern portion of the Oper-ation Utah area of operations. If that is the case, the 12 heli-copters which landed 200 meters from his position were dropping off the Marines of 2/4 and Bravo 1/7 near An

Tuyet(1). Therefore, Doan was part of the attack of the Bravo Company Marines protecting the downed helicopter.

Sometime during the second week of March 1966, *Newsweek* ran a story focusing on the aftermath of Operation Utah which contained a quote from Marine operations officer Major E.M. Snyder. Referring to the 21st NVA Regiment, Snyder said, "I wouldn't be surprised if it was at least three months before we hear from that regiment again. It's just survivors now."

Snyder was mistaken. Just three weeks after Utah, Charlie Company of the 1st Battalion 7th Marines engaged an estimated battalion of the 21st Regiment in a fierce battle at Vinh Loc (2) on Operation Indiana. Charlie Company lost 11 Marines and 55 wounded. The enemy losses were 69 confirmed dead, though the actual count exceeded that figure because the NVA, as was their custom, escaped overnight carrying an unknown number of their dead with them.

The next morning Bravo 1/7, Captain Prewitt's company that held off the NVA assault three weeks earlier, arrived at Vinh Loc (2). The Marines found 19 weapons including three of the deadly 12.7mm machine guns. One of the Bravo Company Marines, Bob "Ira" Frazure, from the state of Washington, discovered one of those machine guns beside the dead body of the NVA soldier who manned it. Judging from the drag trails he saw near the machine gun pit, it was clear to Ira that this man had sacrificed his life holding off the Marines thus giving his comrades the opportunity to escape.

That soldier was Vu Dinh Doan. Lying on his chest was his diary, which Ira picked up and stuck in his pocket. He looked at the photograph of the two girls and noticed there was an inscription written on the back. Of course, he had no way of knowing what it said. The inscription was written by Doan. It read:

"My dear Nhat and Yen. You two gave me this photograph as a memento when I left on 9 June 1965. Now I am living with the people of South Viet Nam and I am still trying to stay alive as of 9 March 1966 here in Quang Ngai. If I am alive when the country is unified, we will all be together again. We will all be happy when our country is unified."

Unlike the families of American servicemen killed in action, families of fallen NVA soldiers received no notification from their government. Vu Dinh Doan's wife and children had no idea what happened to him until the war ended nine years after his death. Of the 50 men from the village who joined the People's Army with Doan, only three survived. One of them was Vu Ba Con who, upon returning to the village, visited Doan's family and told them how he died. Con also wrote a letter to the government verifying that Vu Dinh Doan was killed in action. Consequently, Doan was assigned the title of Martyr, the recognition given to all those who died fighting against the Americans and its allies.

In 1986, after the construction of the village Martyrs Cemetery, Doan's widow urged her grown-up children to find their father's grave site and bring his remains home. Con had told them Doan was killed on Chop Non Hill. Doan's son, Vu Dinh Son, traveled to Quang Ngai Province, but had no luck in locating his father's grave. Chop Non Hill had been destroyed by American bombing. But Son returned to Quang Ngai in 2001. Upon hearing news that a northerner was looking for his father's grave site, some of the local people came to see him. One of the villagers told Son that he resembled one of the soldiers, whose name was Doan or Hoan. Interestingly enough, Son recovered his father's remains because the villagers outside Chop Non Hill remembered Doan because he entertained them with his guitar playing and singing. After receiving an official memorandum from Quang Ngai Province Military Command, Doan's remains were brought home.

With Doan's remains buried beneath his memorial tomb at the village Martyrs Cemetery, the family doubtless believed that was the end of it. Little did they know that Vu Dinh Doan kept a diary and that it was in the possession of a former Marine from Washington state whose company had been pinned down and under attack by Doan's unit, and whose sister company killed Doan; and that a lady from Missouri, whose brother was killed by Doan's unit in that firefight with Ira's company, would take responsibility for them receiving the diary Doan kept.

Ira Frazure came to regret having kept the diary. It was a reminder that somewhere there was a family for whom that diary would mean the world. He had contacted various organizations, but no one showed any interest in helping him. Then he was contacted by Marge Garner who introduced herself as the sister of Gary Sooter, a member of Ira's platoon.

"I liked that kid from the moment I met him," Ira told me. "He had a very pleasant way about him. Everybody in the platoon liked Gary."

Ira was one of the Marines Marge contacted while writing her book about Gary. She and Ira had many telephone conversations. Besides telling Marge what he remembered about her brother, Ira discussed his own life during and after the war. He told her about the diary and how conflicted he had been about keeping it. Being a Gold Star family member, Marge understood what the diary would mean to the NVA soldier's family. She had an idea. There was a PBS series called the *History Detectives* that might be able to help. She sent them a letter requesting their help.

"Her story was immediately compelling," said Series Producer Jennifer Silverman. For months the research team searched for the soldier's family. Their first step, of course, was to translate the diary into English. For that they requested the assistance of Merle Pribbenow who was a Vietnamese language specialist with the CIA during the war. Merle provided all the information required for a proper search: the soldier's name, the village, district, and province where he came from, when he joined the People's Army of Viet Nam, and when he made the march down the Ho Chi Minh Trail. Asked what unit he was with, Merle said, "By all indications he was with the 21st Regiment." Which turned out to be correct.

The person responsible for locating the family was Kyle Horst, a man who speaks Vietnamese like a native and has an abundant supply of contacts, one of whom, Hang, located the family fairly quickly. They also discovered the identities of the two girls in the photo Doan carried—Yen and Nhat. The older girl, Yen, was a member of the cultural troupe, performing patriotic songs, poetry, and skits for the troops. She was reported to have moved to another province. They located Nhet who, at the age of 71 when the diary episode aired in 2012, still lived in the same village. Being shown the photo of herself and Yen, Nhat said, "We presented this photo to him before he went into the Army. In the militia we did a lot of things. I served in an anti-aircraft unit that shot down American aircraft. That's why I was awarded a medal."

The History Detectives diary episode ends with the narrator and researcher, Wes Cowan, meeting with Marge and Ira to report the results of their investigation. They learned that the show sent the diary to Secretary of Defense Leon Panetta, who turned it over to his Vietnamese counterpart. That was not what Ira wanted to hear. "Did they give the diary to the family?," he asked, to which Cowan assured him that it had indeed been returned. Sadly, Doan's widow passed away before seeing the diary. She was, however, grateful for its return. Wes played a video for Marge and Ira of Doan's son speaking on behalf of the family. He is shown speaking in front of his mother's death altar.

"Hello, I am Vu Dinh Son, son of Martyr Vu Dinh Doan. You picked up my father's diary. On behalf of my family, I would like to say thank you. During the war I think you were an ethical person."

Then Ira was presented with a letter from Son to Ira telling him, "Before she died, my mother was very happy to learn the news about my father's diary. This is what she told me: 'In war, if you don't shoot me, I will shoot you. The fact that this man held on to my husband's papers and sought to return them proves that the one who survived is a good man, a moral man.'"

Six years after the airing of that *History Detectives* episode, which I had never seen, someone sent me the link. I received it just as I was in the process of organizing a trip back to Viet Nam. Since five out of the seven Lima Company Marines in our group fought on Hill 50, I desperately wanted us to meet at least one 21st Regiment survivor. I found out that simply is not possible due to the restrictions imposed by the Vietnamese government as to who and what veterans issued tourist visas have access to. That all changed for us the moment I contacted Kyle Horst who agreed to be our guide. Not only that, but he arranged to have a member of the Ministry of Foreign Affairs accompany us so that no doors would be shut in our faces, and no one would refuse to speak to us thinking that doing so would be frowned upon by the government. Thanks to Kyle, we were not issued tourist visas. Our visas stated that we were "Invited Guests of the Socialist Republic of Viet Nam." Toward the end of our journey we visited the Martyr Cemetery in Long Xuyen Village where I met Doan's son, Vu Dinh Son. He was reserved at first, but became instantly animated when I told him, through our interpreter, that I was a friend of Ira Frazure, and that I would be seeing Ira at a reunion three months after our return to the U.S. "Oh, please give him my best regards!" Then together we placed incense at the base of his father's memorial tomb.

The Diary of Vu Dinh Doan

Jose Perez, Jr. in Iwa Kuni, Japan

CHAPTER 18

Harlan and Perez

One week after my discharge on 9 September 1968, I began my college career at Southwestern College in Chula Vista, a suburb of San Diego. The week I began classes, my cousin, who lived in nearby Imperial Beach, gave me a letter that had been delivered to his address. It was from my best buddy, Jose Perez, Jr. I didn't need to open the letter to know he was back in the Nam. In place of postage, he had written the word, "Free." He sounded cheerful:

"I'm the platoon sergeant, so if you need any jungle boots just say so, and I will mail you some when I go on R&R. Write to me and send me some Camels for my enjoyment. Well, that's all I have to say for now. Hey, here's a corny line, "hit those books hard and make me proud of you.""

I did not write back, nor did I send him a carton of Camels for his enjoyment. The reason being: fear. Not only was my friend back in the Nam, the return address read, "Bravo Company, 1st Battalion, 9th Marines."

1/9. The news could not have been worse. Perez was up at the DMZ with the outfit whose nickname was The Walking Dead. Michael Herr wrote of 1/9, "Of all the hard-luck outfits in Vietnam, this was said to be the most doomed, doomed in its Search-and-Destroy days before Khe Sanh, known for a history of ambush and confusion and for a casualty rate which was the highest of any outfit in the entire war." I was certain Perez would not come back alive.

Knowing the month his enlistment ended in 1969, I contacted Headquarters Marine Corps in Washington and learned my worst fear had not materialized. Perez had been discharged on schedule. We reunited in 1984 at the Wall for the unveiling of the *Three Fighting Men* statue. Bob Detty was also there. Detty was a member of the squad Perez led. My first memory of Detty was an event that occurred not long after he and some other replacements joined the platoon.

It was a beautiful springtime morning out in the bush. Perez and I were sitting together enjoying our C-ration breakfast when we received a couple of sniper rounds from the tree line about 200 meters from our perimeter. Detty and the other new guys immediately scrambled about in a panic. Perez and I looked at each other and had the same thought: we would not allow some raggedy VC guerrilla to interrupt our meal. But more than that, we each knew that our non-reaction to the sniper was a way of demonstrating to the new guys that occasional harassing fire was something they would have to get used to.

Perez and I had come a long way since Lima Company's first day in-country. The night before the landing, in the troop compartment of the ship, Lance Corporal Tony Ramirez, from Houston, Texas, posed this question to no one in particular: "Who's gonna be the first one to get killed, Harlan or Perez?"

What could we say? We were, after all, the lowest-ranking PFCs in the platoon. Of course, when it came to actual combat, everyone in the platoon, except our platoon sergeant, Staff Sergeant Gingrich, before he was promoted to gunnery sergeant, were new to combat. Just the same, we had a lot to prove. During our 2019 visit to Vietnam I mentioned that to Detty, who replied, "You definitely succeeded in proving it."

It required much reflection in the years following my Marine Corps service to realize that for Perez and I, something deeper had been achieved over and above proving ourselves as Marines: for the first time in our lives, we were *needed*.

Jose Perez, Jr. was from San Antonio. We reported for duty in Okinawa on the same day. He was 18 and I was 19. We did not have much in common. Perez was a Mexican American from Texas, and I was a white guy from a middle-class family in the Ozarks. Our differences also included our physical appearance: Perez was around 5'8" and I was 6'2". His size made him the more suitable choice for checking out tunnels, yet during our first month in-country we continually argued over which of us would crawl inside a tunnel with a flashlight, armed with a .45.

Perez had an odd sense of humor. After one of our operations we got to spend the day at the battalion area where we could shower, sleep on cots in a tent, eat mess hall chow, and drink a few beers. The company had hair clippers in case someone was in need of a haircut. Perez told one of the guys he'd be willing to cut his hair. The guy asked Perez if he knew what he was doing. "I worked in a barber shop," he said. So the guy said OK. The result was disastrous. It was a horrible haircut. Looking in a mirror, the guy yelled, "Perez, you said you were a barber!"

"No I didn't," Perez replied. "I said I worked in a barber shop. I swept the floor."

Toward the end of Operation Double Eagle II, Perez was medevaced after suffering a non-combat leg injury. He returned to the platoon a few days after Operation Utah. Not being with the platoon during the fighting on Hill 50 was a much bigger deal for Perez than it was for me. He felt guilty about it. If he was fearless before his injury, he became recklessly so afterward.

Fortunately, he was also extremely lucky. Early one evening during an operation, our squads' paths crossed. The platoon had been engaged in a firefight that afternoon. We were getting ready to set up a perimeter for the night. I was about to assign my men their positions when I heard Perez yell, "Hey Gary! Look at this!" He was standing there grinning, holding half of his M-14 in one hand and the other half in the other. An enemy bullet had struck the grip portion of his rifle stock next to the trigger guard, less than an inch from his hand. Not only did the bullet shatter the rifle in two, it also struck the body portion of an M-26 fragmentation grenade that was attached to his web belt.

I had some close calls of my own. One day we were walking across a stream when a sniper with an automatic rifle opened up with a burst of fire. Three rounds struck the water no more than a foot to my right. The downside of being a squad leader was having a radioman walk behind you, thus alerting snipers that you were a leader, an ideal target.

Operation Utah, in which 98 Marines were killed and 278 wounded, was the costliest operation I participated in. Operation Teton, which was my last operation with 3/1, was the most successful. Confirmed enemy casualties were 36 killed, 3 wounded, and 9 captured, along with the apprehension of 27 Viet Cong suspects. Marine casualties were 2 killed and 15 wounded. I was one of the latter.

Unlike Utah, which had been hastily organized, Operation Teton was just the opposite. It was carefully and cleverly planned. Four companies participated: Kilo and Lima from the 3rd Battalion 1st Marines; Delta Company from the 1st Battalion 1st Marines; and Foxtrot Company from the 2nd Battalion 2nd Marines.

The initial mission was to conduct search and destroy operations in the hamlets of Tra Khe(1), Tra Lo, and Cau Ha(2) in order to capture or destroy all enemy personnel, weapons, and supplies. The four rifle companies departed on foot from the 3/1 command post at Cau Ha(1) between 3 and 4 in the morning of 12 October, and by first light we had established a cordon around the three hamlets. Prior to the search, all the villagers were taken to a collection point where food and shelter were provided while the Marines searched the three hamlets. This lasted for three days, during which the results were rather negligible. At 0900 on the 15th, we began marching north, giving the impression that the operation was over, and we were returning the battalion command post. But this was all a ruse. Our main objective was Tra Khe(2).

Tra Khe(2) was a fairly large hamlet covering 1200 meters by 200 meters. When the column was parallel to Tra Khe(2) we quickly moved into position, establishing a cordon around the entire hamlet. There was no collection point set up for the villagers. They all departed for a secure hamlet nearby. Once that was accomplished the search began.

At 1136 hours a Lima Company Marine detonated a land mine resulting in four Marines getting wounded. In the four days we searched the hamlet, Lima Company discovered 62 land mines. Except for the one detonation, they were all discovered and destroyed without friendly casualties.

It was a pretty wild affair. And exhausting. All day we searched for caves and tunnels, and each night the VC tried to fight their way out of the hamlet. I was assigned a dog team—a German Shepherd and his handler. Not only was the dog adept at locating the enemy caves and tunnels during the day, each night he alerted us to the presence of the VC before the fighting began.

If the purpose of this book was to tell my life story, rather than how it was impacted by the war, it would be impossible to do so without a discussion of my fifty-year history with dogs: two Dobermans, three German Shepherds, a Standard Poodle, and a Beagle. My third wife once remarked, "I think your dogs are more important to you than your family." That was not true. For many years, however, it was easier for me to relate to them than to humans.

That fifty-year dog narrative actually began with the scout dog assigned to my squad. As a kid, I was somewhat afraid of dogs. That changed on Operation Teton. We had dug a fighting hole that accommodated me, my radioman, and the dog handler. At 2000 hours the first night, an estimated 50 VC delivered intense small arms fire on our positions in a coordinated attempt to break out of the cordon. 14 VC were killed in the engagement. There were no Marine casualties. We discovered, however, that the fighting hole we dug was not big enough.

When the firing began, the German Shepherd, being the intelligent animal he was, forced his way into the hole. In doing so, he was forcing me out of the hole. I actually punched him in the head. At that moment, a dog bite would have been preferable to a gunshot wound. I won't speculate as to which of us would be considered the least expendable to the Marine Corps. Suffice it to say I was not bitten, and the four of us—three humans and a canine—managed to hunker down together until the next morning when we expanded the size of our fighting hole.

I managed to learn a valuable lesson that night, one that I would re-learn many times over the next five decades. People like to say, "Dogs know when you are afraid of them." That is true. But it is also the case that they know when you are *not* afraid of them.

It was the same routine the following two days. During that operation we discovered 53 caves and tunnels, most of which were built to accommodate 3 men. Just like the tunnels we found on Hill 50, they had well-concealed entrances which were located in heavily vegetated areas along hedgerows. In one area that appeared to be a cemetery, we discovered six caves and tunnels with entrances concealed under cactus plants. The tunnels ran under simulated grave mounds.

Enemy casualties were 36 killed, 3 wounded, 9 captured, and 27 VC suspects. I became a casualty the third night when a piece of shrapnel from an enemy grenade broke the right lens of my glasses and another piece lodged in my right cheek. I was medevaced the next morning. By the next week I was back in the field. I was given a medical document stating that due to my injury I was permitted to wear sunglasses. As for the shrapnel buried in my cheek, the doctor felt there was no need to dig it out. The only downside of is that I am unable to have an MRI.

When I was wounded, my radioman contacted the platoon radioman informing him that Lima 1 Bravo Actual (my call sign) had been wounded. The next thing I knew, Perez appeared at my position. He had run somewhere between 60 and 70 meters from his position to mine, in the midst of an intense firefight.

"What the hell are you doing, Perez?!," I yelled.

"I heard you were wounded," he replied.

"You have a radio, dammit! You could have found out how badly I was wounded without pulling this John Wayne bullshit!"

Oh well. What're you gonna do? That was Perez.

In the after-action report for Operation Teton, our battalion commander stated that "Interrogation of captives from Tra Khe (2) revealed that generally, the VC have very little respect for Marine search abilities. Rather than flee when Marines enter the hamlet, these VC stated they would hide in their caves, confident that they would not be discovered. To counter this tactic, we must be prepared to conduct extensive and meticulous searches of VC controlled hamlets."

The colonel also stated that "Hopefully, now that the VC infrastructure has been destroyed, a secure hamlet may be created." According to the 3/1 Command Chronology for February 1967—four months after Operation Teton—another operation, Operation Searcy, was conducted in Tra Khe(2). Reading the Commander's Analysis, it was as if Operation Teton never happened, that vis-à-vis Tra Khe(2), it was a new world for the 3rd Battalion 1st Marines:

"The Tra Khe(2) area has long been considered a VC base of operations. This vicinity is characterized by a small and predominantly hostile population. The Third Battalion's goal was to: a) capture or destroy enemy forces and supplies in the Tra Khe(2) area and b) deny that area to the enemy for future use as an operating base."

The command's solution to the problem was to relocate the entire population of Tra Khe(2) from their ancestral homes to the village of Nui Kim Son. If they were hostile before Operation Searcy, they were considerably more so now.

A month after Operation Teton, shortly before our tours of duty ended and we were scheduled to return to the States, Perez and I decided to extend our overseas tour six months. We were assigned M.P. Duty at the Marine Air Station, Iwa Kuni, Japan.

Out of the bush and into a military police detachment run by a gung-ho lifer who had not served in Vietnam: Gunnery Sergeant Rodriguez. Gunny Rodriguez was a PT (physical training) fanatic whose five and ten-mile runs first thing in the mornings did not suit Perez and I too well considering we were normally hung over. Our drinking usually took place in the barracks because time and again we would commit some offense the gunny deemed sufficiently egregious as to deny us liberty call. We always kept a supply of one-gallon bottles on hand of Akadama port wine, which the Marines called "typhoon fifths," stored in our lockers.

On one of our morning runs, Perez and I did or said something that rubbed Gunny the wrong way, and he said, "OK, you assholes! Run around the formation twenty times!" When we returned to the barracks, I said to Perez, "You know, we're NCOs. The Gunny doesn't have any right calling us assholes in front of the men. Let's go have a word with him." Perez was naturally apprehensive, but he went along with my ridiculous idea.

The door to the gunny's office was open, and he was busy with some paperwork when I knocked. He looked up long enough to see it was us, returned to his work, and said, "What do *you* want?"

"Well, Gunny," I began, "Perez and I don't think it's right for you to address us as assholes in front of the men."

The gunny quit writing and looked up at us. "You *are* assholes," he said.

I looked at Perez. He looked at me, and I turned to the Gunny and said cheerfully, as though he had just solved a problem for us, "OK, Gunny. Thank you!" And we walked off.

He was right, of course. We *were* assholes. Taking a couple of pissed off grunts fresh from the Nam and making them M.P.s was doubtless a bad idea. One example involves something I did for which I feel guilty about to this day.

I was working the main gate. Enlisted men were required to return to the base by midnight. A taxi pulled up exactly five minutes after 12. The passenger was a young sailor who had taken the taxi from Hiroshima, a good distance away. I instructed him to pay the driver and get out of the taxi. I proceeded to write him up. Five minutes late. Yes, I was clearly an asshole.

The last time Perez and I were together was in 1988 when I hosted a small platoon reunion at my farm north of Springfield, Missouri. Besides Perez, those in attendance were Bob Detty, Dennis Burke, our platoon radioman Jose Escamilla, and Rick DeMarco. We provided a guest room for Perez. Everyone else stayed at a nearby motel.

My wife and I slept in a bedroom with a door that went out to the deck and above-ground swimming pool in the backyard. The reunion took place in late summer, so we kept the door open and used the screen door. It was the first morning after the group arrived the day before when, sometime between 6 and 7, I was awakened by the sound of a can of Budweiser being opened. By the time I got up, which was no more than thirty minutes or so later, two or three more beers had been opened. I had already figured out Perez had a severe drinking problem the day before, when he failed to arrive on his scheduled flight to the Springfield Airport. He arrived on a later flight. He admitted that he missed his flight because he hung out too long in an airport bar in San Antonio.

In September 2006, Rick DeMarco, whom I called "D", who was Perez's squad leader before Perez took over the position when Rick became platoon guide, drove from his home in Ohio to pick me up. We drove to San Antonio to attend the funeral of Jose Perez, Jr. whose death was doubtless caused by alcoholism. A year before Perez's passing, D called to suggest we drive to San Antonio, pick up Perez, and hold him hostage somewhere until he was clean. I appreciated D's concern for our friend, but I did not think that was a workable solution. Just over two years after Perez's death, D died as a result of a brain tumor.

I emailed Bob Detty recently to ask if he had any recollections to share about Perez. His reply:

"You mean like the time Perez took a patrol from An Trac with our fire team and a squad of Pfs.(Vietnamese popular forces)? We set up an ambush, and one of the PFs proceeded to turn on his favorite radio station and light a cigarette. You know what happened next. Perez commenced beating the pf seriously about the head and shoulders. Needless to say, we broke the ambush. This was in June 1966. July 1966, we were set up on the river patrol base, you and the 1st squad were guarding the bridge near Regiment. Perez went on R and R to the Philippines, I think, and didn't return for about 3 weeks. The reason: somehow, he got on one of the hospital ships and didn't know how to get off!!! DeMarco was a little pissed, but mostly laughed. Vintage Perez! Then there was the time Perez and you got into a fistfight. I think this was sometime in August 1966 in battalion rear at Marble Mountain. Anyway, you two started arguing about some sort of brotherly conflict.

Someone pulled you back, and I ended up sitting on Perez until he cooled off. He threatened to write me up, demanded I get off him because he was my squad leader, etc. Just glad he didn't shoot me. That night you guys ate evening chow together.

And lastly, I'm sure you know this, but Perez most assuredly looked up to, respected, and loved you."

The feeling was most assuredly mutual.

Nate Lee, killed on Go Noi Island May 17, 1968.

CHAPTER 19

Sergeant Nate Lee

6 March 2019

Go Noi Island

Day Five of our journey was an open day for most of the group—free to shop, go to the beach, or simply enjoy the sights of Hoi An. As for me, I was going to visit a place I had never been, but one which had haunted my imagination for over fifty years. Accompanied by Bob Detty and Ron Clay, we traveled 12 miles west to that place: Go Noi Island.

Go Noi had been a haven for the VC and the NVA. Any unit sent there could be reasonably certain of heavy fighting. A three-and-a-half-month operation, code-named Allen Brook, took place there in 1968 resulting in 917 enemy dead and 11 captured. 170 Marines and 2 sailors were killed, and 1,124 wounded. A good many more casualties were sustained from non-combat related causes such as heat stroke, disease, snakebite, and accidents. On 17 May India Company, 3rd Battalion 27th Marines suffered 19 KIAs and over 50 wounded.

Unlike the morning of 17 May 1968, when the temperature was somewhere between 110 and 120 degrees, it was a pleasant day as we traced the steps of India Company. They had marched through the village of Le Nam(1). We stopped there for lunch at the My Son Restaurant where we met a man who remembered the battle that took place on 17 May. He was only

14 at the time. Though he did not participate in the battle, he was already a Viet Cong guerrilla.

Leaving the restaurant, we followed India Company's route. We walked through elephant grass until we reached a riverbank overlooking a mostly dry riverbed. On the other side, at least 100 meters away, was a tree line on top of the opposite riverbank. For decades I had wondered how a reinforced rifle company could be ambushed and pinned down. Now that I was there it was obvious how it happened. A more ideal spot for an ambush was inconceivable. The question still remained as to why it happened as it did. Knowing that a sizable NVA force was operating in the area, why would our leaders expose an entire company of Marines in that dry riverbed nearly a quarter of a mile wide without first sending out scouts or a fire team to check it out?

But that is what they did. What the India Company Marines confronted was a battalion of soldiers with the 36th NVA Regiment, well-hidden in fortified bunkers and spider holes all along the tree line atop of the riverbank. There were two deadly snipers on each end of a long line of soldiers armed with machine guns and AK-47s. They waited until the Marines were out in the open and close to their positions below before opening fire. Within the first hour there were dead and wounded Marines lying everywhere. Captain Thomas Ralph, the India Company commander was killed as well as two of the three platoon commanders. One of them had been my own platoon commander, Lieutenant Marcus Fiebelkorn. Also killed that day was Sergeant Nate Lee, who was both an exceptional leader of Marines as well as a morally superior human being. I would never have returned to Vietnam for a second tour had it not been for him.

I would not go so far as to say it was fate that brought me together with Nate Lee, at least not in the supernatural sense of the word. But it was a natural outcome arrived at by a series of personal choices beginning with the choice to leave the reserves, transfer to the regular Marine Corps and volunteer for infantry duty in Vietnam, a choice that resulted in the belief that there was no valid reason for the United States being in Vietnam, and the determination to do whatever I could to avoid being sent back there a second time.

When I proposed the idea of the two of us extending our overseas time six months, I only shared part of the reason with Perez—that there was nothing waiting for us back home, that we would be just a couple of Nam vets among thousands of others. For me, however, there was an underlying reason for extending. The Marine Corps guaranteed every returning Marine one year in the States before being redeployed. Extending my overseas tour six months meant that by the time I was eligible for redeployment to the Nam, I would only have four months before my discharge, making it unlikely they would send me back.

As previously mentioned, I spent the first couple of months back at Camp Pendleton in a state of inebriation. Oddly enough, I became sober thanks to an ancient philosopher named Socrates. Browsing in a San Diego bookstore one night I picked up a book containing four works—known as Socratic dialogs--by Plato titled The Last Days of Socrates.

Thus, I gave up drinking for reading. I was not interested in establishing friendships in my new outfit. For some reason, probably having to do with my standoffish behavior, a couple of the Marines, who were apparently pot smokers, suspected me of being a narc, working for the CID (the Criminal Investigation Division). I could care less what they thought.

Then one day I received orders for Sea School in San Diego. I was appalled. Sea School meant dress blues and spit and polish. I was a rifleman, a grunt. After reporting to Sea School, I read a document that made me very happy. It listed the prerequisites for Sea School, one of which was having served Stateside at least one year before admission. "Excuse me, Gunny, I'm not supposed to be here." So back to Pendleton I went. My new orders sent me to India Company, 3rd Battalion, 27th Marines. I was one of a dozen corporals who were Nam vets. So was the platoon sergeant, Nate Lee.

Sergeant Lee was a gung-ho type whom I immediately dismissed as a typical lifer. But a couple of things happened during my second week that changed my opinion of the man. The first was the morning one of the PFCs showed up for formation badly beaten. When Sergeant Lee asked him, what happened the kid told him he had been beaten up by the bouncer at the Playgirl Club in Oceanside. Before dismissing the platoon, Sergeant Lee announced there would be a platoon meeting at 1630. I figured he was going to advise everyone to stay away from the Playgirl Club. Instead, he announced that all members of the platoon were to assemble at the Playgirl Club at precisely 1900, that we were to proceed there in twos and threes so as to avoid to drawing attention to ourselves.

Though Sergeant Lee made it clear that our participation was voluntary, the entire platoon showed up at the entrance of the Playgirl Club at 1900. Sergeant Lee called out the bouncer whom the PFC identified as his attacker. The bouncer was a big guy about 6-foot 5, several inches taller than Sergeant Lee. It didn't take long for the MPs to arrive ordering us to disperse, but before we did, Sergeant Lee got in the man's face and informed him that if he ever beat up another one of his men we would come back and level the place. Clearly, this was not your everyday by-the-book lifer.

The second change occurred two days later when I learned I had been promoted to sergeant and became a squad leader. This meant I would move into the sergeant quarters with Sergeant Lee and Sergeant Haugen, one of the other squad leaders. The other squad leader, Sergeant Chavis, and the platoon guide, Sergeant Day were married and lived in base housing.

Tom Haugen was a squared-away Marine from Arizona who had served two tours in Nam. In 1965 he was among the first Marine snipers when they were organized. He had recently returned from his second tour with the 5th Marines.

I soon discovered Nate Lee was the kind of person whose friendship was ideally suited for someone like myself who desired to become a student of philosophy and literature. He was a devout Catholic who was both well-read and worldly. In his first enlistment from 1956 to 1960 he played first trumpet with the Marine Band at Parris Island. The band traveled through Europe, performing at the Brussels World's Fair in Belgium and the Edinburgh Castle in Scotland.

During their two-week stay in Scotland he met Frances Trotman, a Scottish lass who fell deeply in love with the tall, good-looking Italian American Marine. According to one of Nate's four brothers, the two would have gotten married had it not been for the fact that their alcoholic father was on the verge of losing their house. Nate returned to the States and saved the home by arranging to have it refinanced.

After completing his enlistment Nate worked as a courier with the CIA and was a jazz trumpeter on the side. When it became obvious that America's involvement in Vietnam was getting serious, he reenlisted as an infantryman and served a tour of duty with the 2nd Battalion, 4th Marines from 1965 to 1966 under the legendary Bull Fisher. He fought on Operation Starlite, the action that prompted me to join the regular Marine Corps and volunteer for duty in Vietnam. One thing was certain: Nate's first tour did not diminish his belief in the military's mission in Vietnam. The war was one of many issues we argued over. And we argued frequently, much to the enjoyment of those around us. We did not abide by the precept that it is best not to avoid discussions of politics and religion. Whatever faith I had in a divine being was destroyed on Hill 50. Sitting around a campfire up in the hills of Camp Pendleton one night, enduring one of my anti-religion rants, Nate advised me to read the works of a 19th Century German philosopher named Nietzsche so that I might at least acquaint myself with some coherent thoughts on the subject.

As 1968 rolled around, the future was looking bright. In nine months, I'd be going to college and letting my hair grow. Meanwhile the war was still raging. At the end of January, the NVA and VC launched coordinated attacks throughout South Vietnam that we now know as the Tet Offensive of 1968, when Walter Cronkite informed his viewers that in his opinion the best we could hope for in Vietnam was a stalemate. Westmoreland disagreed. He said he needed an additional 200,000 troops for a counter-offensive. He may or may not have been granted that many, but a decision was made to activate troops from the Army's 82nd Airborne Division and my regiment, the 27th Marines. I received word of this the night of 12 February. I was returning to the base from San Diego. Tom Haugen had let me borrow his Volkswagen Bug for a date. The MP at the gate asked me what unit I was with. When I told him India 3/27, he told me I needed to report back immediately, that 3/27 was being activated for Vietnam.

The following morning the company clerk posted a list containing two columns: Deployables and Non-Deployables. As expected, my name was among the non-deployables. The Marines I was closest to—Nate Lee, Tom Haugen, and my first fire team leader, Corporal Leroy Gonzales, who fought on Operation Utah with India 3/1—were deployables. Tom Haugen was a non-deployable who signed a waiver, giving up his right to remain Stateside.

There was a GI Resistance movement going on at the time with service members refusing to serve in Vietnam because they believed that American intervention in Vietnam was morally unjustified. I shared that belief, yet I felt a moral obligation to go back when I didn't have to. Had I not received orders to Sea School and remained in that outfit in which I had no friends, I would have watched them ship out without a second thought. And even when my promotion to sergeant came through and I became a squad leader, making it obvious that I was not after all a narc with the CID, they would have been no more than comrades to me. As Professor J. Glenn Gray wrote, "The essential difference between comradeship and friendship consists in a heightened awareness of the self in friendship and the suppression of self-awareness in comradeship." That was precisely what I had received from Nate Lee: an awareness of a higher self. To have watched him ship out to the Nam without me would have constituted abandonment. If the motto *Semper Fidelis* meant anything it was that you do not abandon your friends.

Instead of signing a waiver, I chose to go back in a weaselly manner. I told the company clerk if he were to re-post the list with my name on the deployable side, I wouldn't say a word to the contrary. He complied. Without telling them what I had done, I called my parents to inform them my outfit had been activated for Vietnam.

Except for Leroy Gonzales the rest of my squad were non-deployables. The Marine Corps always claimed that despite what MOS (military occupation) a Marine is assigned upon graduation from boot camp, every Marine is a basic rifleman. In our case they made good on that promise. The Marines they sent me were mostly men with non-infantry MOSs including a cook, a mechanic, a truck driver, and a water pump engineer. I would later learn that three-quarters of the battalion that went over were non-infantry Marines. Back home the reserve unit I was with was a rifle company. One might wonder why the reserves weren't called up, and the answer was simple: politics. 1968 was an election year.

We picked up Marcus Fiebelkorn, our new platoon commander, who had just graduated from Basic School. During his first meeting with the sergeants he told us he understood we had all served tours in Vietnam and until he knew the ropes, he would be counting on us for guidance. "Sir," I replied, "you are probably the smartest second lieutenant I've ever met."

The battalion boarded six-bys (six-by-six three-axle trucks). We were on Interstate 5 on our way to the El Toro Marine Air Station when suddenly the convoy turned around and drove back to the base. The platoon had assembled back in the barracks when Lt. Fiebelkorn came in and announced that we would not be flying out until that evening because President Johnson would be sending us off at 1800 hours.

"If that son-of-a-bitch tries to shake my hand I'll refuse," I said, to which the lieutenant replied, "Now, don't make a scene, Sergeant Harlan," to which I replied, "What are they going to do, sir, send me to Vietnam?"

The battalion stood in formation for hours waiting for the arrival of Air Force One. LBJ finally arrived, delivered a bullshit patriotic speech and proceeded to inspect the troops, walking up and down the ranks accompanied by General Lew Walt. I was the only member of my squad whom he stopped in front of. Extending his hand, he said, "Good to see you. God bless you and keep you." Naturally, I shook his hand. For one thing, we needed no distractions where we were going. For another, I wouldn't dream of embarrassing Lew Walt.

At last it was time to board the C-141 transport jet. As we marched in formation to the jet a woman yelled, "Go get 'em, tigers!" It was not encouraging. Sitting next to Lee I said, "At least we're finished with this bullshit!" But no sooner had I said that than a couple of Secret Service guys came aboard followed by the president.

"Men, if those Marines at Khe Sanh were here and you were there, you know they would want to go over to help you." Yeah, sure they would. Guess I spoke too soon about the bullshit being over.

We were not sent to Khe Sanh, or even northern I-Corps. We were sent to the Quang Nam Province. Not only that, but to the same battalion compound I said good-bye to in November 1966. When 3/1 was there we was called it the battalion area. When we took the compound over from 2/3 it was referred to as Cau Ha base command post. When 3/27 left and 2/1 took over they called it Camp 413. One of those 2/1 Marines was Lieutenant Lewis B. Puller, Jr., son of Chesty Puller, who led a Golf Company platoon.

The place was nastier than ever. Guenter Lewy was right when he wrote that the Quang Nam defied meaningful pacification. The booby traps were much worse than before. During March, the first full month of combat, the battalion suffered 136 wounded and 6 killed. The battalion's strength was down 10% from wounds caused by booby traps. There were so many casualties the Division began questioning the battalion's competence. Saigon sent an Army major to investigate the reason for so many casualties. His investigation yielded the conclusion that our patrolling area had a higher saturation of booby traps than any other sector in the history of land warfare. There were Marines who had served up north, including Khe Sanh, who requested transfers back after patrolling the Quang Nam death trap.

A few days before we left California Nate Lee was replaced by Staff Sergeant Frank Cortez as platoon sergeant and reassigned as platoon guide. As such he was responsible for seeing that we were adequately supplied with ammunition and rations. Whatever Sergeant Lee experienced during his first tour it was not the booby-trap infested Quang Nam Province where the civilians supported the VC and NVA and wanted us out of their country. Consequently, his spirit was gradually dwindling by the day. It got even worse one day when we returned from the field after suffering two casualties only to learn that back home Martin Luther King had been assassinated. Three weeks later the platoon's morale took a hit when Loyd Kinsorthy, a 19-year-old in Leroy Gonzales's fire team, was killed by a booby trap. Back home in San Jose, Loyd's wife was pregnant with the son he would never know.

I was furious. And I was looking for payback. I got my opportunity three days later on a sweep along the Song Vinh

Dien River. Dale Camp and another Marine were floating down the river on some device they procured when they noticed a cleverly camouflaged tunnel dug into the side of the riverbank concealed with bamboo. I said I would go in myself with the usual flashlight and a .45. Tom Haugen got a rope and tied it to my ankle. After the first few feet straight ahead, the tunnel took a sharp turn to the left. That's when I saw two figures dressed in black. I shot the first one in the chest. I didn't have a chance to shoot the other one because Haugen pulled me out. I crawled back in and tossed a grenade inside. Once the dust and smoke settled, I went in after their bodies. I discovered one of them, the one I had shot, was a young woman.

A dozen or more Marines were standing on the bank watching below as I retrieved the corpses. As I was pulling out the male, his foot separated from his leg. I held the foot over my head and asked, "Anybody missing a foot?" The Marines above me laughed—all of them except Sergeant Lee. Later that night I spoke with him privately, explaining that the bit with the foot was a contrived effort on my part to get the troops out of the funk that had firmly settled into the platoon.

What was happening with Nate Lee went much deeper than a temporary funk. The man who projected more spirit than anyone I had ever met had descended into a state of complete despair and hopelessness. Without his having to say as much, Nate Lee had come to agree with the opinions I expressed in our arguments about the war back at Camp Pendleton, that except for the South Vietnamese who profited from our being there, we were unwanted invaders. I reminded him that we had an obligation to the men to bring them home alive. But I wasn't getting through to him.

A week later, as the platoon was forming up for another sweep, the company clerk came running up shouting, "Sergeant Harlan, you need to get your gear together. A jeep is taking you to Da Nang. You've got orders for Stateside!"

I should have been thrilled by the news, but I wasn't. Sergeant Lee must have noticed my ambivalence because he said, "Sergeant Harlan, get back there and make something of your life." Before getting on the jeep I gave Lt. Fiebelkorn my book of Dostoevsky short stories.

Later I learned why I received the sudden unexpected orders home. Unbeknownst to me, my father demanded to know why his son had been sent back to Vietnam after being back from overseas eight months. First, he wrote to our congressman, Representative Durward Hall, who apparently had more important matters to attend to. Then he wrote to Missouri Senator Stuart Symington who took the time to contact Headquarters Marine Corps which concluded that my Vietnam orders must have been an administrative error.

Three days after my departure, 3/27 was notified that it would be deployed on an operation code-named Allen Brook. They were helilifted to Hill 148 in the Que Son Mountains overlooking Go Noi Island. It was not literally an island. It was called that because it was surrounded by rivers, streams, and roads. The local population supported the Viet Cong and the NVA. The enemy units on the Island that month included the 36th Regiment of the 308th NVA Division and elements of three Viet Cong battalions—R-20, V-25, and the T-3 Sappers.

India Company suffered two casualties that first day shortly after they began establishing a perimeter on Hill 148. Lance Corporal Tim Davis detonated a booby trap while hauling sandbags left by the 7th Marines with which to fortify the fighting hole he was to share with PFC. Tom Hansen. He lost both legs. The chopper that had dropped them off returned to medivac him to Da Nang. Seeing a boot near his head, Tim asked the door gunner who else was being medevaced. The gunner told him it was just him, that that had been his leg. Asking if it could be reattached, the gunner replied, "No man." Tim told the gunner to kick it out the door. The gunner did so and said, "That should feed a family of six!"

301

Tim was sent to the hospital in Guam where he shared a room with Bill Gostlin who had lost a leg four days earlier. The head nurse was a lady they called Miss K. One day Tim fell out of his wheelchair. Miss K refused to help him, and Tim shouted that he would report her. "You're a Marine," the nurse said. "Get back in the chair yourself!" When he did, Miss K began clapping and the others in the ward joined in. Twenty-five years later, Tim, Bill, and Mark Smith, who had also lost his legs, came to Washington for the dedication of the Vietnam Women's Memorial. Tim arranged for a meeting with Miss K. He gave her a large bouquet of roses. Bill Gostlin gave her his Purple Heart, explaining that the guys on the Wall would want her to have it.

In 1994 I drove to Kansas City to watch Tim compete on the basketball court at the National Veterans Wheelchair Games. There were a number of spills. Each time play would stop until someone came on the court to lift the chair back up. Not so with Tim. Because of his aggressive performance he took more spills than anyone, but each time he would somehow flip the chair upright on his own. There was a banquet on the last day of the Games. Tim was presented with the "Spirit of the Games Award."

Shortly after Tim was medevaced, India Company was preparing to move off the hill. Dale Camp, the Marine who spotted the camouflaged hill the previous month, was with his squad as they were moving out. In Robert Simonsen's book, *Every Marine*, Dale describes what happened:

"As we moved across the top of the hill there was a huge explosion and I was knocked on my face. As I lay there, big pieces of earth and rocks were coming down on us. I thought it had been a mortar and anticipated another. When it didn't come, and the rocks quit falling I looked up. There right in front of my face was the top pallet of someone's mouth. The teeth were still in it and it was burned and smoking. That was just too much for my mind, and I blanked that scene out for many years. Sometime in the 70s while thinking about Nam for the millionth time it all came back to me. I wonder how many other things are still hidden inside there?"

Dale yelled for his squad leader, Corporal Zucroff, but there was no answer. Zucroff and another Marine had died from the blast. Zucroff had been blown off the hill. Dale and his platoon commander, Lieutenant Stephen Thompson, slid down the hill to retrieve what was left of Corporal Zucroff. "His clothes were gone," recalls Dale. "His face was gone, his arms and legs were gone, and he was split wide open from his crotch to his sternum. The only way we knew it was him was that he was balding and had red hair."

One wounded and two dead before arriving at the area of operations, Go Noi Island. The second and third day they were on the Island, but there was little action. On the fourth day they engaged the NVA in a firefight. PFC Juan "Speedy" Gonzales was the first casualty. He was shot in the leg. Corporal Robert Simonsen was firing into the tree line when the men on his right and left were killed by gunfire. A round struck Simonsen's helmet sending fragments into his head. He was moved to a safe area alongside Speedy had who not only been shot three times but was also hit by friendly fire—shrapnel from an air strike. When they were medevaced there were ten dead and ten wounded on the chopper. The load was so heavy they had to throw off all extra gear in order to take off.

The enemy unit they were up against had recently marched down the Ho Chi Minh Trail and infiltrated Go Noi Island. They were an elite outfit that took part in the final assault against the French at Dien Bien Phu. The next day one of their battalions would have the upper hand against the Americans when they ambushed India Company.

In addition to the deadly fire brought down on them, there was the scorching heat. Water was scarce and very much needed for the wounded. Nate Lee was among the first ones hit. The snipers kept the wounded alive so they could pick off the Marines who attempted to rescue them.

"Bullets were hitting all around us," recalls Dale Camp. "We were laying in some shallow tank tracks. There was no cover at all. The bodies of dead and wounded were laying all over."

Sergeant Lee was lying in a depression. Others, including Sergeant Ray Allison, thought he had been killed. Allison had a machine gunner attached to his platoon, PFC Robert Burke, who Ray was told intended to go after one of the bunkers. "Burke was on the far-left hand edge of the riverbank. I told him not to leave the riverbank. He had an M-60, and somebody came and told me that Burke was going out to get one of the sniper positions. I said, 'No! Stay here at the bank and provide us with security.' The next thing I knew they said Burke had left."

Bob Simonsen describes Burke's actions:

"In one sector of the action, PFC Robert C. Burke began a one-man assault against the enemy. He climbed to the edge of the riverbank and singlehandedly started assaulting various bunkers and delivering such a high volume of suppressive fire that he temporarily relieved the pressure on the forward elements of the company enabling some of the casualties to be pulled to safety. Observing an NVA bunker that was pinning down one of the friendly elements, Burke, oblivious to the rounds hitting around him, aggressively assaulted this fortification with such deadly accurate fire that three NVA were seen fleeing from the position. These soldiers were quickly killed by Burke with a burst of machine gun fire.

"At this time, a group of hidden snipers began directing all their fire on this Marine. Although suffering from the 110 degree plus heat, he began covering the area with fire by walking laterally up and down the line of fire. He suppressed much of the enemy fire until his M-60 machine gun malfunctioned. Moving back to a covered position, he handed his weapon to a wounded comrade and took a casualty's M-16 rifle and magazines and grabbed as many grenades as he could carry. He proceeded back up the bank into the midst of the enemy fire. Disregarding his own safety, he repeatedly exposed himself to the enemy fire as he lobbed grenades at the enemy bunkers and positions with little effect because of the heavily fortified complex.

"Seeing yet another pocket of resistance, Burke aggressively assaulted it, firing his M-16 rifle from the hip until he knocked out the position.

"Observing that his M-60 machine gun was now functioning, he threw two belts of ammunition over his shoulder, grabbed his repaired machine gun, and once again returned to his precarious position at the top of the riverbank. He again made a valiant stand as he saturated the area with well-placed bursts of machine gun fire. It was there that an NVA sniper found his mark and mortally wounded PFC. Burke."

Robert Burke would receive the Medal of Honor posthumously. He was eighteen years-old, the youngest recipient of the medal in the Vietnam War.

Ray Allison would discover that Nate Lee was not killed:

"Late in the afternoon the heat started getting really intense and we were hurting for water. Then across the way I saw Nate starting to move. We yelled at him to stay still because the snipers were still shooting and picking us off. As he was moving, he was shot again, and he died right there. Nobody knew that he was even alive until he started moving. He had probably laid there for two or three hours in the sun. I thought that he had probably been shot and lost consciousness before trying to move."

Nate Lee was killed on his mother's birthday. The family had gathered that evening to celebrate the occasion. Two days later Mrs. Lee was babysitting a couple of her grandkids when one of them came to her in the kitchen saying, "Grandma, there are two cops at the front door." But the two men were not wearing police uniforms. They wore Marine uniforms, and they were there to convey the tragic news.

The reality of survivor's guilt became apparent after the war ended, when there was nothing left to fight, neither the communists nor the U.S. government. I was not alone in having survivor's guilt over Nate's death. Tom Haugen was not with the platoon on the day of the ambush. He was back in the battalion compound. He had less than a month before the end of his enlistment and the Marine Corps deemed it necessary to keep him out of the field. Thus, he blamed himself for not being there at Nate's side. I am fully convinced that had Tom not signed the waiver and served the remainder of his enlistment in the States, he would have lived a normal, peaceful existence. He was smart and he was squared-away. But by 1975 he had slipped into the deep end, involving himself in various criminal activities. He was shot and killed by a low life he was after in Phoenix, Arizona.

My own feelings of guilt over Nate's death had nothing to do with the fact that I was not at his side on May 17. My survivor's guilt was based on a moral comparison between the two of us. Nate was the guy who once he came to understand that the war was a tragic mistake, that we were killing and dying for no good reason, lost his will to fight. I was the guy who could argue with conviction that our intervention in Vietnam was morally unjustified one moment, and then cast aside moral considerations and return to the combat zone to kill more communists the next.

For two years I taught beginning philosophy courses at the University of Wyoming. The first four weeks or so was devoted to Socrates--using the same book that attracted me to the discipline, *The Last Days of Socrates*. In an effort to broaden the students understanding of Socrates I would draw from other dialogs as well. One day I began reading a passage from the *Symposium*--specifically, Alcibiades' account of Socrates on the battlefield. I began reading the part where

Alcibiades says, "And then, gentlemen, you should have seen him when we were in retreat from Delium." Suddenly things started getting weird when I continued reading the passage: "He was walking with the same 'lofty strut and sideways glance' that he goes about with here in Athens."

I started losing it! I was struggling to get through the passage without completely losing my composure. You would have thought I was speaking at the funeral of my closest friend! Can you even imagine what those students were thinking? What the hell! This guy is breaking up over a philosopher who's been dead for over two-thousand years!

But it wasn't Socrates I was thinking about. It was Nate Lee.

Leroy Gonzales and Gary Harlan, having just returned from the field, and sustaining several casualties, were informed of the assassinatin of Martin Luther King, Jr. back home.

CHAPTER 20

Please Do Not Thank Me for My Service

It was sometime in March, 1968, the month after President Johnson bid us farewell at the El Toro Marine Air Station when, after days of wandering around out in the bush looking for VC and doing our best to avoid booby-traps, we had returned to the battalion compound for cold showers and hot chow. That evening four of us—myself, Nate Lee, Tom Haugen, and Leroy Gonzales—were having a beer together when Leroy, always the optimist, suggested we reunite at his home in Rawlins, Wyoming in the summer of '69. Each of us would be civilians by then, and we all agreed to be there.

Haugen and I fulfilled our promise. He arrived from Phoenix with his girlfriend, Elleen, and I drove up from San Diego with my girlfriend, Elaine. We were treated like royalty by Leroy's parents, Manual and Emma. Looking back on those three days, one thing was conspicuously absent—namely, any discussion of Nate Lee. In the years that followed, it became apparent why that was so: each of us blamed himself for Nate's death, and believed he bore his guilt alone.

Tom and I were both active in the antiwar movement at our respective colleges. I lived in a two-story house in San Diego with a group of like-minded longhairs, one of whom was my friend, Harry, who had the misfortune of having a high number in the draft lottery making it inevitable that he would be drafted. Harry was not soldier material. It was not in his nature. He was a genuine pacifist. There had doubtless been plenty of young guys like Harry who had been drafted and sent off to war. But Harry was my friend and I did not want him to be one of them.

Tom Haugen knew of a physician in Phoenix who was sympathetic to the cause. Tom invited Harry to move to Phoenix and take up residence at his home. Harry accepted the offer, had an appointment with the doctor, and stayed out of the Army with a bad knee.

I suspect there are other combat veterans like Tom and me—guys with PTSD symptoms that did not fully manifest themselves as long as we were engaged in the fight. But once the troops were withdrawn, the fight was over. The Vietnamese were left to settle matters on their own, and we were left to confront our ghosts and demons.

While I am not one of those who glibly assure others that everything happens for a reason, there have been times when it has seemed that some things have happened to me for a reason. In my senior year at Sonoma State University, for instance, I applied to several graduate programs back east. I had just been accepted at Duke, but with only partial financial assistance. Then I received a call from a gentleman identifying himself as Dr. Richard Howey, philosophy department head at the University of Wyoming. I hadn't applied to Wyoming, but earlier in the year I sent a copy of a bachelor's thesis I had written on the German philosopher, Martin Heidegger to my Uncle Art's sister-in-law who was an English professor there. I didn't expect her to have much, if anything, to say about the philosophical content of the paper. I just wanted her assessment of the writing. Instead of replying to me she shared the paper with Dr. Howey, who had recently published a book on Heidegger. He called to offer me a teaching assistantship that not only covered tuition and fees but paid $3,000 a year teaching two beginning philosophy courses a semester while earning my master's degree.

The *it happened for a reason* scenario did not involve the education I received at Wyoming, which was superb. It involved moving to Laramie, Wyoming, an hour away from Leroy Gonzales in Rawlins. Had that not occurred I would have continued to think I was alone in my guilt over Nate Lee's death. Had it not been for the opportunity of seeing Leroy regularly, I would never have learned the truth—that he carried a burden of guilt much heavier than mine.

Leroy told me something he had never disclosed to anyone. Two nights before the company was ambushed on Go Noi Island, they had set up a perimeter around Liberty Bridge. Nate informed Leroy that he was finished, that he was through with fighting in that war. Leroy, who would have followed Nate Lee anywhere, said that if Nate was quitting, so was he.

A jeep took them to battalion headquarters where they were taken to the office of Lt. Colonel Tullis Woodham, the commanding officer of the battalion. The Colonel told Sergeant Lee that given his exemplary record, he would leave the office for a few minutes to give them both time to reconsider, and if they did, they would be returned to their platoon and the matter would be forgotten. During that time Nate implored Leroy to go back, telling him, "Look, I'm single. I can spend five years in prison, get out and go on with my life. You have a wife and child back home." Because Leroy refused to leave his side, Nate picked up his rifle and the two of them returned to the platoon. Two days later, Nate was killed in the ambush on Go Noi Island. For years I felt I contributed to his downfall with all my arguments about the war being morally unjustified when we were at Camp Pendleton. Now I learned that Leroy assumed the blame for Nate's death due to his refusal to return to the outfit and allow Nate to bear the consequences alone.

Leroy told me this sometime in early February of 1975, around the time I experienced the Nate Lee flashback during my lecture on Socrates. On the 12th of February I called Tom Haugen. It had been four years since we were in contact. I suggested the three of us get together. He agreed to come up to Wyoming in June. Though I wasn't thinking of it in those terms, what I had in mind was a support group. We could benefit from Tom's stability right then.

Tom had always been the stable one. Making the landing with the 9th Marines on 8 March 1965, he was among the first ground troops committed to the Vietnam War. In November of that year he was one of twelve Marines selected for the newly formed sniper unit that would operate throughout I-Corps for the next six years.

In December 1966, eight months after returning from his Vietnam tour, Tom volunteered to go back. According to his brother, Gerry, Tom had read somewhere about the difficulties new guys faced who were sent over as replacements. Tom thought he could be of service to these men whom we derisively referred to as FNGs, fucking new guys.

Tom was assigned to Kilo Company, 3rd Battalion, 5th Marines. He was wounded on Operation Swift on 4 September 1967, the same day the "Grunt Padre", Navy Chaplain Vincent Capodanno, discussed earlier in this book, was killed during the same battle. Tom and six others were wounded by shrapnel from an enemy 60mm mortar round. They were transported to the hospital ship, the USS *Repose*.

In January 1968, after recovering from his wounds, Tom received orders for India Company, 3rd Battalion 27th Marines at Camp Pendleton. He was sent to our platoon where he took over leadership of the 3rd squad. When the battalion was activated for Vietnam, Tom, like me, was not deployable. He signed a waiver, waiving his right to spend a year Stateside before being sent back over for his third tour of duty.

Tom sent me a three-page letter after our conversation. "It's ironic," he wrote, "that you called this time of year. Seven years ago, you, Leroy, Dawson, Sgt. Lee, and I were getting ready to go back to Vietnam." The first part of the letter seemed to indicate he was living a normal life with his wife and their adopted daughter. "We own our home, have two cars and one truck, 2 TVs (one color), washer, dryer, refrigerator, new furniture and a dog. I'm turning into a regular Marvin Middle-Class." As the next portion of the letter revealed, all the talk of cars, TVs, new furniture, etc. was just a facade.

"Usually I break up the monotony by terrorizing bars, burglary, and cattle rustling. My partner and I are supposed to go out tomorrow and get another cow. About every two months we go out and shoot a cow and then take it over to this old man's house where we butcher it. The last time I bought meat was April of last year." His words were truly alarming. This was not the squared-away Marine I had known.

Our summer reunion never took place. On the 31ˢᵗ of March while watching the NCAA championship game between Kentucky and UCLA, I received a call from Gerry Haugen informing me that Tom died four days earlier. He was being paid $750 to recover a man's motorcycle which had been stolen. Certain as to who had stolen it, Tom broke into the man's home and beat him up. Around midnight two days later, Tom climbed over the fence in the suspected thief's backyard in an effort to recover the stolen bike. But the man was waiting on his roof with a .22 rifle. Tom was shot in the eye. For nearly a month he lay unconscious at the hospital where Elleen was a nurse.

I called Leroy with the news of our friend's death. The funeral was scheduled for the next day so there was no way we could be there. But that weekend we made the flight to

313

Phoenix to spend the day with Elleen and their daughter, Lori. For Leroy and I, it was one of the darkest experiences of our lives. Leroy, the most gregarious and upbeat individual I've ever known, did not speak a word during the flight back to Denver. He said one thing after we took our seats on the plane. He asked, "What's it mean?"

It was a powerful question. I had no answer. But now that I've had 45 years to think about it, I'll give it a shot.

Unpacking the meaning of Tom Haugen's death at the age of 28 requires an understanding of two causal factors, the first having to do with how a squared-away Marine sergeant with an unblemished military record, a man who exemplified the fourteen traits of a Marine NCO, including Integrity, Knowledge, Courage, Dependability, Unselfishness, Justice, Loyalty, and Judgment, became a reckless, law-breaking civilian; and the second having to do with the decisions made by the politicians responsible for setting up the whole thing.

The question about Tom's out-of-control behavior stemmed from the death of Nate Lee. According to his brother, Tom blamed himself for not being there for Nate when the company was ambushed on Operation Allen Brook even though the reason was beyond his control. Tom was taken out of the field because his enlistment was about to end, and he was ordered to prepare for his flight back to the States.

Even if he had been with Nate and Leroy on Go Noi Island that day, Tom would still have suffered the same survivor guilt that Leroy and I were going through because even though we each had our own reasons for bearing responsibility for Nate's death, the common factor was: how could I possibly deserve to return to civilian life and be happy when a morally superior man like Nate Lee died on the battlefield?

I believe that had Tom reunited with Leroy and I in Wyoming that summer the experience would have lessened the rage he was acting out. For one thing, he would have known he was not alone in possessing those emotions. Furthermore, being the type of person naturally disposed to helping others, had he hung on a few years more he would doubtless have been active in the Vietnam veteran movement that began in the late '70s and picked up steam in the '80s. He could have joined Leroy and I in 1983 when we visited the Wall and then onto Hazelton, Pennsylvania to meet the Lee family.

To this day I cannot claim to have discovered the complete answer to Leroy's question, What's it mean? However, in 1979 I read an article in *Harper's* by a journalist and historian that provided a clue as to the identity and motivation of the people who gave us the Vietnam War. The article was titled, "The Two Americas". Its author was Walter Karp, a man who waged a relentless war on what he called "the official version of things." Lewis Latham, longtime editor of *Harper's*, said of Karp, "He believed that in America it is the people who have rights, not the state, and that the working of a democratic republic requires a raucous assembly of citizens unafraid to speak their minds. He thought that if only enough people had the courage to say what they meant, then all would be well."

"Even as a schoolboy reciting the Pledge of Allegiance," Karp wrote, "I thought America an odd sort of place." Odd because there seemed to be two Americas. The children were required to pledge allegiance to the flag of the United States of America--"one nation, indivisible, with liberty and justice for all." That was one America. But then there was also the "republic for which it stands," a second America resulting in two separate objects of a patriot's devotion. One is the nation. The other is the American republic. "At every juncture of our public life," Karp observed, "these two Americas conflict with each other."

Karp was unable to understand why it was much of a rivalry to begin with. After all, he wrote, "The republic is the great central fact of American life. It is the constitution of liberty and self-government, the frame and arena of all American politics. The republic is what Americans founded when they founded America. The nation, by comparison, is a poor, dim thing, for the nation is merely America conceived as a corporate unit, a hollow shell. The flag is its emblem, 'Uncle Sam' is its nickname; yet there is virtually nothing in the internal life of America that can bring that abstract entity to life."

According to Karp, we have two Americas with two corresponding types of patriotism. The first is republican patriotism: "To love America because you cherish the Constitution of liberty is republican patriotism. We were citizens of the republic long before we saw ourselves as members of a nation." Karp recalls Abraham Lincoln's praise of Henry Clay: "Lincoln lauded his hero Henry Clay for being a patriot in two sorts of ways. Clay loved his country, Lincoln said, 'partly because it was his own country, but mostly because it was a free country."

When Nate Lee, Leroy Gonzales, Tom Haugen and I enlisted in the Marines we were required to take an oath, an oath that made no reference to the nation or the flag, but rather, a pledge to protect the Constitution from all enemies foreign and domestic. At boot camp recruits were issued the *Guidebook for Marines*. That 500-page book covered everything from Marine Corps history and traditions to military discipline; rank structure; battalion organization; tactics; weapons; and perhaps most importantly, Marine Corps leadership. That chapter discusses in detail the 14 NCO leadership traits, one of which is courage which, it explains, comes in two forms: physical and moral.

"As for moral courage, know what's right and stand up for it. Marines are not plaster saints by any means. But they serve God, Country, and Corps—in that order." Had Nate Lee gone through with his decision to quit fighting, he would have been court martialed. But he would have stood up for what he knew was right.

The underlying meaning of both Nate Lee's diminished spirit and the question of how a dependable, stand-up guy like

Tom Haugen went completely off the rails and ended up getting killed by some low-life in Phoenix, Arizona begins and ends with their decision to join the Marines. They joined for the same reason each and every one of us discussed in this book joined: republican patriotism. The decision had nothing to do with the flag or the cult of the nation. It had everything to do with the fact that like Henry Clay, we loved our country, not just because it was our country, but because it was a free country worth protecting at all costs, even if that meant sacrificing our own lives in the process. Unlike a fringe of the antiwar movement that placed the blame for the Vietnam War on the warriors, Karp understood who the real culprits were. Tom Haugen's downfall began with his good faith decision to join the Marines and serve three tours of duty in Vietnam. It ended with his complete disillusionment, caused by the proponents of the second form of patriotism, *nationism*.

What brings that hollow shell called the nation to life? Karp asked, and the answer is war. "It is most fully a nation, most intensely alive as an entity, when it wages war against other nations. Even in peacetime it is the memory of past wars and the menace of future wars that keep the idea of the nation alive in America. *War and the cult of the nation are virtually one and the same.*" (italics mine)

Consider a recent example of how the memory of past wars keeps nationism alive in America—the controversy over NFL players kneeling during the National Anthem, a gesture many, including President Trump, condemned as unpatriotic. From Karp's perspective, there was a group of athletes standing up for the republic by kneeling or sitting down during the National Anthem protesting injustices that have been, and continue to be, targeted against a minority of our citizenry. Lest I leave the impression that I am unsympathetic to the feelings of those who regarded the players actions as an insult to the memory of those who died in combat, let me share my own experience with the Anthem performed at a sporting event.

Always Faithful

I am a diehard fan of the St. Louis Cardinals. Two or three times a season I make the two-and-a-half-hour drive to St. Louis to see a Cards game. Standing with thousands of fans, I get emotional when the National Anthem is performed. Every time. Why? Because there is no other moment in my life when I feel more alive and more grateful to be alive. The second the "Star Spangled Banner" begins, I am overcome with emotion stemming from two sources: The joy of being there with my fellow fans, conjoined with the memory of all the Marines I served with who didn't make it out of Vietnam to root for *their* favorite teams. A lot of people who have never served in combat, including the president, subscribe to the warped notion that we fought for the flag. Nothing could be further from the truth. We fought and died for each other.

By the way, when I say each other I am referring to White Marines, Black Marines, Hispanic Marines, and Asian Marines. Several times in this book I have stated that I am proud of my service in Vietnam. Let me be clear about the source of that pride. Sure, much of it has to do with having met the standards of a combat Marine. But more than that, I am proud to have lived in a world in which the veil was lifted, where all the ethnic and cultural differences that folks back home considered important were exposed for what they truly are—superficial. No one talked about diversity. We *lived* diversity. So when I imagine one of my Marine brothers—who served in the Vietnam War or in the current War on Terror—being stopped and searched by a cop because of the color of his skin, that disturbs me a lot more than the image of a millionaire athlete kneeling during the National Anthem.

All right, I will concede that the kneeling controversy represents an honest disagreement between the two Americas. Besides, I was just warming up to, skirting around the edges as it were, of my real beef with America which has nothing to do with sporting events and high-priced athletes. It's about how the proponents of nationism have taken control of the narrative, encouraging us to ignore the dictates of a self-governing republic. In Karp's words:

"The republic is more than the form of our government plus a few rudimentary maxims and memories. It embodies a profound principle of political action—an 'energizing' principle, as Jefferson called it. It is supposed to operate at all times and under all conditions against oligarchy, special privilege, and arbitrary power. *The energizing principle is the preservation and perfecting of self-government, the securing of each citizen of an equal voice in his own government.*" (italics mine)

For a while it appeared that the memory of Vietnam was a deterrent to the employment of arbitrary power and misadventures overseas. It was called "the Vietnam syndrome," and the nationists were none too pleased about it. Here's how Karp describes the nationist zeal leading up to the Vietnam War:

"By 1961 the only way Americans could demonstrate our 'will' to defend what was dear to us was to shed the blood of our youth over trifles. That way lay madness, but that was the way eagerly taken. Corrupted by fifteen years of unchallenged power and determined at all costs to maintain the empire of menace, the imperial republic under President Kennedy was losing every last link to common sense and prudence."

In the course of organizing our group's 2019 trip I researched the subject of vets returning to Vietnam. Time and again I came across the words, "healing and reconciliation" as applied to the goal and purpose behind making the long journey back to Southeast Asia. I understood the healing part, but reconciliation? Didn't that word imply a restoration of friendly relations? Exactly who were we reconciling with? The communists, with whom we were never friends to begin with? Speaking for myself, since I am the only Vietnam vet for whom I have an absolute right to speak, the reconciliation I have sought, and continue to seek, is with America, not Vietnam. All right, you ask wearily, what's your beef with America?

319

Let me begin by saying what it is not about. It is most definitely not about the lack of a hero's welcome upon returning home. My set of grievances center around the conflict between the two Americas and the country's confusion about what patriotism entails. Of course, as an 18 year-old from the Ozarks who left home for Marine boot camp in 1964, I was not interested in anyone's nuanced take on the meaning of patriotism, and certainly not willing to entertain the notion that our charismatic fallen leader, the original darling of identity politics, lacked common sense. He explained quite clearly what patriotism entailed in his inaugural address. President Kennedy told us it meant asking what we could for our country, not what our country could do for us. Moreover, it demanded that we "pay any price, bear any burden, and meet any hardship" to assure the survival and success of liberty abroad. So, what better choice could a patriotic teenager make than join the U.S. Marines and fight for the cause of liberty—even if it was 10,000 miles away in a country he'd never heard of?

But our dashing leader had certainly heard of it. On June 1st, 1956, Kennedy, then a senator from Massachusetts, addressed the Conference on Vietnam sponsored by the American Friends of Vietnam. The senator began his speech with a rundown of the Domino Theory, stating that if Communism were not contained it would spread to other countries. Vietnam, he declared, was "the cornerstone of the Free World in Southeast Asia." Later, his remarks took, to my mind at least, a rather bizarre twist. Kennedy described the Vietnamese as needy children: "If we are not the parents of little Vietnam, then surely we are the godparents. We presided at its birth, we gave assistance to its life, we have helped to shape its future. This is our offspring. We cannot abandon it."

In his book, *American Reckoning: The Vietnam War and Our National Identity*, Christian Appy characterized these remarks about the parent/child relationship as "an appealing image—

flattering to every generous impulse of a great and wealthy nation."

I find Appy's praise for such paternalistic drivel perplexing given the historical context at the time of Kennedy remarks. For over fifty years prior to World War Two the Vietnamese people had suffered under French colonial rule. After the Japanese invasion into Indochina, the French, just as they had done with the Nazis in France, retained nominal control of the country with the understanding that there would be 30,000 Japanese troops occupying Indochina and the Japanese military would take control of all Vietnamese airports, thus making it the strongest staging area for the Japanese in Southeast Asia. It would have been fresh in Kennedy's mind that the only allies the U.S. could count on in the area were the Vietnamese—specifically, the Viet Minh, led by Ho Chi Minh. In December 1944, after American pilot William Shaw was shot down near the Vietnam and China border, Ho personally helped the pilot return to the American airbase located in Kunming, China. Ho met a number of Americans in Kunming including Charles Fenn, a Marine lieutenant who introduced him to Major General Claire Chennault, commander of the 14th Air Force.

Another American impressed with Ho and his organization was Lt. Colonel Archimedes Patti who headed the OSS (precursor of the CIA) office in Kunming. "We saw what kind of troops the Viet Minh were," Patti recalled in 1980. "They were willing, fine young nationalists, what we used to call 'gung-ho' type. They were willing to risk their lives for their cause, the cause of independence against the French."

There was a desperate need at the time to find someone willing and capable of destroying a three-hundred-mile railway line between Kunming and Hanoi, thus depriving the Japanese of a vital communication link. As Patti later recalled, "The Chinese couldn't do it and the French wouldn't do it." Representing the Viet Minh, General Vo Nguyen Giap agreed to carry out the mission. To prepare them properly, Patti deployed seven Americans, code-named The Deer Team, who parachuted into the Cao Bang Province where the Viet Minh were headquartered. They trained 85 Viet Minh in the use of small arms and 60mm mortars.

The Viet Minh did everything the Allies asked of them—and more. They gathered intelligence, protected downed pilots, and destroyed the railway line. They never asked for weapons or expected America to help them rid their country of the French. All Ho Chi Minh wanted was a relationship with the U.S. When the war ended, the Americans went home. Ho wrote six letters to President Truman, asking for his support. He never received a reply. "This was disappointing to Ho Chi Minh," recalled Henry Prunier, a member of the Deer Team. "He thought because he had collaboration with the Americans against the Japanese, he could get American collaboration against the French."

Ho wrote this letter to Charles Fenn:

"Dear Lieutenant Fenn,

The war has ended. That's good for everyone. I just feel sorry that our American friends have left us so soon. Your departure from this country means that our relationship will be more difficult. War has ended in victory, but we small and dependent countries have no parts, even a very small share in the victory of freedom and democracy. To have a worthy part, we must continue to fight. I believe you and the great American people will always support us."

And fight they did. Two years before Kennedy's address to the Conference on Vietnam, the Viet Minh defeated the French at Dien Bien Phu. The French agreed to negotiate the end of the war in Geneva. The Geneva Accords, as it was called, divided the country in two. This was intended as a stopgap measure until an election that was to be held in 1956 which would result in the unification of Vietnam. The election never took place. The U.S. and the leaders in the south, knowing that Ho Chi Minh would more than likely win, opted for two Vietnams. Apparently, "our offspring", the "little Vietnam" whose "future we shaped," was South Vietnam, a government in name only. This point was made explicit by Paul Warnke in Christian Appy's oral history, *Patriots: The Vietnam War Remembered from All Sides.*

In 1966 Defense Secretary Robert McNamara, asked Warnke to be general counsel for the Department of Defense. "I'd love to," Warnke told him, "but you have to realize that I do not think this war in Vietnam is a good idea," to which McNamara, oddly enough, told him that didn't make any difference.

Warnke's first trip to Vietnam took place in 1967. "The first house I went to had two pictures on the wall. One was of Jack Kennedy and the other was Ho Chi Minh. I thought, we're in trouble. The people I talked to didn't seem to have any feeling about South Vietnam as a country. We fought the war for a separate South Vietnam, but there wasn't any South and there never was one. I think that was our big mistake. We used to talk about nation-building, but no outside force is going to build a nation. There just wasn't a government in South Vietnam that had any popular support."

Five years after the end of the war called the Vietnam War and the Vietnamese called The Resistance War Against the Americans, Archimedes Patti stated:

"Ho Chi Minh was on a silver platter in 1945. We had him. He was willing to be a democratic republic if nothing else. Socialist, yes. Really, we had Ho Chi Minh, we had the Viet Minh. We had the Indochina question in our hand. But for reasons that defy good logic, we find today that we supported the French for a war they themselves dubbed, 'la sale guerre', the dirty war, and we paid to the tune of 80% of the cost of the French war and 100% of the American-Vietnam War."

One year before his death in 2013, Henry Prunier echoed Patti's view. He recalled a time during the war when he was asked his opinion. The opinion he offered did not sit well with supporters of the war effort. "I said we could never win over there because the Vietnamese knew what they were doing. They were fighting for a cause. They were fighting for their life."

In November 1980 the Harris Firm released the results of a survey of the public's attitude toward Vietnam veterans. It stated that a "substantial 64-27 percent majority of Americans agrees with this view that "Vietnam was the wrong war in the wrong place at the wrong time," and that "veterans of the Vietnam War were made suckers, having to risk their lives in that war."

It also stated that "by an overwhelming 97-2 percent, Americans feel that "veterans who served during the time the Vietnam War was going on deserve respect for having served their country in the armed forces."

At the time, this struck me as a positive development. At last, the public was able to separate the war from the warrior. But it was a good thing if and only if the public remained vigilant against the nationists who comprised the thing Eisenhower had warned us of, namely the military-industrial complex: those who were predisposed to give us another wrong war in the wrong place at the wrong time.

"By God, we've kicked the Vietnam syndrome once and for all," proclaimed President George H.W. Bush shortly after America's swift defeat of Saddam Hussein in the Persian Gulf War. Of course, anyone with any knowledge of the two wars would be reluctant to mention them together in the same breath. As Jim Webb pointed out at the time, "Not to denigrate what we accomplished against Hussein, but Hussein was no military strategist. If Ho Chi Minh had put sixty percent of his army in one spot where there were no trees, we would have blown them away in forty days too."

Of course, the so-called "Vietnam syndrome" had less to do with U.S. military capability than it did with Americans attitude toward war. Viet Thanh Nguyen characterized the Vietnam syndrome as "the fear of failure and the moral revulsion to war that have plagued Americans since their defeat in Vietnam."

Time and again during the build-up leading to the quick prosecution of the Gulf War, Bush and his spokespersons promised us that this *would not be another Vietnam.* Clearly, their intention went further than simply assuring the public that this was a just cause that would not result in another quagmire. That aspect alone might persuade the public to support the military action against Saddam Hussein, but it was not sufficient for accomplishing the ultimate goal of "kicking the Vietnam syndrome." That would require that the public not only separate the war from the warrior, but to make the case that supporting the warrior demanded that we support the war. In his book, Vietnam Shadows: The War, Its Ghosts, and its Legacies, Arnold Isaacs summed it up as follows:

"To the extent that the country remembered its treatment of Vietnam vets as shameful, the chance to expiate that shame in this new war was welcomed. And, as was no doubt intended by the Bush administration and its publicists, to the extent that opposing the *policy* in Vietnam had been interpreted (particularly after the fact) as dishonoring the soldiers who fought there, this time support for the soldiers would have to be expressed as support for the policy as well. Groups supporting the administration distributed millions of red-white-and-blue bumper stickers proclaiming, 'Support Our Troops'. Forests of U.S. Flags flew in front of homes and public buildings; miles of yellow ribbon—previously an emblem of love and loyalty for hostages or prisoners, not soldiers—festooned mailboxes and storefronts."

In May 1980, around the time the Harris Survey was published, The Washington Post organized a symposium which they called, "Voices of a Wounded Generation." The contributors included, in the words of the moderator, Richard

Harwood, "warriors and war resisters." One of the resisters was James Fallows, a writer for The Atlantic who argued for the need of a dialog between "the different camps of our generation." There was, he told the group, "deeply and sometimes not so deeply suppressed resentment and grudges" that needed to be addressed. "And unless those are examined and brought out," he said, "I think we'll be in trouble in the long run. I fear a backlash if these things aren't talked about fully enough. People will become big militarists to try to prove that this part of their background is not something to be ashamed of."

Unfortunately, we never had that national dialog, though one of those people who became a diehard militarist after avoiding military service (with five deferments) when he was of draft age—Dick Cheney, Secretary of Defense during the Gulf War—did explain why he didn't serve in Vietnam: "I had other priorities."

As the 20th Century came to a close the Vietnam Syndrome was still hanging on for life. It died on 11 September 2001.

It's a shame Walter Karp left us before 9/11. We need voices like his, reminding us of our responsibilities as citizens of a republic, of the energizing principle of self-government, warning us of the enemies of popular self-government who have "striven to erect and strengthen the rival cult of the nation, by war if possible, by the menace of war when there is a perilous lull in the fighting."

In 2007 I visited Gerry Haugen, the brother of Tom Haugen, who lives in Fallbrook, California, a town adjacent to Camp Pendleton. Gerry's niece was dating a Marine stationed there. Gerry invited him over to meet me. His name was Brad. A handsome Marine about 6 foot 4 inches tall, Brad would make the ideal subject for a Marine recruiting poster.

I asked Brad what outfit he was with. I was genuinely thrilled to hear him say Lima Company, 3rd Battalion, 1st Marines. "That's was the outfit I served with in Vietnam," I told him. Throughout the fighting in Iraq I had received emails from retired Marine officers I had served under who had inside information to share about Marine operations. I kept up with the whereabouts of my old unit.

"So you fought in the battle of Falluja?", I asked.

"Yes."

At that point in the conversation Gerry said, "Gary is against the Iraq War."

Though I had no idea why Gerry found it necessary to bring that up right then, I said, "That's right, Brad. I was opposed to the Iraq invasion from the start. But let me tell you this: anyone who claims that you cannot support the troops without supporting the war is completely mistaken."

How could I *not* support Brad and his brothers? They are *my* brothers. In an article he wrote for *The Atlantic* in 2015, thirty-five years after his comments in "Voices of a Wounded Generation," James Fallows wrote, "Everyone 'supports' the troops, but few know very much about them." Prior to working on this book, I had never heard the expression, "moral injury." But it immediately hit home. It explained my own struggles. It took Nate Lee's life as much as the bullets of the NVA sniper. It was what drove Tom Haugen to his death.

In her book, *Afterwar*, Nancy Sherman examines the issue of moral injury. She writes:

"With 2.6 million service members having gone to war in Iraq and Afghanistan, and most of them now home with the draw-down of those wars, moral injuries are a part of that homecoming. Unlike lost legs and missing eyes, these wounds can often go unnoticed. And soldiers may keep them that way. For one year, for two, with stone silence. In some cases, for forty or fifty years, buried deep inside, untouchable, until perhaps another group of vets come home from war and they see themselves, now at sixty or seventy, in the faces of those twenty-year-olds."

According to Sherman, moral wounds require moral healing, something that is not limited to therapists and other professionals. We can all play a part simply by listening. As one of those old vets Sherman alludes to, I have not seen their faces, but I have paid close attention to their words. In an article published in the *Washington Post*, Timothy Kudo, a Marine captain who served in Iraq and Afghanistan, explains his struggle with having "held two contradictory beliefs: Killing is always wrong, but in war, it is necessary. How could something be both immoral and necessary?"

A rebuttal to Kudo's article appeared in the *National Review*. Written by Dennis Prager, it was titled, "A Morally Confused Marine".

"War makes us killers," wrote Kudo. "We must confront this horror directly if we are to be honest about the true costs of war," to which Prager responds, "Other than the author, are there many Americans who enter the military in time of war without confronting the fact that they are likely to kill?"

The correct question should have been, are there any Americans entering the military more aware than Captain Kudo that he will be likely to kill? After all, he makes that clear in the first two sentences of his article:

"When I joined the Marine Corps, I knew I would kill people. I was trained to do it in a number of ways, to pulling a trigger to ordering a bomb strike to beating someone to death with a rock."

Prager also ignores the next sentence in which Kudo writes, "As I got closer to deploying for war in 2009, my lethal abilities were refined, but my ethical understanding of killing was not."

I would like to give Mr. Prager the benefit of the doubt, excusing him for his abysmal ignorance on the subject. In fact, I would give him a pass if it were simply a case of his lack of understanding one basic fact, that for the person who has undergone extensive combat training prior to being deployed, the idea of killing another human being in actual combat is just that, an abstract idea. For many of us, it remained so until we returned home from the battlefield and began processing our experience. As Viet Tranh Nguyen wrote, "All wars are fought twice, the first time on the battlefield, the second time in memory."

I cannot excuse Prager's arrogant dismissal of Captain Kudo's moral struggle because his rebuttal was not written in good faith. For Prager, Captain Kudo's article represented a means with which to advance his own ideological agenda. "Captain Kudo," Prager writes, "has been infected with the dominant religion—leftism." What he wrote for the leftist *Washington Post* was, accordingly, "a fine example of the moral confusion leftism has wrought over the last half century."

Even more telling is the fact that Prager completely ignores the experience that had the greatest impact on Captain Kudo's life. One day in 2010 his patrol killed two teenagers riding a motorcycle. They learned afterward that they had killed two unarmed civilians. Kudo writes, "It's been more than two years since we killed those people on the motorcycle, and I think about them every day. Sometimes its when I'm reading the news or watching a movie, but most often it's when I'm taking a shower or walking down my street in Brooklyn."

"Veterans are the only ones who can explain the ethical impact of war," wrote Captain Kudo. This made me curious about Dennis Prager's background. He identifies himself in his website as "one of America's most respected radio talk show hosts." I learned he was roughly my age, meaning he was a draft-age male during the Vietnam War. But this self-proclaimed expert on war has no military service to his credit. Like Dick Cheney, Prager, who was studying in England in 1969, apparently "had other priorities."

Prager, and those of his ilk, are perfect examples of the folks James Fallows had in mind when he stated in his 2015 article that if he was writing a history of the war that has been conducted the past two decades, he would call it...

"*Chickenhawk Nation*, based on the derisive term for those eager to go to war, as long as someone else is going. It would be the story of a country willing to do anything for its military except take it seriously. As a result, what happens to all institutions that escape serious scrutiny and engagement has happened to our military. Outsiders treat it both too reverently and too cavalierly, as if regarding its members as heroes makes up for committing them to unending, unwinnable missions and denying them anything like the political mindshare we give to other major public undertakings, from medical care to public education to environmental rules...For democracies, messy debates are less damaging in the long run than letting important functions run on autopilot, as our military essentially does now. A chickenhawk nation is more likely to keep going to war, and keep losing, than one that wrestles with long-term questions of effectiveness."

America, unless you are willing and able to listen dispassionately and non-judgmentally to the stories of returning veterans like Captain Kudo; until you begin to heed the warnings of the damage endless war is inflicting on our society from people like James Fallows, and decide for yourselves that enough is enough, do me a favor:

PLEASE DO NOT THANK ME FOR MY SERVICE.

Bibliography

Abuza, Zachary. Renovating Politics in Contemporary Vietnam (Boulder: Lynne Rienner Publishers, Inc., 2001)

Appy, Christian. American Reckoning (New York: Penguin Group, 2015)

Camus, Albert. Resistance, Rebellion, and Death (New York: Alfred A. Knopf, Inc., 1960)

Fallows, James. "The Tragedy of the American Military," The Atlantic, January/February 2015 issue.

Gardner, Lloyd. Iraq and the Lessons of Vietnam: Or, How Not to Learn From the Past (New York: The New Press, 2007)

Goldstein, Gordon. Lessons in Disaster: McGeorge Bundy and the Path to War in Vietnam (New York: Henry Holt and Company LLC, 2008)

Greenway, H.D.S. Foreign Correspondent (New York: Simon & Schuster, 2014)

Gray, J. Glenn, The Warriors: Reflections on Men in Battle (New York: Harper & Row, 1959)

Horne, A.D. The Wounded Generation: America After Vietnam (Englewood Cliffs, 1981)

Isaacs, Arnold. Vietnam Shadows: The War, its Ghosts, and its Legacy (Baltimore: The Johns Hopkins University Press, 1997)

Karp, Walter. Buried Alive: Essays on Our Endangered Republic (New York: Franklin Square Press, 1992)

DeShazo, Claude and Latting, Charles. Once a Marine: Collected Stories by Enlisted Marine Corps Veterans—Their Lives 35 Years Later (Bloomington: Author House, 2005)

Lee, Alex. Utter's Battalion (New York: Ballantine Books, 2000)

Lewy, Guenter. America in Vietnam (New York: Oxford University Press, 1978)

Meagher, Robert Emmet. Killing From the Inside Out: Moral Injury and Just War Eugene: Cascade Books, 2014)

Nguyen, Lien-Hang. Hanoi's War (Chapel Hill: University of North Carolina Press, 2012)

Nguyen, Viet Thanh. Nothing Ever Dies: Vietnam and the Memory of War (Cambridge: Harvard University Press, 2016)

Schwenkel, Christina. The American War in Vietnam: Transnational Remembrance and Representation (Bloomington: Indiana University Press, 2009)

Shay, Jonathon. Achilles in Vietnam: Combat Trauma and the Undoing of Character (New York: Simon & Shuster, 1994)

Sherman, Nancy. Afterwar: Healing the Moral Wounds of Our Soldiers (New York: Oxford University Press, 2015)

Simonsen, Robert. Every Marine: 1968 Vietnam, A Battle for Go Noi Island (Westminster: Heritage Books, 2004)

Tai, Hue-Tam Ho. The Country of Memory: Remaking the Past of Late Socialist Vietnam (Berkeley: University of California Press, 2001)

Turner, Fred. Echoes of Combat: The Vietnam War in American Memory (New York: Doubleday, 1996)

Wells, Jack. "Full Circle," Vietnam magazine, June, 2017

Made in the USA
Monee, IL
22 July 2020